Command on Trial

Command on Trial

Japanese Officers, War Crimes, and Command Responsibility

Paul Taucher

HKU PRESS
香港大學出版社

Hong Kong University Press
The University of Hong Kong
Pok Fu Lam Road
Hong Kong
https://hkupress.hku.hk

ISBN 978-988-8946-82-2 (*Hardback*)

British Library Cataloguing-in-Publication Data
A catalogue record for this book is available from the British Library.

Digitally printed

Contents

Abbreviations

ICTY	International Criminal Tribunal for the former Yugoslavia
IJA	Imperial Japanese Army
IJN	Imperial Japanese Navy
IMTFE	International Military Tribunal for the Far East
JAG	Judge Advocate General
NAA	National Archives of Australia
NARA	National Archives and Records Administration (USA)
NCO	Non-Commissioned Officer
NLA	National Library of Australia
POW	Prisoner of War
SCAP	Supreme Commander of the Allied Powers (Tokyo)
TNA	The National Archives (UK)

Conventions

Japanese personal names are usually given in the text with surname first, in accordance with Japanese custom, and using macrons to indicate long vowels as appropriate. The war crimes trial records, however, are erratic in their recording of Japanese names, sometimes putting the surname first and sometimes not. Their spelling of Japanese names in English varies, and they do not use macrons. When quoting from the trial records, I have maintained the order and spelling as it appears in those records. Japanese place-names are given without macrons.

The formal titles of trial records include the names of all defendants in a case, which produces exceedingly long citations for the larger trials. I have therefore cited these records in an abbreviated format in footnotes and the bibliography, giving the name of the first defendant and the total number of defendants but not listing all the names.

Introduction

The 1941–1945 war in the Pacific between Japan and the Allies was a brutal conflict, in which members of the Japanese military committed many crimes against Allied soldiers and civilians. Prisoners of war (POWs), civilians in areas occupied by the Japanese military, and guerrilla fighters were illegally tortured and killed. Captives were provided with inadequate food and medicine, housed in poor accommodation, and forced to work in arduous conditions, even when sick. The Allies received information about these crimes during the war and repeatedly warned that the perpetrators would face justice. After Japan's unconditional surrender in August 1945, the Allies set out to fulfil this promise by punishing those who had committed war crimes, using the mechanism of war crimes trials.

At the trials, the Allies were determined not only to prosecute direct perpetrators of atrocities, who were usually enlisted soldiers, non-commissioned officers, and civilian auxiliary employees, but also officers who had been in a position of command when war crimes were committed. They were conscious that even if comparatively junior personnel had been directly responsible for offences, their crimes nevertheless had been carried out within a military hierarchy. That is, Allied authorities believed that the structure of the Japanese military had allowed the crimes to occur, and thus, that pursuing guilt for war crimes should extend to those who had been in positions of command. For the trials to become a lasting precedent and a lasting deterrent, officers – as well as direct perpetrators – needed to be held accountable.

To achieve this goal, the Allied authorities made use of a major new legal doctrine: that of command responsibility, which is the focus of this book. The new doctrine was developed by extending to military tribunals legal concepts and principles that existed in domestic criminal and civil law. It was used to hold commanding officers responsible for the crimes of their subordinates, even in cases where the officer had not ordered the crimes to occur or did not know that the crimes had happened. Command responsibility, which came to be used throughout the war crimes trials held after the Second World War in Europe and Asia, was first applied in the Allied trials of Japanese war criminals.

In addition to achieving justice for victims and punishing the guilty, the trials were designed to act as a deterrent to misconduct in any future conflicts. When the Second World War began, the laws, rules, and customs of war had not yet been clearly defined, and it was questionable to what extent they could be applied either to nation-states or to individuals.[1] The post-war trials offered an opportunity to establish an international consensus on how wars should be fought. Holding military officers liable for the crimes of their subordinates would mean, in theory, that officers would take greater care to prevent, halt, or punish the commission of war crimes in the future. Within this greater goal of deterrence, Allied legal personnel also hoped that the trials themselves would serve as a form of broad precedent for future war crimes trials programs.[2]

Literature on the trials of alleged Japanese war criminals has focused primarily on the trial of senior Japanese civilian and military leaders before the International Tribunal for the Far East (IMTFE), also known as the Tokyo trial, but scholarship on the national trials has recently become more plentiful. Works on the national trials generally focus on individual prosecuting countries. Many of these works are concerned with the question of whether the trials were fair, though Aszkielowicz and Chamberlain examine the political significance of the trials on the prosecuting countries. Two works examine the trial programs of multiple nations. Piccigallo's pioneering work discusses each Allied government's trial processes, rules, procedure, and outcomes, comparing the different approaches and results. Wilson, Cribb, Trefalt, and Aszkielowicz cover the national trials from the early planning and investigation stages through to conviction, punishment, and release of those convicted. They argue that at both an international and national level, politics and justice were intimately connected at all stages of the war crimes trial program. In addressing whether the post-war trials were fair, they acknowledge different understandings of fairness, making use of the distinction between 'procedural' and 'substantive' justice.[3] In procedural justice, which is usually the chief concern of domestic criminal trials, the focus is on the steps taken to achieve the result itself. Substantive justice, by contrast, aims for an outcome where the right people are investigated, prosecuted,

1. Sandra Wilson, Robert Cribb, Beatrice Trefalt, and Dean Aszkielowicz, *Japanese War Criminals* (Columbia University Press, 2016), 29–31.
2. National Archives and Records Administration, College Park MD (hereafter NARA), RG331, Supreme Commander of the Allied Powers, Legal Section, Administrative Division, War Crimes File, 1945–49, Publications, 'The Yokohama War Crimes Trials: December 1945–September 1947', Box 1350, 15.
3. Wilson, Cribb, Trefalt, and Aszkielowicz, *Japanese War Criminals*, 4–10.

found guilty, and given an appropriate sentence for the right crime.[4] *Japanese War Criminals* points out that for the Allies, substantive justice, rather than procedural justice, was the clear goal. In this book, I show how the doctrine of command responsibility was used to achieve that goal.

Though existing works have examined command responsibility trials in the Pacific, most of these analyse the trials of high-ranking officers, and such studies rarely situate such trials within the broader aims of the Allied post-war trial program.[5] Such works acknowledge the national trials of Japanese war criminals as the foundation of the doctrine and largely treat the first command responsibility trial, that of Lieutenant-General Yamashita Tomoyuki, as basic precedent. Accordingly, there is a considerable body of scholarly work on Yamashita's trial, and its implications and consequences.[6] Taken as a whole, the most striking feature of the literature on the Yamashita proceeding is the level of disagreement among the authors as to why Yamashita was convicted. Beyond the Yamashita trial, three other command responsibility cases have received broad scholarly attention: two US trials of multiple high-ranking German officers conducted in Germany, known as the Hostages Trial (1947–1948) and the High Command Trial (1947–1948), and the US prosecution of the Japanese Admiral Toyoda

---

4. On substantive justice, see Wojciech Sadurski, *Giving Desert Its Due: Social Justice and Legal Theory* (Reidel, 1985), 49–56.
5. John Pritchard, 'The Historical Experience of British War Crimes Courts in the Far East, 1946–1948', *International Relations* 6 (1978): 311–26; Suzannah Linton, ed., *Hong Kong's War Crimes Trials* (Oxford University Press, 2013); Sharon Chamberlain, *A Reckoning: Philippine Trials of Japanese War Criminals* (University of Wisconsin Press, 2018); Barak Kushner, *Men to Devils, Devils to Men: Japanese War Crimes and Chinese Justice* (Harvard University Press, 2015); Dean Aszkielowicz, *The Australian Pursuit of Japanese War Criminals, 1943–1957: From Foe to Friend* (Hong Kong University Press, 2017); Georgina Fitzpatrick, Tim McCormack, and Narrelle Morris, *Australia's War Crimes Trials, 1945–51* (Brill-Nijhoff, 2016); Caroline Pappas, 'Law and Politics: Australia's War Crimes Trials in the Pacific, 1943–1961' (unpublished PhD thesis, University of New South Wales, 1998); Michael Carrell, 'Australia's Prosecution of Japanese War Criminals: Stimuli and Constraints' (unpublished PhD thesis, University of Melbourne, 2005); Jamie Fellows, 'Law at a Critical Juncture: Retribution and Criminal Responsibility at the US Army War Crimes Trials in the Philippines, 1945–1957' (unpublished PhD thesis, James Cook University, 2020); Fred L. Borch, *Military Trials of War Criminals in the Netherlands East Indies, 1946–1949* (Oxford University Press, 2017).
6. A. Frank Reel, *The Case of General Yamashita* (University of Chicago Press, 1949); Richard L. Lael, *The Yamashita Precedent: War Crimes and Command Responsibility* (Scholarly Resources, 1982); Allan A. Ryan, *Yamashita's Ghost: War Crimes, MacArthur's Justice and Command Accountability* (University Press of Kansas, 2012); Anne-Marie Prévost, 'Race and War Crimes: The 1945 Trial of General Tomoyuki Yamashita', *Human Rights Quarterly* 14 (1992): 303–38; Courtney Whitney, *The Case of General Yamashita: A Memorandum* (Supreme Commander of the Allied Powers, Government Section, 1949); George F. Guy, 'The Defense of General Yamashita', *United States Academy of Legal Studies* 6 (1950): 215–36; Bruce Landrum, 'The Yamashita War Crimes Trial: Command Responsibility Then and Now', *Military Law Review* 149 (1995): 293–302.

Soemu (1948).[7] For the most part, analysis of these other command responsibility trials have treated the outcome of the trial as either reinforcing or altering the interpretation of command responsibility as applied in Yamashita: that is, that the trials collectively form some kind of precedent.

In contrast, this book examines the trials of junior and middle-ranking Japanese officers, who constituted the great majority of defendants in command responsibility trials. The trials are from the US, Australian, UK, and Philippine programs because documentation of these proceedings is the most fully available. Records of the other three sets of trials – the French, Chinese, and Netherlands Indies proceedings – are either inadequate in the first place, or are currently unavailable.[8] This book closely examines twenty command responsibility trials for the four main types of crime for which command responsibility was relevant – summary execution, massacre, torture, and mistreatment of captives – and analyses the use of the doctrine in trials pertaining to those crimes.

Identifying trials that used command responsibility can be a difficult task. The charges against accused officers rarely mentioned command responsibility, even when it was the basis of the case. Instead, officers were commonly charged with directly committing a crime, even when it was their subordinates who had carried out the offending action, or else they were charged with the vague accusation that they had been 'concerned in' a crime. Moreover, the national trials of the four countries examined here did not need to, and frequently did not, publish a reasoned decision for their judgments. These factors mean that, in order to determine whether or not command responsibility was the basis of a trial, it is necessary to analyse the entire record of the trial and all associated legal activities: that is the transcript itself, plus legal reviews, petitions, and affidavits from witnesses and potential witnesses.[9]

---

7. Kevin Jon Heller, *The Nuremberg Trials and the Origins of International Criminal Law* (Oxford University Press, 2011), 263–71, 392–94; Guénaël Mettraux, *The Law of Command Responsibility* (Oxford University Press, 2009), 220–23, 231–37, 263; Peter MacGuire, *Law and War: International Law and American History* (Columbia University Press, 2010), 126, 132–34; Gary D. Solis, *The Law of Armed Conflict: International Humanitarian Law in War* (Cambridge University Press, 2010), 386–87; L. C. Green, 'Command Responsibility in International Humanitarian Law', *Transnational Law and Contemporary Problems* 5 (1995): 36–37.
8. The French and Nationalist Chinese trial records are brief. The Netherlands Indies trial records opened in January 2020 but closed because of the COVID-19 pandemic, and at the time of research, offered limited services.
9. For other legal studies that use this approach, see Suzannah Linton, 'Introduction', in *Hong Kong's War Crimes Trials*, ed. Suzannah Linton (Oxford University Press, 2013), 2; Gideon Boas and Lisa Lee, 'Command Responsibility and Other Grounds of Criminal Responsibility', in *Australia's War Crimes Trials 1945–51*, ed. Georgina Fitzpatrick, Tim McCormack, and Narrelle Morris (Brill, 2016), 171–72; Jamie Fellows, 'Law at a Critical Juncture: The US Army's Command Responsibility Trials at Manila, 1945–1947', *American Journal of Legal History* 60 (2020): 192–222; Nina B. Jørgensen, 'On Being "Concerned" in a Crime: Embryonic Joint Criminal Enterprise?', in *Hong Kong's War Crimes Trials*, 149, 156.

One of the key findings of this study is that the new doctrine was applied much more widely than is generally recognised. Because trial records usually do not specifically identify command responsibility cases, it is difficult to arrive at an overall number of officers who were prosecuted under the doctrine. I estimate that approximately 25 to 35 per cent of lower-ranking officers – that is, lieutenants through to colonels, and equivalent ranks in the navy – who appeared as defendants in the US, Australian, UK, and Philippines trials of suspected Japanese war criminals were tried under command responsibility.[10] This estimation is based on an examination of more than two hundred trials of lower-ranking officers from the four jurisdictions treated in this book. Therefore, command responsibility was one of the central mechanisms of the Allied war crimes trials, rather than a specialised tool used only or primarily to try senior officers.

Furthermore, this study shows that the doctrine of command responsibility was applied inconsistently in the Allied trials in the Asia-Pacific region, not only across the different national jurisdictions, but also within each country's trial program. The circumstances of the trials and of the war were partly responsible. First, the new doctrine turned out to be a more complex legal tool than had initially been expected. Although command responsibility sounded in principle like a relatively simple and natural extension of war crimes law and domestic criminal law, in practice it proved to be exceedingly complicated, with the result that trials applied the doctrine inconsistently and unpredictably. Second, the scope of the trials was vast, in the number of proceedings, their geographical locations, the range of offences prosecuted, and the length of time it took to complete the program. As a result, different interpretations and applications were likely to appear, opportunities for communication among different courtrooms was limited, and over time, what the trials meant to the Allies, and indeed to the Japanese population, evolved alongside broader political and diplomatic developments. Third, there was an overwhelming desire amongst many tribunal members to secure convictions, the effect of which was to override attention to the complexity of cases.

Beyond these immediate difficulties, however, lay an even greater obstacle to the goal of producing consistent results in command responsibility proceedings: namely, the fact that the Allies did not enter the trials with any agreed understanding of what behaviour could and should be expected of a commander. The legal proceedings raised difficult questions about what command was, and what it had or should have meant in the context of the Pacific War. At the deepest level there was simply no moral or philosophical consensus on these matters among the Allied authorities. Exercising command had been no simple matter in a conflict that had been fought over great distances by large and disparate forces,

10. For a table of ranks, see Appendix A.

and understanding afterwards what had happened and what should have happened during the conflict proved equally difficult. Uncertainty over which interpretation of command responsibility should be applied in any specific case was, ultimately, the result of uncertainty about how commanders could be expected to behave. In this sense, the deployment of the doctrine of command responsibility in prosecutions of suspected Japanese war criminals brought to the fore the enduring problem of how to attribute credit and blame to individuals in complex military hierarchies.

Some tribunals held commanders to exceptionally high objective standards and treated command as something that could not be derogated, either by an officer's rank or capability, or by external factors. Other trials took the view that command came with onerous duties and responsibilities that nonetheless could be mitigated by a range of factors. The different interpretations and applications of command responsibility were, thus, not primarily a result of the circumstances of the war, the trial program, or a desire for vengeance. Rather, differences arose because of varied understandings of what command meant. Beyond setting out that commanders could be held responsible for the crimes of their subordinates, the command responsibility trials never created a coherent precedent about how the doctrine actually operated in practice.

The command responsibility prosecutions pushed the limits of what the war crimes trials could achieve. The doctrine attempted to turn what appeared to be the straightforward legal and political goal of prosecuting officers who had not directly participated in a crime into a unified principle with the full force of recognised law. The Allies assumed that the familiar legal concepts upon which command responsibility was built, including duty, responsibility, liability, and guilt, were easily applicable to the unfamiliar crimes that had occurred during the war, and, further, would naturally develop into a clear definition of what effective command looked like. The results of the courtroom proceedings, however, were mixed. The command responsibility trials succeeded in the basic goal of prosecuting all levels of the Japanese military for war crimes and convicting officers who could or should have prevented war crimes. However, they did not succeed in developing a clear legal framework for future prosecutions under the doctrine, and at times came close to applying broad collective responsibility upon the Japanese military, something that the Allied policy and legal experts were reluctant to do. In other words, the Allies' immediate policy goals were met, but the longer-term goals of establishing a recognised body of relevant international law failed.

The War, the Crimes, and the Trials

Japan and China had been engaged in full-scale war since July 1937. On 7/8 December 1941, in an effort to secure access to resources to continue fighting in China until Japan could claim victory, Japanese forces attacked British Malaya and the Philippines. They also attacked Pearl Harbor in Hawai'i, the headquarters of the US Pacific Fleet, in an attempt to prevent US counterattacks in Southeast Asia. Over the next six months, the Japanese military was wildly successful, conquering British, Dutch, Portuguese, and US territories across Southeast Asia and the Pacific. In addition to capturing large swathes of territory, the Japanese military also captured large numbers of Allied soldiers as POWs.

From June 1942, however, Japan began to lose control of the war, following a naval defeat at the Pacific island of Midway that helped to return naval superiority to the US, and a defeat of its ground forces during fighting on Guadalcanal in the Solomon Islands between August 1942 and February 1943.[11] From then on, the Allies began to recover Japanese-occupied territory in the Pacific. From mid-1943 the US navy wreaked havoc on Japanese supply ships and began blockading Japanese-occupied islands. By the end of the war, over 70 per cent of Japanese shipping had been destroyed.[12] Beginning in late 1944, US air raids systematically destroyed Japanese cities in a campaign that culminated in catastrophic fire-bombing raids from early 1945 and the dropping of atomic bombs on Hiroshima and Nagasaki in August 1945.[13] The bombings, combined with the Soviet Union's declaration of war on Japan and invasion of Japanese-occupied Manchuria and Korea, led to Japan's unconditional surrender on 15 August 1945. By this time, the Japanese military had already suffered disastrous defeats in Burma and the Philippines and had been forced out of most of the Pacific islands, though large portions of China and Southeast Asia, including British Malaya and much of the Netherlands Indies, remained under Japanese control until Japan's surrender.

Japanese forces had committed atrocities during fighting in China from 1937 onwards. On 13 December 1937 the Imperial Japanese Army (IJA) captured the Chinese capital, Nanjing. Over the next six weeks, the IJA looted and burned large portions of the city, raped tens of thousands of women, and murdered up

11. Ronald H. Spector, *Eagle Against the Sun: The American War with Japan* (Vintage Books, 1985), 1–3, 167–77.
12. Edward Drea, *Japan's Imperial Army: Its Rise and Fall, 1853–1945* (University Press of Kansas, 2009), 33; B. F. Johnston, *Japanese Food Management in World War II* (Stanford University Press, 1953), 141.
13. See E. B. Kerr, *Flames Over Tokyo: The US Army Air Force's Incendiary Campaign Against Japan, 1944–1945* (D. I. Fine, 1991); David H. James, *The Rise and Fall of the Japanese Empire* (Routledge, 1951), 316–23.

to 200,000 civilians and surrendered soldiers.[14] Japanese soldiers continued to commit atrocities throughout the war in China. Even though they knew about these atrocities, Allied authorities were hopeful at the outbreak of the conflict in the Pacific in 1941 that the Japanese military would comply with international laws and customs relating to war. On 18 December 1941, the US Secretary of State, Cordell Hull, expressed to the Japanese Foreign Minister, Tōgō Shigenori, the Allies' expectation that Japan would abide by the Third Geneva Convention of 1929, which regulated the treatment of POWs. The Japanese government had signed but not ratified the treaty, meaning that its provisions were not legally binding on Japan. The Japanese Foreign Ministry nevertheless replied that the government and military would observe the spirit of the treaty, while changing what needed to be changed to accommodate the circumstances of the war (*mutatis mutandis*).[15]

By early 1942, however, it was clear that Japanese forces were committing widespread crimes against POWs and civilians in occupied territories in Southeast Asia and the Pacific. Following their capture of Singapore in February 1942, Japanese soldiers killed doctors, nurses, and patients at the Alexandra Barracks Hospital, and, over the course of three weeks, killed thousands of Chinese men whom they considered to be a security threat.[16] In the Philippines, following the final surrender of US and Philippine forces in April 1942, more than 600 US and an unknown number of Philippine soldiers died on a forced march from the front line to POW camps, known as the Bataan Death March.[17] Then, from September 1942 to December 1943, approximately 70,000 civilian labourers and 12,000 POWs died working in harsh conditions on the infamous Thailand-Burma Railway.[18] Throughout the rest of the war, the Allies received reports of inhumane treatment of captives, brutal treatment of local civilians, and the denial of protections to surrendering soldiers.

The wartime Allied response to reports of Japanese atrocities was a mixture of outrage and repeated warnings. Allied media coverage of the crimes portrayed not only the Japanese military, but the entire Japanese population, as barbaric. Constant emphasis on Japanese barbarism in the media fostered

14. Daqing Yang, 'Convergence or Divergence? Recent Historical Writings on the Rape of Nanjing', *The American Historical Review* 104 (1999): 844–53; Peter Li, 'The Nanking Holocaust: Memory, Trauma and Reconciliation', in *Japanese War Crimes: The Search for Justice*, ed. Peter Li (Transaction Publishers, 2003), 234–35.
15. Wilson, Cribb, Trefalt, and Aszkielowicz, *Japanese War Criminals*, 12–13.
16. Yoji Akashi, 'Japanese Policy Towards the Malayan Chinese 1941–1945', *Journal of Southeast Asian Studies* 1, no. 2 (1970): 66–69.
17. Spector and others suggest that 5,000–10,000 Philippine soldiers died on the march, but these figures seem questionable. See Spector, *Eagle Against the Sun*, 396–98.
18. Paul H. Kratoska, 'General Introduction', in *The Thailand-Burma Railway, 1942–1946: Documents and Selected Writings*, ed. Paul H. Kratoska (Routledge, 2006), 11.

a desire, amongst both Allied civilians and military personnel, for vengeance against Japan.[19] At the same time, Allied governments and militaries repeatedly warned the Japanese authorities that war criminals would face punishment after the conflict ended. In anticipation of later trials, Allied authorities also began to collect evidence of war crimes, but these investigations remained secret to avoid Japanese reprisals against Allied prisoners.[20] Allied warnings to Japan culminated in the Potsdam Declaration, issued on 26 July 1945 and signed by the UK, the US, and China, which insisted on the unconditional surrender of Japan and promised that war criminals would face 'stern justice'.[21] By this point, Allied political and legal planners had concluded that using Allied principles of law and justice, rather than delivering some form of summary punishment, was the only legitimate way of dealing with the atrocities committed by Axis forces during the war.[22] Once Japan surrendered, and with the decision to hold war crimes trials made, Allied legal planners set about creating an international tribunal in Tokyo, the International Military Tribunal for the Far East (IMTFE), and a separate set of national trials to be run by Allied military authorities.

Each of the seven Allied governments that elected at that point to run national trials created military tribunals under its own jurisdiction, but these tribunals loosely co-operated with each other and all had the same basic format. Each court proceeding had a panel of judges, usually three, but sometimes five in more complicated or high-profile trials. The judges were not required to, and often did not, have legal training. Because of this, all the national trials had a post-trial review stage, where professional military lawyers went over the proceedings to identify any potential errors or concerns. The review lawyer could also recommend changing any sentence that had been passed; however, this recommendation was not binding. After the review, the proceedings were sent to a confirming officer, who would confirm or modify the verdict and sentence. Death sentences had to be confirmed by the head of the national government or the head of the military running the trial. Some verdicts were overturned entirely, many sentences were reduced, and in a handful of cases, a retrial was ordered.[23]

Lawyers for both prosecution and defence were initially drawn from Allied militaries. Many had worked in war crimes investigation teams. As the trials progressed, Japanese criminal lawyers overwhelmingly took over the defence.

19. Wilson, Cribb, Trefalt, and Aszkielowicz, *Japanese War Criminals*, 24–25; John Dower, *War Without Mercy: Race and Power in the Pacific War* (Pantheon, 1986), 37.
20. Wilson, Cribb, Trefalt, and Aszkielowicz, *Japanese War Criminals*, 19.
21. 'Proclamation by the Heads of Governments, United States, China and the United Kingdom'.
22. Wilson, Cribb, Trefalt, and Aszkielowicz, *Japanese War Criminals*, 19.
23. Piccigallo, *The Japanese on Trial*, 36–37, 98, 125, 188; Wilson, Cribb, Trefalt, and Aszkielowicz, *Japanese War Criminals*, 75–76, 96–98.

Prosecutors had certain advantages over the defence lawyers. If they had worked in investigation teams, they might possess extra evidence, which sometimes appears to have been withheld if it could have prevented a conviction or lessened a potential sentence.[24] As they were better resourced, prosecutors also had greater chances of producing witnesses who were overseas, whereas the defence had to make do with witnesses who were locally available.[25] Proceedings were conducted in the native language of the prosecution, which was English except in the Chinese, French, and Netherlands Indies trials, while Japanese defence lawyers had to rely on translators and interpreters to understand complicated legal arguments.

The national trials operated under rules and procedures that were designed to expedite proceedings. Hearsay evidence and unsworn testimony were readily accepted in most proceedings. There was no requirement to produce witnesses: some trials were conducted solely on documentary evidence, even when direct witnesses were alive and available to give evidence. Tribunal judges were not required to, and generally did not, give reasons for their decisions. Three factors were probably responsible. First, the judges usually did not have formal legal training, so would likely have struggled to deliver legally reasoned decisions. Second, the trials were intended to be expeditious and drafting judgments is often a time-consuming process. Third, the trials were not bound by precedent – ironically, in view of the planners' desire that these trials themselves should act as precedents in the future – which meant that later trials did not have to consider how points of law had been interpreted and applied in earlier trials.[26]

Contemporary and later commentators have expressed misgivings about the differences in rules and procedures between, on the one hand, the military tribunals and the IMTFE, and on the other hand, civilian criminal courts in the home countries of the prosecuting powers, arguing or implying that these differences undermined the fairness of the trials. How evidence was used, the competence of defence counsel, and, in some cases, lack of impartiality on the bench, have all been raised as flaws of the trials.[27] Determining what would have been fair when dealing with war crimes, however, is a vexed matter. Allied planners were convinced that without changes in procedure, many suspects would never face prosecution because the right kind of evidence was not available; and they feared

24. Wilson, Cribb, Trefalt, and Aszkielowicz, *Japanese War Criminals*, 83.
25. Wilson, Cribb, Trefalt, and Aszkielowicz, *Japanese War Criminals*, 83.
26. Wilson, Cribb, Trefalt, and Aszkielowicz, *Japanese War Criminals*, 80–90.
27. Wilson, Cribb, Trefalt, and Aszkielowicz, *Japanese War Criminals*, 6; Prévost, 'Race and War Crimes', 315–18; Lisette Schouten, 'Colonial Justice in the Netherlands Indies War Crimes Trials', in *Trials for International Crimes in Asia*, ed. Kirsten Sellars (Cambridge University Press, 2016), 86–87; Pritchard, 'The Historical Experience of British War Crimes Courts', *International Relations* 6 (1978): 319.

that without expedited trials, the process would take an inordinate amount of time. Even with the changes made, the trials ran for over five years, far longer than the ten months that British authorities initially expected.[28]

One of the most significant consequences of the prolonged trial program was that the trials were subject to changing political goals. As well as achieving some form of justice for crimes committed during the war, the trials were part of a broader political goal to democratise and demilitarise Japanese society. The IMTFE in particular removed key leaders from both the military and government who would likely oppose the Allies' goal. The national trials also served to remove military leaders, particularly from the officer corps, from Japanese society. However, from mid-1947 onwards, the Allied goals for Japan shifted away from democratisation and demilitarisation towards limiting the influence of communism and creating a more resilient Cold War partner. This change in policy, commonly referred to as the 'Reverse Course', resulted in many politicians and military personnel who had essentially been purged from public office returning to public life.[29] With this change in direction, it was difficult to argue that convicted and suspected war criminals should be barred from Japanese society, particularly when Japan had been demilitarised, meaning that it was highly unlikely that Japanese personnel would commit future war crimes.[30] In this book, I further argue that the 'Reverse Course' also played a role in reducing the severity of sentences of those found guilty under command responsibility. The grander political objectives of the Allies in Japan necessarily impacted the attribution of guilt within the post-war justice system.

Command responsibility was an important tool in achieving the kind of justice that the Allies wanted. In domestic criminal law in most Western countries, a person cannot be held criminally responsible for the acts of another, unless there is some level of direct participation or encouragement.[31] In other words, a commander could have been held culpable for murder if he had ordered a subordinate to commit a war crime, but simply being in a position of power and control, without some positive act relative to the substantive crime, could not have attracted liability. In view of the widespread atrocities committed by Japanese military personnel during the Second World War, however, investigators and prosecutors could not apportion guilt solely to direct perpetrators

28. Wilson, Cribb, Trefalt, and Aszkielowicz, 64.
29. Michael Schaller, *Altered States: The United States and Japan Since the Occupation* (Oxford University Press, 1997), 7–31; Takemae Eiji, *Inside GHQ: The Allied Occupation of Japan and Its Legacy*, trans. Robert Ricketts and Sebastian Swann (Continuum, 2002), 45–48; Aszkielowicz, *The Australian Pursuit of Japanese War Criminals*, 72–73.
30. Wilson, Cribb, Trefalt, and Aszkielowicz, 126–27.
31. Arthur O'Reilly, 'Command Responsibility: A Call to Realign the Doctrine with Principles of Individual Accountability and Retributive Justice', *Gonzaga Law Review* 40 (2005): 127–28.

if they hoped to achieve their goals: they also needed to target those who had permitted crimes to happen or failed to punish crimes when they were committed. Command responsibility allowed tribunals to mete out justice where something fundamentally wrong had occurred, even in circumstances under which traditional domestic criminal law would have decreed that the accused had not committed any crime. Command responsibility was, thus, a utilitarian theory of liability, deployed to achieve justice as comprehensively as possible for the widespread war crimes committed by Japanese forces during the war. In practice, however, it was used in widely different and sometimes contradictory ways according to the type of crime prosecuted, the position of the accused officer within the military hierarchy, and the amount of evidence available.

1

Establishing Courts and the Principle of Command Responsibility

By the first half of 1942, Allied governments had begun to receive reports that Japanese soldiers had committed war crimes against Allied soldiers and civilians. In March 1942, the UK government informed the House of Commons that in December 1941, the Japanese army had captured and massacred fifty British soldiers in Hong Kong.[1] Reports of atrocities continued to arrive. In April 1943, the International Red Cross warned the Australian government that war crimes were probably occurring in Japanese-run prisoner of war (POW) camps but could not confirm the information due to the limited access the Japanese government had given it to the camps. The Australian government suppressed this information to limit damage to civilian and military morale.[2] Also in April 1943, the US government received reports from US and Philippine escapees of POW camps about crimes committed during the April 1942 Bataan Death March, but, like the Australian government, it suppressed the news until six months later.[3]

Throughout 1944 and 1945, as the Allies took back Japanese-occupied territory in Southeast Asia and the Pacific, they gathered more evidence of war crimes, and it became clear that crimes had been widespread. The question for Allied authorities became how to respond to such atrocities. Taking immediate action during the war would likely lead to reprisals against Allied captives. Therefore, cataloguing the evidence and pursuing justice after the war ended seemed to be the best option, though exactly how justice would be achieved was not clear at the time.[4]

---

1. 'Japanese Barbarism at Hong Kong', *Tweed Daily* (NSW), 12 March 1942, 4.
2. Dean Aszkielowicz, *The Australian Pursuit of Japanese War Criminals 1943–1957: From Foe to Friend* (Hong Kong University Press, 2017), 26.
3. John Dower, *War Without Mercy: Race and Power in the Pacific War* (Pantheon, 1986), 39.
4. Sandra Wilson, Robert Cribb, Beatrice Trefalt, and Dean Aszkielowicz, *Japanese War Criminals: The Politics of Justice After the Second World War* (Columbia University Press, 2017), 43.

By the end of the conflict, Allied governments had decided that prosecuting suspected war criminals in courtrooms was the best way of achieving their goals. The decision to prosecute was only the first of a long series of determinations that were necessary before courts could be set up. The various Allied powers had to decide what the scope of the trials would be, what procedures they would follow, and who would be tried. The result was a mix of one international tribunal and many national military tribunals. I argue in this chapter, however, that all the prosecuting authorities were determined from the beginning to equip themselves to deal with every level of the Japanese military, rather than contenting themselves with prosecuting only the direct perpetrators of atrocities. I show that the principle of command responsibility was at the forefront of legal planning, and it influenced the structure and form of the trials.

For Allied authorities, the principle of command responsibility was essential because the whole of the Japanese military was potentially culpable for war crimes. Many legal personnel seem to have believed that virtually all members of the Japanese military were guilty.[5] Allied authorities treated the Japanese military, and especially the army, almost as if it were a criminal organisation. It was hence vital to be able to prosecute military personnel from anywhere in the chain of command. This attitude can be seen in the statements of William Webb, Australian jurist, war crimes investigator, and president of the International Military Tribunal for the Far East (IMTFE). Webb did not participate in the national trials as a jurist, but had investigated potential war crimes in New Guinea on behalf of the Australian government during the conflict itself.[6] In 1945 he argued that the purpose of the national trials was to demonstrate the kind of war that Japan had fought, and to show that criminal actions at an individual level had been perpetrated throughout the chain of command.[7] Webb's position makes it clear that he, like other prominent Allied figures, thought that responsibility for the Pacific War and the crimes that occurred during the conflict, existed throughout the Japanese military's chain of command and possibly extended to the whole of Japan.

The idea that commanders could be held criminally responsible for the conduct of their subordinates was not new at the end of the Second World War. In 1474 the Archduke of Austria had used the same basic premise to prosecute and execute an enemy nobleman for crimes committed by mercenaries in the town of Breisach in the Rhine Valley, in what was then the Holy Roman Empire.[8] The US military took the same approach in the aftermath of the Civil War in

5. Wilson, Cribb, Trefalt, and Aszkielowicz, *Japanese War Criminals*, 90.
6. Aszkielowicz, *The Australian Pursuit of Japanese War Criminals*, 3–4.
7. National Library of Australia (hereafter NLA), Folder 28, Box 3. 'Webb Cable to External Affairs', No day/month, 1945, Papers of D. C. S. Sissons 1956–2006.
8. Guénaël Mettraux, *The Law of Command Responsibility* (Oxford University Press, 2009), 1–5.

1865 to try a former Confederate officer who had been in command of POWs, alleging that the officer had participated in a conspiracy to injure the health and lives of the prisoners.[9] An 1895 British parliamentary report on violence against Armenian Christians in the Ottoman Empire suggested that a local military commander must have known that atrocities were taking place and asserted that his failure to act to prevent the crimes made him criminally culpable.[10] In all of these examples, however, the commander in question had had some degree of personal involvement in the crime, by either ordering or actively encouraging it – command responsibility meant an officer was held responsible for the orders he gave. Furthermore, these instances were all isolated events, not part of a broad trend, and the legal principles used against the commanders were not embedded in any wider system of related laws.[11] The command responsibility trials in the Pacific in the mid-twentieth century, by contrast, operated within a complex web of international and domestic law.

The system that the Allies created to deal with suspected Japanese war criminals was founded on a mix of existing international treaties, laws and customs, existing domestic court procedure and doctrines within the relevant countries, and a foundational belief amongst the Allies that they had a broad mandate to punish and reform Japan. This foundational belief provided Allied authorities with justification to interpret or modify existing treaties, customs, laws, and procedures as they saw fit. They waived existing procedural requirements governing how evidence could be applied and weighed in court, and which legal defences could be used. They also created new legislation and legal norms, and applied them retroactively. To bring senior leaders to justice, the prosecuting authorities reinterpreted and extended the scope of international treaties to broaden the range of defendants who could be brought to court. Taken as a whole, these changes meant that all suspects, from low-ranking enlisted soldiers through to senior civilian and military leaders, not only could face trial, but also were liable for harsher sentences than if the changes had not been made.[12]

The trials of Japanese war crimes suspects extended the concept of command responsibility beyond its previous limits by applying it to officers who had not directly ordered or participated in a crime. Without the adjustments to normal procedure that are discussed in this chapter, it would have been extremely

9. Lewis L. Laska and James M. Smith, 'Hell and the Devil: Andersonville and the Trial of Captain Wirz, C.S.A. 1865', *Military Law Review* 68 (1975): 125.
10. Jan Martin Lemnitzer, 'International Legal History: From Atrocity Reports to War Crimes Tribunals – The Roots of Modern War Crimes Investigations in Nineteenth Century Legal Activism and First World War Propaganda', in *War Crimes Trials and Investigations: A Multi-Disciplinary Approach*, ed. Jonathan Waterlow and Jacques Schuhmacher (Palgrave Macmillan, 2018), 132–34.
11. Mettraux, *The Law of Command Responsibility*, 5.
12. Wilson, Cribb, Trefalt, and Aszkielowicz, *Japanese War Criminals*, 26–30.

difficult to do this. The changes made to normal court procedure highlight Allied assumptions about how the Japanese military had committed war crimes. Though individuals, often low-ranking enlisted men, were the actual perpetrators of the crimes, Allied authorities clearly believed that commanding officers were potentially collectively guilty for allowing the crimes to occur in the first place, or for failing to stop them from happening.

Early Warnings and an Early Framework

In setting up war crimes trials in Asia and the Pacific, the Allies followed the fundamental principle they had already established to deal with Nazi war crimes. In January 1942, Allied leaders had issued the St James Declaration, which proposed the use of 'organised channels of justice' to prosecute German war criminals. The government of Nationalist China quickly extended the St James Declaration to Japanese military personnel.[13] In August 1942 the US president, Franklin D. Roosevelt, issued the first of multiple warnings to the Japanese government that war criminals would be pursued once the conflict ended. Other Allied governments echoed these statements, which eventually culminated in the Potsdam Declaration of 26 July 1945, setting out the terms for Japanese surrender. The Potsdam Declaration stated that 'stern justice' would be meted out to war criminals: it made no distinction regarding rank.[14]

It was initially unclear to Allied authorities how the justice that was first envisaged in the St James Declaration and later in the Potsdam Declaration would be meted out. War crimes trials had been held in various places after the First World War, but the results were widely considered to have been unsatisfactory. German authorities had prosecuted German war crimes suspects in the German Supreme Court in Leipzig in 1921. Only seventeen suspects were tried. Ten were found guilty and received light sentences, ranging from a few months to four years.[15] At the insistence of the French and UK governments, the Ottoman government tried approximately two hundred of its own officers and low-level officials for the massacre of Armenians during the war, of whom three were executed. The Turkish government had forewarned many other suspects,

13. United Nations War Crimes Commission, *History of the United Nations War Crimes Commission and the Development of the Laws of War* (His Majesty's Stationery Office, 1948), 87–91.
14. Philip R. Piccigallo, *The Japanese on Trial: Allied War Crimes Operations in the East, 1945–51* (University of Texas Press, 1979), 4.
15. *History of the United Nations War Crimes Commission*, 47. See also Jürgen Matthäus, 'The Lessons of Leipzig: Punishing German War Criminals after the First World War', in *Atrocities on Trial: Historical Perspectives on the Politics of Prosecuting War Crimes*, ed. Patricia Heberer and Jürgen Matthäus (University of Nebraska Press, 2008), 3–23; James F. Willis, *Prologue to Nuremberg: The Politics and Diplomacy of Punishing War Criminals of the First World War* (Greenwood Press, 1982), 133–39.

allowing them either to destroy evidence or to escape before they were arrested.[16] By 1926, both the Belgian and the French governments had tried and sentenced German suspects in their domestic courts in absentia, which meant that the accused never faced their punishment.[17] The fact that both the German and the Ottoman governments conducted trials of their own war criminals contributed to the relatively low number of suspects prosecuted and the lenient sentences for most of those found guilty.[18] For the Allied governments in 1945, the main lesson taken from these trials was, therefore, that this time they must administer justice themselves.

At the London International Conference on Military Trials in June 1945, representatives of the USSR, France, the US, and the UK clarified how and on what basis justice would be meted out to Nazi war criminals. US representative and Associate Justice of the Supreme Court of the United States, Robert Jackson, argued that the only viable option was to try accused war criminals before a dispassionate court.[19] Jackson's recommendation was in stark contrast to ideas previously floated by both Roosevelt and UK Prime Minister Winston Churchill, who had – apparently genuinely –considered drafting a list of senior Axis war criminals who would be arrested on sight and summarily executed.[20]

Jackson's comments at the conference changed the tone of the discussion about war crimes. He insisted that the prosecuting powers begin from the principle that courts would be used because they are examples of the highest principles of Western justice, and that as many war criminals as possible would be prosecuted, including civilian leaders who had advocated war. Jackson's recommendation that suspects be tried in war crimes courts met the St James Declaration's call for a channel of organised justice. It was a breakthrough in designing Allied policy that built on the initial calls for justice and formulated them as concrete legal principles. Having a legitimate foundation was important for the trials, as the Allied authorities, especially US authorities, sought to use them to show Japan's population that the war, and the actions of the Japanese military, had been illegitimate.[21] The representatives of the USSR, the UK, the US, and French gov-

16. Alan Kramer, 'The First Wave of International War Crimes Trials: Istanbul and Leipzig', *European Review* 14 (2006): 444–46.
17. Willis, *Prologue to Nuremberg*, 145; R. John Pritchard, 'The Parameters of Justice: The Evolution of British Civil and Military Perspectives on War Crimes Trials and Their Legal Context (1942–1956)', in *International Humanitarian Law: Prospects*, ed. John Carey, William V. Dunlop, and R. John Pritchard (Brill, 2006), 289–90.
18. Timothy McCormack, 'From Sun Tzu to the Sixth Committee: The Evolution of an International Criminal Law Regime', in *The Law of War Crimes: National and International Approaches*, ed. Timothy McCormack and Gerry Simpson (Kluwer Law International, 1997), 48–50.
19. Wilson, Cribb, Trefalt, and Aszkielowicz, *Japanese War Criminals*, 19.
20. Wilson, Cribb, Trefalt, and Aszkielowicz, *Japanese War Criminals*, 28.
21. Wilson, Cribb, Trefalt, and Aszkielowicz, *Japanese War Criminals*, 20.

ernments accepted Jackson's recommendations. The International Conference on Military Trials led to the creation of the International Military Tribunal, better known as the Nuremberg Tribunal, where senior Nazi leaders were tried for war crimes, and then to the establishment of the IMTFE in Tokyo.[22]

Legitimising the Trials and Closing Loopholes

Organising trials on the scale envisaged for German and Japanese war crimes suspects was a monumental task, without precedent in legal history, and it raised difficult legal problems. In the Japanese case, the military's apparently widespread brutality during the war – and the Allied commitment to undertake prosecutions across a broad range – meant there were many thousands of potential defendants. Prosecuting all of them would be a tremendous undertaking. Problematic, too, was that some of the acts committed by Japanese personnel during the war had not been considered to be war crimes at the time they were committed, so if the Allied legal authorities wanted to prosecute these acts, retroactive law would need to be applied, a strategy that could diminish the legitimacy of the trials.

In fact, it was questionable which parts of international law applied to the Japanese military and government. On 2 September 1945, the Japanese government had formally accepted the terms of the Potsdam Declaration, which meant both that the country had unconditionally surrendered, and that the government had accepted that war criminals would be punished.[23] Nevertheless, legal issues still arose in the prosecution of crimes committed against both POWs and civilians. While the Japanese government was party to the 1899 Hague Convention, and the subsequent 1907 Hague Convention, which established basic protections for POWs, it had only signed but not ratified the 1929 Third Geneva Convention, which greatly expanded the protections granted to POWs. It was possible to conclude that the 1929 treaty therefore did not apply to Japan, and thus, much of the ill-treatment of POWs was not strictly illegal in international terms. As we have seen, however, the Japanese Foreign Ministry had informed the US Secretary of State after war broke out that Japan would observe the treaty to the extent possible.[24] This statement by the Japanese government overcame one legal hurdle for the post-war prosecutions of war crimes suspects.

---

22. Neil Boister and Robert Cryer, *The Tokyo International Military Tribunal: A Reappraisal* (Oxford University Press, 2008), 19–23.
23. Ronald H. Spector, *Eagle Against the Sun: The American War with Japan* (Vintage Books, 1985), 559.
24. 'Indictment, Appendix D', in *Documents on the Tokyo International Military Tribunal*, ed. Neil Boister and Robert Cryer (Oxford University Press, 2008), 58; 'Majority Judgment', in Boister and Cryer, *Documents on the Tokyo International Military Tribunal*, 106.

In respect to crimes against civilians, there was no treaty equivalent to the Geneva Convention, though attempts had been made to codify similar provisions at the 1919 Versailles Conference.[25] Allied legal authorities approached this problem with two arguments. The first was that the acts committed by Japanese military personnel were so horrific that any objections to the application of retrospective laws to enable their prosecution were invalid, as the acts were never innocent, and contravened established customs that were widely recognised. The second was that the crimes contravened natural law, a form of law that required neither precedent nor codification but was readily apparent. Generally, both arguments were used, and both served to bolster the legitimacy of the Allied prosecutions and to establish the clear illegitimacy of the Japanese crimes.[26]

These legal arguments affirmed that the Allies could use trials to punish perpetrators of conventional war crimes, but problems remained. For the national trials, it was necessary to revise existing laws to cover the prosecution of ordinary soldiers, rather than national leaders. In particular, if the trials were to have a reasonable chance of securing convictions, the Allied authorities needed to diminish the scope of defences upon which the accused might have been able to rely under existing international and national criminal law.

One of the most significant changes made by the Allies was to the defence of superior orders. Junior rank was to be no defence against prosecution in the war crimes trials, and the chain of command was not to be a shield. At the start of the war, Allied military manuals and conventional legal thinking had held that if soldiers committed a war crime under the orders of a superior, the defence of superior orders operated to find the subordinates not guilty.[27] The rationale behind this defence is clear. When waging war, militaries rely on soldiers' unquestioning obedience to orders. The defence of superior orders acknowledges this reality. Furthermore, low-ranking enlisted soldiers were generally not given formal training in international criminal law. Instead, enlisted soldiers relied on their superior officers to ensure that the acts they carried out were legal. Most Allied militaries, however, anticipating that many accused German and Japanese war criminals would use the defence during their trial, revised their military manuals in 1943 and 1944 to make the defence of superior orders only a partial defence.[28] The change meant that even if defendants could show that they had acted under

25. McCormack, 'From Sun Tzu to the Sixth Committee', 46–47.
26. Wilson, Cribb, Trefalt, and Aszkielowicz, *Japanese War Criminals*, 25–27; Gillian Triggs, 'Australia's War Crimes Trials: All Pity Choked', in McCormack and Simpson, *The Law of War Crimes*, 141–43.
27. Hilaire McCoubrey, *International Humanitarian Law: The Regulation of Armed Conflicts* (Dartmouth Publishing Company, 1990), 219–21.
28. Alan M. Wilner, 'Superior Orders as a Defence to Violations of International Criminal Law', *Maryland Law Review* 26 (1966), 136–37; Aszkielowicz, *The Australian Pursuit of Japanese War Criminals*, 55.

orders when carrying out a crime, their guilt was only mitigated rather than fully absolved.[29] In articulating a diminished form of the defence of superior orders to be used at the trials, the Allied militaries removed a significant barrier to apportioning guilt at multiple levels of the military command structure. The decision to remove the claim of superior orders as a total defence was part of the Allies' goal to reframe personal responsibility within militaries: an accused could no longer rely on the military hierarchy to avoid guilt for war crimes.

Though the Allied militaries had changed how the defence of superior orders would work in courts, the idea that low-level enlisted soldiers were not criminally responsible for acting under orders influenced the selection of defendants, as well as the sentences of those who were tried and convicted. Many enlisted soldiers who had obeyed a direct order to commit a crime escaped prosecution, while Korean guards in camps were only brought to trial if they had been identified as especially violent.[30] The decision not to prosecute large numbers of enlisted soldiers, whether they were acting under superior orders or not, demonstrates that Allied legal personnel were more interested in prosecuting those who had held some form of command during the war.

Lack of appropriate evidence seemed likely to be another significant barrier to convictions of war criminals. Legal experts were aware that collecting evidence in the aftermath of a chaotic and destructive war would be difficult. Many documents had been destroyed during the war, either as collateral damage, or wilfully by Japanese personnel anticipating prosecution.[31] Many witnesses were dead or missing. Without evidence from such sources, suspected war criminals throughout the chain of command might never face trial or might be found not guilty. To overcome this hurdle, tribunals allowed the submission of evidence that would not ordinarily be admissible in domestic courts, or even courts-martial, especially hearsay evidence.[32] Hearsay evidence usually refers to evidence which relies on the claim by a witness that another person made a statement outside of court. If the person who made the alleged statement is not available to be cross-examined, the witness' claim cannot be proved. Hearsay evidence

29. Bing Bing Jia, 'The Plea of Superior Orders in the Hong Kong Trials', in *Hong Kong's War Crimes Trials*, ed. Suzannah Linton (Oxford University Press, 2013), 173–75; Monique Cormier and Sarah Finnin, 'Obedience to Superior Orders and Related Defences', in *Australia's War Crimes Trials, 1945–51*, ed. Georgina Fitzpatrick, Tim McCormack, and Narrelle Morris (Brill-Nijhoff, 2016), 182–86.

30. Wilson, Cribb, Trefalt, and Aszkielowicz, *Japanese War Criminals*, 63, 86; Sandra Wilson, 'Koreans in the Trials of Japanese War Crimes Suspects', in *Debating Collaboration and Complicity in War Crimes Trials in Asia, 1945–1956*, ed. Kerstin von Lingen (Palgrave Macmillan, 2017), 19–40.

31. See Kazufumi Hamai and Peter Mauch, 'The Wartime Destruction of the Japanese Diplomatic Record in Historical Perspective', in *Defamiliarizing Japan's Asia-Pacific War*, ed. W. Puck Brecher and Michael W. Myers (University of Hawaii Press, 2019), 17–33.

32. Wilson, Cribb, Trefalt, and Aszkielowicz, *Japanese War Criminals*, 81–83.

may also consist of a document, such as a diary or affidavit, whose author is not available to be cross-examined. In the difficult circumstances immediately after the war, Allied governments felt that it was improper for a suspect to be found not guilty merely because standard forms of evidence were unavailable.[33]

As well as greatly expanding the type of evidence that could be produced in court, the regulations governing the investigation and prosecution of Japanese suspects also allowed a broader interpretation of how such evidence could be applied to suspects before trial and to the accused. The Australian and UK regulations provided for a form of group responsibility for war crimes in certain circumstances. Where there was evidence that a war crime had occurred through the concerted action of a unit, then evidence given upon a charge connected to that crime could be received by the tribunal as *Prima Facie* evidence of the responsibility of each member of the group for the crime.[34] The US regulations made the same provision.[35] Despite the fact that there was nothing similar within the Philippines regulations, comparable arguments were accepted in court.[36]

Though the point was never made explicit, the regulations and arguments that broadened the range of admissible evidence and allowed evidence against one accused to be brought against other members of his unit were particularly important for command responsibility to operate effectively. Evidence inculpating officers could be particularly hard to find, because in many cases there was no clear evidence of a commander having ordered or taken part in a crime. The modifications that the Allies made to standard courtroom procedures were therefore necessary to establish a connection between commanding officers and the actions of their subordinates.

33. Caroline Pappas, 'Law and Politics: Australia's War Crimes Trials in the Pacific, 1943–1961' (unpublished PhD thesis, University of New South Wales, 1998), 94–97.
34. Regulation 9 (2) *War Crimes Act 1945* (Cth), archived at Federal Registrar of Legislation [https://www.legislation.gov.au/Details/C1945A00048]; Regulation 8 (ii) *Royal Warrant 0160/2498*, 18 June 1945, archived at The Avalon Project [https://avalon.law.yale.edu/imt/imtroyal.asp]. See also Nina H. B. Jørgensen, 'On Being "Concerned" in a Crime: Embryonic Joint Criminal Enterprise?', in Linton, *Hong Kong's War Crimes Trials*, 137–68; Nina H. B. Jørgensen, 'Theories of Joint Criminal Responsibility at the Asian Tribunals', in *Trials for International Crimes in Asia*, ed. Kirsten Sellars (Cambridge University Press, 2015), 318–40.
35. United Nations War Crimes Commission, *Law Reports of Trials of War Criminals* (His Majesty's Stationery Office, 1947), vol. 1, 119.
36. National Archives and Records Administration, College Park, MD (hereafter NARA), Supreme Commander for the Allied Powers, Legal Section, Prosecution Division, *Philippines versus Various Japanese War Criminals*, Case File, 1947–1949, Box 1690, *Philippines vs Nakamura Hideichi and Twelve Others*, 997.

Creating Tribunals and Regulating Procedure

The changes to normal procedure made by Allied legal authorities helped to create a foundation for the trials and to remove some standard protections from both direct perpetrators and military commanders. Prosecuting Japanese military personnel was the next step. At the national level, courts were created that maintained a resemblance to domestic criminal courts and military courts-martial yet could still successfully dispense justice for war crimes.

The UK, US, Philippine, and Australian courts were underpinned by different legal instruments,[37] but nevertheless shared many similarities in the way they operated, as they were all designed to achieve the same result and targeted the same types of people. The US and UK governments made easy decisions to create tribunals under their own powers. For the Australian and Philippine governments, however, it was more complicated. Australia had the option of adopting the UK form as its own, pending royal assent. In the end, Australian authorities decided that using their own legislation to prosecute war criminals was preferable, as part of a broader policy of the Australian government at the time to act more independently of Britain.[38] Indeed, Dr Herbert Vere Evatt, the Australian Minister for External Affairs, had written his doctoral thesis on why the Australian government ought not to rely on UK Royal Warrants in exercising Commonwealth power.[39] Meanwhile, the Philippine government at first enabled the US to conduct trials, again through executive power, with an understanding by both governments that the Philippines military would eventually take control of the prosecutions in the newly independent country.

The regulations that created the tribunals partially defined what the accused could be charged with. The US, Philippine, and UK regulations covered violations of the laws of war, which consisted of established war crimes, as well as violations of the customs of war. The latter category enabled prosecutors to charge individuals with crimes that had not been recognised in international treaties as crimes at the time of commission. The Australian *War Crimes Act* listed crimes that could be prosecuted. The list, however, was not designed to be exhaustive, and provided for prosecution of other offences that were not stipulated.[40]

37. On the UK courts, see A. P. V. Rogers, 'War Crimes Trials Under the British Royal Warrant: British Practice, 1945–1949', *The International and Comparative Law Quarterly* 39, no. 4 (1990): 787–89; Pritchard, 'The Parameters of Justice', 282–89. On the US courts, see United Nations War Crimes Commission, *Law Reports*, vol. 1, 111–13, and Piccigallo, *The Japanese on Trial*, 34–36. On the Philippine courts, see Sharon W. Chamberlain, *A Reckoning: Philippine Trials of Japanese War Criminals* (University of Wisconsin Press, 2019), 41–43 and Piccigallo, *The Japanese on Trial*, 188–89, 197–98. On the Australian courts, see Aszkielowicz, *The Australian Pursuit of Japanese War Criminals*, 37–38 and Piccigallo, *The Japanese on Trial*, 124–25.
38. Aszkielowicz, *The Australian Pursuit of Japanese War Criminals*, 37–38.
39. Herbert Vere Evatt, *The Royal Prerogative* (The Law Book Company, 1987).
40. Aszkielowicz, *The Australian Pursuit of Japanese War Criminals*, 37–38.

Standard Allied charges against an accused included mistreatment of prisoners, massacre, and murder. More unusual charges included causing 'mental and emotional harm' to prisoners.[41]

Prosecution staff were often sourced from the relevant army's legal department. Many of these army lawyers had been civilian lawyers before the war and drew heavily upon their domestic legal training to inform their legal strategies.[42] Some prosecutors had been part of war crimes investigation teams before the trials had started; they proved to be particularly dogged in their pursuit of suspected war criminals.[43]

At the trials, the accused always had access to a defence lawyer, whether Allied or Japanese. Some of the Japanese lawyers had served as legal officers in the accused's unit, some had been legal officers in Japanese occupation administrations in conquered territories, and some were civilian lawyers sent from Japan. Japanese lawyers, whether they had civilian or military training, generally struggled during the proceedings. The trials were conducted in the language of the prosecuting nation, which meant that time-consuming translation and interpreting were necessary for most of the defence counsel, so less effort could be spent crafting a defence strategy.[44] Furthermore, defence lawyers were often provided with limited resources and poor accommodation, especially in trials outside of major towns.[45] Allied defence lawyers sometimes worked alongside Japanese counsel. Their presence generally made proceedings run more smoothly and efficiently. Allied defence lawyers, however, could still struggle in presenting cases: there were many unfamiliar features in a system designed to deliver substantive justice, rather than the procedural justice to which they were accustomed.

All the national tribunals considered here had a minimum of three military officers sitting as judges of fact and law. There was therefore no jury, and every issue at the trial, including the admissibility of evidence, the relevance of legal arguments and lines of questioning, and findings of guilt, was decided by the bench. In theory, the judges were of a rank equivalent to or higher than that of

41. National Archives of Australia (hereafter NAA), Canberra, War Crimes Trial of Tahara Susumu and Sixteen Others (hereafter Trial of Tahara), volume 1, Charge Sheet, 1–3, archived at [https://recordsearch.naa.gov.au/SearchNRetrieve/Interface/ViewImage.aspx?B=739675].
42. NLA, Major H. F. Dick to D. C. S. Sissons, 17 September 1976, MS 0392, Papers of D. C. S. Sissons, Box 22.
43. Wilson, Cribb, Trefalt, and Aszkielowicz, *Japanese War Criminals*, 79; J. M. Williams, 'Australian War Crimes Trials 1946–1951: National Sentiment, Australian Ethos, their Historical Genesis, and Impact on the Trials' (MA coursework paper, University of Sydney, 1988), 30–34, Sissons Papers, Box 21.
44. On issues of interpreting and translating at the IMTFE, see Kayoko Takeda, *Interpreting the Tokyo War Crimes Tribunal: A Sociopolitical Analysis* (University of Ottawa Press, 2010).
45. Munemiya Shinji, *The Account of Legal Proceedings of Court for War Criminal Suspects*, trans. Kazuo Yoshioka (Horitzu Shimpo Press, 1946), 34–37.

the accused, as was normal in military courts, though this requirement was not strictly followed. Having judges of an equivalent or higher rank meant that those passing judgment presumably had at least a basic understanding of the accused's duties and of what could be expected from them, a consideration that would be especially important in command responsibility trials. Proceedings with higher-ranking defendants usually had five judges sitting.[46]

While the UK and Australian tribunals formally required that at least one of the judges should have legal experience, they did not always have such experience in practice.[47] Where there was no legal experience on the bench, or in trials that were expected to be more complex, a legal advisor, called a Judge Advocate, would be present in the court to assist the bench on points of law and to provide advice on the admissibility of evidence and on what weight ought to be attached to different pieces of evidence.[48] In the Philippine and US trials, there was no requirement for the judges to have legal experience, and no legal advisor was present in court. Instead, one of the judges would be nominated as the Law Member, to make rulings on points of law and the admissibility of evidence. There was no requirement for the law member to have legal experience or legal qualifications.[49]

Tribunals were not required to publish reasons for their decisions, and they usually did not.[50] Practical reasons were largely responsible, but in addition, considering that the trials were a new step in international criminal law, there was a benefit in allowing the courts wide discretion in applying doctrines, including command responsibility. The Philippines tribunals more often provided written reasons than the tribunals of other nations, especially when the accused's crimes were particularly egregious. Such judgments, however, were generally more concerned with elaborating the moral failings of the accused, rather than the legal implications of the trial.[51]

There was no formal system of appeal, but if the accused was found guilty, he could lodge a basic appeal against the verdict or sentence of the court in a petition document. Petitions usually contained character references from members

46. Piccigallo, *The Japanese on Trial*, 36–37, 98, 125, 188.
47. John Pritchard, 'The Historical Experience of British War Crimes Courts in the Far East, 1946–1948', *International Relations* 6 (1978): 322–23; D. C. S. Sissons, 'The Australian War Crimes Trials and Investigations (1942–51)', in *Bridging Australia and Japan Volume 2: The Writings of David Sissons, Historian and Political Scientist*, ed. Keiko Tamura and Arthur Stockwin (ANU Press: 2020), 83.
48. Sissons, 'The Australian War Crimes Trials and Investigations (1942–51)', 22.
49. Piccigallo, *The Japanese on Trial*, 37, 188; Chamberlain, *A Reckoning*, 64.
50. Suzannah Linton, 'Introduction', in Linton, *Hong Kong's War Crimes Trials*, 1.
51. NARA, RG331, Supreme Commander for the Allied Powers, Legal Section, Prosecution Division, *Philippines versus Various Japanese War Criminals*, Case File, 1947–1949, Box 1688, *Philippines v Sato So*, Trial Transcript, 550–51.

of the accused's family and community in Japan, occasionally from senior officers, and in at least one instance, from a member of the Japanese royal family.[52] Petitions would often argue that the procedure of the tribunal had been manifestly unjust, usually in regard to the type of evidence submitted to the court: objections were made, for example, to the reliance on hearsay or on written affidavits. The substance of a petition was naturally limited, however, as there was no written judgment to argue against. As the tribunals were not bound by precedent, moreover, there was no basis for comparison that might have enabled an argument that doctrines had been improperly interpreted and applied, or that sentences were too harsh.

All four national jurisdictions examined here used a post-trial review to balance the limited legal experience of the bench, as well as the lack of dissemination of reasoned decisions. For the UK and Australia, the review was conducted by the Judge Advocate, who had legal training. The Judge Advocate wrote a summary of the proceedings, which was then forwarded, along with any petition, to the Judge Advocate General (JAG), a senior legal expert. The JAG would provide a thorough review of the summary, as well as the trial transcript, together with a report of the trial and a non-binding recommendation on whether the sentence should be upheld. The JAG's report was then sent to a Confirming Officer, who could reject, accept, or modify the sentence of the court. For the Australian trials, the Confirming Officer was the commander-in-chief of the army. In the UK, it was the military commander of the district in which the trial had been held, usually a major-general. The recommendations within the JAG's report were often followed, but not always.[53]

The US and Philippine post-trial review followed the same broad steps as for UK and Australian trials. A team of civilian and military lawyers would review the trial transcript and evidence to identify any errors that might have prejudiced the accused's case. This review was then sent to the military's staff advocate general, who made his final recommendations before sending the trial material and reviews to the convening authority, who was usually the general or admiral in command of the area in which the trial had been held. The convening authority could alter the sentence in any way he felt was necessary. Death sentences for US trials had to be signed off by General Douglas MacArthur, in his capacity as Supreme Commander for the Allied Powers, and for Philippines trials by the Philippine president.[54]

52. NARA, RG153, Records of the Office of the Judge Advocate General (Army), War Crimes Branch, Case Files 1944–49, Box 881, *USA v Ichinoe Kimiya and Six Others*, Petition of Ichinoe Kimiya, 12–13.
53. Aszkielowicz, *The Australian Pursuit of Japanese War Criminals*, 46–47; Pritchard, 'The Historical Experience of British War Crimes Courts in the Far East, 1946–1948', 322–23.
54. Piccigallo, *The Japanese on Trial*, 36–38; Chamberlain, *A Reckoning*, 94–95.

The level of oversight offered by the post-trial reviews was inconsistent. Some reviews displayed a careful analysis of the arguments used in court and a detailed discussion of what evidence had been raised and how it had been used. Other reviews were little more than a restatement of the prosecution's closing argument. Some reviewers complained about the length and complexity of the trials, on the grounds that it was almost impossible to keep track of what had happened in court. Interpretations of command responsibility were also inconsistent: some reviewers considered that convicted war criminals should have their sentence reduced because of a particularly strict interpretation of the doctrine, while others did not.

The command responsibility proceedings were a major component of the trial program, so it is surprising that neither review staff, nor more senior policymakers, ever issued clear directions on how the doctrine should be interpreted and applied. While it is true that many tribunal judges did not have legal training, this was not the determinative factor in the inconsistent application of the doctrine. Rather, inconsistency arose primarily because, at multiple levels within the investigation and trial process, the question of exactly what duties, responsibilities, and expectations could be placed on a commander was never settled.

Refining Command Responsibility on the Run: The Yamashita Case

By the time of the Japanese surrender in August 1945, the Allied authorities had established the legal basis of the trials and created a framework that would be flexible enough to prosecute suspects across the chain of command to achieve substantive justice. Despite all the months of planning, however, the doctrine of command responsibility remained uncertain at the beginning of the trials. Only the application of the principle in actual proceedings could clarify how it would work. The key case was the prosecution in Manila of Lieutenant-General Yamashita Tomoyuki for failing to control his subordinates, who had committed war crimes in the Philippines in February 1945.[55] The fact the first major Allied war crimes trial in the Pacific centred on command responsibility highlights the importance to the Allied authorities of bringing senior commanders to justice for Japanese war crimes.

During the Battle of Manila (February–March 1945), approximately 100,000 civilians died, many at the hands of Japanese soldiers carrying out summary executions of suspected guerrillas. Thousands of civilians were tortured and raped.[56]

55. Anne-Marie Prévost, 'Race and War Crimes: The 1945 Trial of General Tomoyuki Yamashita', *Human Rights Quarterly* 14 (1992): 307–9.
56. Antony Beevor, *The Second World War* (Little, Brown, and Company, 2012), 695; Richard Connaughton, John Pimlott, and Duncan Anderson, *The Battle for Manila: The Most Devastating Untold Story of World War II* (Bloomsbury, 1995), 13.

During this time, moreover, Allied POWs under the control of Yamashita's subordinates throughout the Philippines were starving and had little access to medicine.[57] Yamashita was charged not with directly committing war crimes himself, but rather with having done nothing to prevent, halt, or punish his subordinates who had committed atrocities. The Yamashita trial created a crucial basis for numerous other prosecutions of commanders who had not directly taken part in war crimes.

Yamashita was tried before a bench of five generals from the US military, none of whom had commanded armies in the field or had any legal training.[58] Yamashita's conduct during the Japanese defence of the Philippines, and the overall tactical situation, were heavily scrutinised in the trial. Yamashita had assumed formal command of Japanese forces in the Philippines, which had been occupied by Japan since 1942, in October 1944, just eleven days before the US counter-offensive began. His headquarters, located near the city of Baguio on the island of Luzon, were some 250 km from Manila, and his command had been severely hampered by poor planning at higher levels and by serious logistical difficulties. He had had little time to familiarise himself with the command structure of Japanese forces in the Philippines or with the existing Japanese defence plans. Many of Yamashita's soldiers were poorly trained and ill-disciplined.[59]

Furthermore, Yamashita shared his command with the Imperial Japanese Navy, which had partial responsibility for the defence of the Philippines. Yamashita's command structure controlled the land operations conducted by the navy's troops. The naval commander, Rear Admiral Iwabuchi Sanji, however, retained control over other naval operations, including mining of the harbour at Manila and the destruction of Japanese supplies that could not be removed from the city.[60] Because of these duties, a sizeable naval ground force stayed in Manila to support naval operations, despite original plans to maintain only a small military force in the city. Yamashita's orders to abandon the city were never fully carried out, largely due to Iwabuchi's intransigence. US forces, moreover, had surrounded straggling Japanese forces in the city.[61]

Like most other US offensives in the Pacific at this late stage of the war, the American attack on the Philippines was characterised by overwhelming firepower and air supremacy. Japanese supply lines and communications were cut, leaving many units isolated from Yamashita's command. Yamashita's headquarters were

57. Chamberlain, *A Reckoning*, 31–34.
58. Richard Lael, *The Yamashita Precedent: War Crimes and Command Responsibility* (Scholarly Resources, 1982), 88.
59. Bruce Landrum, 'The Yamashita War Crimes Trial: Command Responsibility Then and Now', *Military Law Review* 149 (1995): 293–95.
60. Prévost, 'Race and War Crimes', 313.
61. Spector, *Eagle Against the Sun*, 523–24; Lael, *The Yamashita Precedent*, 27.

also repeatedly bombed.[62] US forces advanced on Manila in January 1945 and had fully encircled the city by 12 February. The naval forces were trapped in the city, and heavy fighting began. Many of the defenders, aware that they were fighting to the death, drank heavily, and began to rape, torture, and murder civilians. US forces relied on heavy artillery to dislodge the defenders.[63] It is likely that a significant proportion of the civilian death toll was caused by the mass artillery used by the US army, but all deaths were nonetheless attributed to Japanese actions.[64]

Outside of Manila, Philippine guerrillas, buoyed by the US invasion, inflicted heavy losses on Japanese soldiers and their supplies. In response, the Imperial Japanese Army conducted widespread counter-guerrilla raids. Under international law, guerrillas were not considered as legitimate combatants and could face summary execution if they were captured. Thus, such operations did not necessarily constitute a war crime. The Japanese army, however, conducting operations in circumstances in which it was unclear who was a civilian and who was a guerrilla, undoubtedly killed thousands of non-combatant civilians alongside legitimate targets.[65]

As well as committing widespread crimes against Philippine civilians, units under Yamashita's command had also mistreated POWs. The army personnel under Yamashita's command included units responsible for the care of POWs, most of whom had been captured in 1942 following the initial Japanese victory in the Philippines. Many prisoners had suffered during the war from insufficient food and medicine. By the time US forces invaded the Philippines in 1944, supplies for POWs were already stretched. The further destruction of Japanese supply lines exacerbated the shortages. The imminent prospect of the US invasion had sometimes heightened the danger for POWs. On 14 December 1944, on the Philippine island of Palawan, some of Yamashita's subordinates killed 139 US POWs in an infamous massacre. The killings were apparently carried out after Japanese scouts spotted a possible invasion fleet, to prevent the captives from being liberated and possibly aiding the invasion force.[66]

Like defendants at many other war crimes trials, Yamashita faced only a single charge. In his case, the charge was that he had 'unlawfully disregarded and failed to discharge his duty as commander to control the operations of the members of his command, permitting them to commit brutal atrocities and

62. Beevor, *The Second World War*, 695.
63. Spector, *Eagle Against the Sun*, 520–24.
64. Allan A. Ryan, *Yamashita's Ghost: War Crimes, MacArthur's Justice, and Command Accountability* (University Press of Kansas, 2012), 41–49.
65. Landrum, 'The Yamashita War Crimes Trial', 294.
66. Richard C. Looman, 'Escape from Palawan', *Leatherneck: Magazine of the Marines* 28 (1945): 66–68.

other high crimes'. This charge was then elaborated through particulars, also known as specifications, which gave the details of the alleged crimes, such as murder or torture. At Yamashita's arraignment, the prosecution detailed sixty-four particulars of the charge, with an additional fifty-nine particulars provided two weeks later.[67] The decision to split the delivery of the particulars in two, and to provide the second half later, was controversial, as it limited the amount of time the defence had to draft an answer to part of the prosecution's case.[68]

The charge against Yamashita had two components. The first was that he had 'unlawfully disregarded and failed to discharge his duty as commander to control the operations of the members of his command'. When read in isolation from the rest of the charge, the legal implication is that Yamashita was held responsible for what was essentially criminal negligence. However, when this part is read in conjunction with the second component of the charge, 'permitting them to commit brutal atrocities and other high crimes', the nature of the crime changes: because 'permitting' constitutes an action, the implication is that Yamashita performed a key role in the crimes of his subordinates. This wording suggests that the prosecutors did not see Yamashita's failure to control the members of his command as a mistake or oversight, but rather as a necessary component of a wilful plan by Yamashita to commit atrocities. It is likely that the prosecutors divided the charge into the two components to increase the chances of securing a conviction against Yamashita. If the tribunal agreed that Yamashita had wilfully allowed his subordinates to commit war crimes, then prosecutors would secure a harsher sentence. If, however, the tribunal did not find that Yamashita's negligence had been wilful, it could still find that it was criminal in its extent.

The prosecution brought forward large amounts of documentary evidence against Yamashita, as well as over 200 witnesses.[69] The evidence showed that members of Yamashita's command had committed widespread war crimes during the defence of the Philippines. The reason the prosecution tendered so much evidence was most likely that no single piece of evidence showed that Yamashita had actual knowledge that the crimes had occurred. The prosecution argued that the sheer number of crimes, perpetrated over several weeks and across multiple geographical locations, meant that it was impossible for Yamashita not to have known that the crimes had been committed.[70] From the prosecution's viewpoint, the scale of the crimes meant that since Yamashita must have known of them yet

67. *United States of America vs Tomoyuki Yamashita*, vol. I, archived at [https://www.legal-tools.org/doc/dda9f9/pdf/], 38–51.
68. Reel, *The Case of General Yamashita*, 76–77; Prévost, 'Race and War Crimes', 317.
69. *United States of America vs Yamashita Tomoyuki*, vol. XXXIV, archived at [https://www.legal-tools.org/doc/578212/pdf/], 4061.
70. Courtney Whitney, *The Case of General Yamashita: A Memorandum* (Supreme Commander for the Allied Powers, 1949), 61–62.

had done nothing to stop them, he must have ordered them. Alternatively, his failure to stop the crimes meant that he had permitted them to occur, and thus his failure to halt the crimes was essentially the same as ordering them.

The prosecution's argument was novel in the field of modern international criminal law and thus was entirely unfamiliar to the defence lawyers. Faced with charges they had never encountered, the defence lawyers responded with a multi-faceted argument. The first part of the defence's case was that the charge did not specify the carrying out of an actual war crime that was recognised in international law. According to the defence, the charge was invalid because it was supported by no precedent. The second part was that the prosecution had failed to raise any evidence that showed Yamashita had known of the crimes, which was true. This aspect of the defence's case ignored the basic premise of the prosecution's argument. For the prosecution, the fact that there was no direct link between Yamashita and the crimes was irrelevant. One of two things must have been true, in this view. The very fact that the crimes were so widespread may have given Yamashita constructive knowledge that the crimes were occurring; that is, he may have had enough information before him to deduce that his subordinates were committing crimes. In this circumstance, Yamashita had had a duty to stop the crimes. The other possibility, for the prosecution, was that Yamashita had ordered the crimes. Finally, the defence argued that the circumstances in which the crimes took place meant that Yamashita could not have known that crimes were being committed. US forces had destroyed Japanese lines of supply and communication, and Yamashita's command post was far from Manila by road. Yamashita had thus been cut off from Manila, where crimes had been most widespread, and therefore had had no reasonable way of knowing that the crimes were occurring or of preventing them, in the defence's view.[71]

The tribunal found Yamashita guilty and sentenced him to death. The Yamashita case was one of the few US trials where a written judgment was provided.[72] The bench probably felt it necessary to explain how the evidence had been applied and how the doctrine of command responsibility had operated because both the tribunal procedure and the charge itself were ground-breaking, and it was clear that they would serve as the basis for other prosecutions.

The written judgment shows that the tribunal applied command responsibility through two modes of reasoning.[73] The first was that the scope of the crimes was so significant and widespread that Yamashita must have known that they were occurring yet had failed to take steps to stop them. Thus, the very fact

71. Reel, *The Case of General Yamashita*, 152–62.
72. *United States of America vs Yamashita Tomoyuki*, vol. XXXIV, 4053–63.
73. Andrew D. Mitchell, 'Failure to Halt, Prevent, or Punish: The Doctrine of Command Responsibility for War Crimes', *Sydney Law Review* 22 (2000): 390.

that the crimes were widespread necessarily meant that Yamashita had actual knowledge of them. The second line of reasoning was that widespread crimes could only be committed because Yamashita had failed in his duty to uncover the earlier instances of atrocities.[74] According to the tribunal, because the crimes were widespread in nature and had occurred across multiple areas and during several months of Yamashita's command, his failure to uncover and halt or punish them was criminally negligent.[75]

Yamashita's defence lawyers appealed the decision of the tribunal to the Supreme Court of the United States on the basis that the Manila tribunal had been unconstitutional, and that the US military did not have jurisdiction to try Yamashita. The defence argued that since the US and Japan had now ceased hostilities, and in view of the fact that the US government was functioning normally at the time of the trial, using a military commission, rather than a civilian court, had been improper. Furthermore, since the charge against Yamashita was without precedent, the trial was invalid, according to the defence, because without an established charge, Yamashita had nothing to answer to.[76] The appeal failed. In 1942, the Supreme Court had already endorsed the prosecution of foreign nationals before military tribunals when there was an established government. The Supreme Court also held that the charge against Yamashita was valid even without specific precedent, on the grounds that international laws and customs required military units to be led by a responsible commander, and that that necessarily meant a commander could be held legally responsible for the acts of his subordinates.[77] The fact that the Supreme Court even considered an appeal, however, was a matter of concern for the US military. The regulations governing the trials were subsequently changed to limit further appeals to civilian courts.[78]

Applying Yamashita

The Yamashita trial was crucial for two reasons. The first and more basic was that it showed that commanders could be held liable for crimes committed by their subordinates. The trial thus played an important part in the significant change to the operation of international criminal law in the immediate post-war years. Not only could individual leaders of a nation be held responsible for acts of

74. W. H. Parks, 'Command Responsibility for War Crimes', *Military Law Review* 62 (1973): 30–46.
75. *United States of America vs Yamashita Tomoyuki*, vol. XXXIV, 4061–63.
76. George F. Guy, 'The Defence of General Yamashita', *United States Air Force Academy Journal of Legal Studies* 215 (1995): 228–31.
77. Lael, *The Yamashita Precedent*, 101–8; *Gideon Boas and Lisa Lee, 'Command Responsibility and Other Grounds of Criminal Responsibility', in Fitzpatrick, McCormack, and Morris, ed., Australia's War Crimes Trials 1945–51, 145.*
78. Lael, *The Yamashita Precedent*, 99.

aggression and war crimes, as shown in the Tokyo and Nuremberg tribunals, but so too could individual military officers. The Yamashita case served not only as a strictly legal precedent, but also as a sign of a transition in international criminal law to a greater emphasis on substantive justice, where responsibility for war crimes is shared between actual perpetrators and those who ordered the crimes or had been in a position to stop the crimes from happening.

Second, the way in which the Yamashita trial was conducted served as a loose framework for further command responsibility prosecutions. The basic premises of the prosecution and defence arguments in the Yamashita proceedings were used frequently at other command responsibility trials run by the Allies, including at the IMTFE, at subsequent national trials, and at Allied trials of German suspects; indeed, the Yamashita trial was sometimes cited as a specific precedent.[79] The doctrine of command responsibility is deployed when there is no clear evidence of a commander ordering or taking part in a crime: if clear evidence existed, the defendant would have been charged with directly committing the ordered crime. When strong evidence is not present, the prosecution needs to show that there are nevertheless reasons to hold a commander liable. The Yamashita trial demonstrated how a commander could be convicted even in the absence of strong evidence of his guilt.

In subsequent trials, as in the Yamashita case, prosecutors would usually amass an overwhelming amount of evidence to show that the commander must have known, or ought to have known, that the alleged crimes were taking place. Alternatively, the prosecution would attempt to use the same tactic as in Yamashita, arguing that the commanding officer must have ordered the crimes, because they were numerous or widespread. In such cases, the prosecution would contend that although there was no direct evidence to show that the accused had ordered the crimes, strong circumstantial evidence pointed towards such a conclusion. For the defence, the only tactic with a chance of succeeding, other than establishing that the commander had been misidentified, was to show that he had not in fact known that the crimes were occurring and could not reasonably have known.

At the end of 1945, Allied militaries were well positioned to begin large-scale prosecutions of suspected Japanese war criminals, including commanders. Prosecutors had a framework that enabled the trials to proceed, even where there was no clear evidence that would have sustained a *Prima Facie* case in domestic

79. National Archives of Australia, Canberra, R125: War Crimes Trial: Proceedings of Military Tribunal, Lieutenant General Baba Masao, Part B, archived at [https://www.legal-tools.org/uploads/tx_ltpdb/ICWC24329MasaoBaba01.pdf], Prosecutor's Opening Address, 41; NARA, RG331, Supreme Commander for the Allied Powers, Legal Section, Prosecution Division, *USA versus Japanese War Criminals*, Case File, Box 1579, *United States of America vs Akira Nagahama*, 915.

courts. The standard of what constituted acceptable evidence had been relaxed, and the scope of the targets against whom such evidence could be applied had been greatly broadened by the doctrine of command responsibility. The US prosecution of Yamashita had created a framework for further command responsibility trials, including at the IMTFE. The Yamashita trial had also supported an application of the doctrine that was vague enough to allow considerable latitude in the courtroom. Such latitude would serve to make the doctrine a powerful prosecution tool in subsequent trials.

2
Summary Execution

During the Second World War, Japanese military personnel carried out summary executions in several different circumstances. A summary execution takes place when there is no trial before a sentence is carried out, or when a trial does take place, but the conduct of the trial is so improper that no result can be classed as a genuine judicial finding. Without a proper trial, the execution is classified as murder, rather than as a legitimate punishment. Japanese soldiers summarily executed Allied airmen who were captured after crash-landing in Japanese-occupied territory.[1] At prisoner of war (POW) camps, Japanese guards sometimes illegally killed captives. These executions were usually carried out as an example of what could happen if prisoners broke camp rules, especially if they escaped, stole food, or communicated with people outside the camp.[2] Civilians in occupied territories could be killed if they were suspected of being spies or guerrillas, or during military reprisals for guerrilla attacks.[3]

Summary executions differed from massacres for two interrelated reasons. Summary executions were generally carried out as a form of quasi-judicial punishment for real or perceived breaches of Japanese laws and rules. For this reason, there were only a small number of victims, usually under ten. Massacres, on the other hand, were used to dispose of potentially dangerous groups, as in

1. Tristan Moss and Georgina Fitzpatrick, 'Crimes Against Captured Airmen', in *Australia's War Crimes Trials 1945–51*, ed. Georgina Fitzpatrick, Tim McCormack, and Narrelle Morris (Brill-Nijhoff, 2016), 239; Timothy Lang Francis, 'To Dispose of the Prisoners: The Japanese Execution of American Aircrew at Fukuoka, Japan, During 1945', *Pacific Historical Review* 66 (1997): 469–501.
2. National Archives of Australia (hereafter NAA), War Crimes Trial of Ichise Shinichi, and Five Others, archived at [https://recordsearch.naa.gov.au/SearchNRetrieve/Interface/ViewImage.aspx?B=722845]; NAA, War Crimes Trial of Hoshijima Susumu, archived at [https://recordsearch.naa.gov.au/SearchNRetrieve/Interface/ViewImage.aspx?B=1900164]; National Archives (UK), Kew (hereafter TNA), WO 235/862, Trial of Takasaki Shinji and One Other.
3. Sharon W. Chamberlain, *A Reckoning: Philippine Trials of Japanese War Criminals* (University of Wisconsin Press, 2019), 29–35; Geok Boi Lee, *The Syonan Years: Singapore Under Japanese Rule 1942–1945* (National Archives of Singapore, 2005), 308.

the Singapore *sook ching* massacre of February–March 1942, in which at least 5,000 Chinese civilian men were killed because they were considered likely to rebel against the Japanese occupation.[4] Massacres also occurred when there were large numbers of inconvenient prisoners, as in the killing of approximately 150 wounded Australian soldiers at Parit Sulong, Malaya, on 23 January 1942, at a time when Japanese forces were rapidly advancing towards Singapore and did not have enough men or material to care for such a large number of prisoners.[5]

Allied prosecutors brought large numbers of Japanese suspects to trial for summary executions. Command responsibility served as an important tool in prosecuting officers who had been in command of the soldiers who had actually carried out such killings. Many commanders were held responsible for the orders they had given to execute prisoners. These prosecutions reflected a foundational understanding of command responsibility: the officer was held criminally responsible for a command he had given. Some officers chose to admit their responsibility, probably in an attempt to protect other personnel by discouraging investigations into their fellow officers and asserting that their subordinates had acted under superior orders. In these circumstances, Allied prosecutors could rely on assessments of responsibility and guilt that derived from domestic criminal law and common understanding. In other cases, however, officers were prosecuted for their failure to prevent, halt, or punish subordinates who had apparently carried out an execution independently of the commander's orders. The interpretation of command responsibility on which this approach was based had first been used in the Yamashita trial. In such cases, Allied war crimes investigators and prosecutors seem to have used command responsibility because they strongly suspected that a superior officer had ordered or in some other way had sanctioned the execution but had no evidence to prove it.

In this chapter I show that in using command responsibility to achieve justice for the victims of summary executions, prosecutors, and, in many cases, tribunals, held Japanese officers to extremely high standards that pushed the limits of what could reasonably be expected of the commander of a combat force. As demonstrated in the previous chapter, command responsibility had been used for the first time in the Yamashita trial because, in the view of prosecutors, Yamashita's subordinates had committed crimes on such a wide scale that either Yamashita must have known and done nothing, or he had been criminally negligent in failing to uncover the crimes. In most of the summary execution trials,

4. Hayashi Hirofumi, 'The Battle of Singapore, the Massacre of Chinese and Understanding of the Issue in Postwar Japan', *The Asia-Pacific Journal: Japan Focus* 7 (2009): 2; Yuma Totani, *Justice in Asia and the Pacific Region, 1945–1952: Allied War Crimes Prosecutions* (Cambridge University Press, 2015), 145–47.
5. Lynette Ramsay Silver, *The Bridge at Parit Sulong: An Investigation of Mass Murder* (The Watermark Press, 2004); Gilbert Mant, *Massacre at Parit Sulong* (Kangaroo Press, 1995).

by contrast, commanders were held criminally responsible for a single execution. Thus, there usually was no established pattern of criminal behaviour that should have alerted a commander to the fact that his subordinates were committing war crimes. The decision to hold such officers responsible for a single, isolated crime which they had not personally committed, and possibly in the absence of evidence that the commander had ordered the execution, is perhaps the most prominent example of the 'stern justice' that Allied governments had foreshadowed in the 1945 Potsdam Declaration. The severe punishment meted out to many officers who were found guilty reflects an understanding of command that assumed complete control over subordinates.

Holding commanders absolutely liable for isolated crimes reflected two elements of the war crimes trials. First, Allied personnel working on the trials often harboured an underlying suspicion that officers had in fact ordered the executions, even when insufficient evidence was presented in court to support this level of involvement. As a result, command responsibility was deployed in a way that allowed Allied courts to punish accused officers as if they had ordered the execution to take place. The suspicion or assumption that accused officers had ordered the crime made such an approach appear acceptable. Second, in cases where there was no such suspicion, holding an officer strictly or absolutely liable for the crimes of his subordinates gave the Allies an opportunity to create a lasting deterrent, in keeping with one of the key goals of the trials.[6]

The summary execution trials highlight the difficulty of defining what command was, and how that definition affected responsibility for war crimes. Many of the lower-ranking officers charged with command responsibility for summary executions seem to have had little control over what happened: the evidence presented in court often showed that the killings were isolated events that frequently were perpetrated as retribution for Allied attacks and Japanese losses. Though the accused repeatedly testified that they had had limited control over the crimes and that the circumstances in which executions took place had been chaotic and uncertain, the tribunals nearly always found that the accused officer nonetheless had exercised or could have exercised some kind of control over the situation. The assessment of the tribunals, in deeming that an officer had had control over a summary execution, points towards an understanding of command as absolute. The summary execution trials also highlight the fact that the tribunals could interpret and apply command responsibility in a variety of ways to reach the desired outcome, or to respond to different conceptions of command amongst tribunal staff. Overall, the summary execution trials suggest that the post-war proceedings were incapable of achieving uniformity in

6. *Report of Robert H. Jackson, U.S. Representative to the International Conference on Military Trials, London, 1945* (Washington DC: US Department of State, 1949), 46–49.

defining what command was and what it entailed, and in turn, how command responsibility should be interpreted and applied.

Trials for Summary Executions of Captured Airmen

Many Allied trials of Japanese military personnel for summary executions resulted from the killing of Allied flight crew who had crashed in Japanese-occupied territory during the war. Such trials held special importance for Allied authorities because wartime Japanese military regulations had legitimised the killing of downed aviators.[7] The Allies wished to reject this line of argument decisively by labelling such killings as summary executions, and to bring those who had ordered them to account. Yet, direct evidence of commanders' complicity was often lacking. In these circumstances, command responsibility was a very useful doctrine for prosecutors, who might need to do no more to secure a conviction than to prove that an officer had been formally in charge of subordinates who had carried out the execution.

The first Japanese executions of crashed Allied flight crew occurred early in the war. On 18 April 1942, sixteen US bombers launched from an aircraft carrier in the western Pacific and bombed six cities across Japan in the famous Doolittle Raids, so named after the commanding officer, Lieutenant-Colonel James Doolittle. Following the raids, one bomber landed in the Soviet Union, and fifteen crash-landed in Japanese-occupied China, where Japanese forces captured eight fliers.[8] Three of the captured airmen were charged before a Japanese military tribunal with strafing and bombing civilians. They were found guilty and executed in October 1942. A post-war Allied tribunal found that the Japanese military proceedings had been illegitimate, on the grounds that legal representation for the defendants had been inadequate, meaning that any verdict reached by the Japanese court should be considered void and that the resulting executions were effectively murders. Unlike many other Allied trials for the summary execution of captured airmen, those tried for killing the Doolittle fliers were sentenced to terms of imprisonment of five to nine years, principally because the accused were deemed to have acted under the superior orders of then Prime Minister Tōjō Hideki.[9]

---

7. Philip R. Piccigallo, *The Japanese on Trial: Allied War Crimes Operations in the East, 1945–1951* (University of Texas Press, 1979), 69–74; Jonathon F. Vance, 'Doolittle Raid', in *Encyclopedia of Prisoners of War and Internment*, ed. Jonathon F. Vance (Grey House Publishing, 2nd ed., 2006), 109–10.
8. Kramer J. Rohfleisch, 'Drawing the Battle Lines in the Pacific', in *The Army Air Force in World War II: Plans and Early Operations January 1939 to August 1942*, vol. 1, ed. Wesley F. Craven and James L. Cate (Chicago: University of Chicago Press, 1983), 442–44.
9. Piccigallo, *The Japanese on Trial*, 71–73.

To enable the prosecution of the Doolittle fliers, in August 1942 the Japanese military authorities retrospectively amended their military law, so that aircrew who attacked civilian targets could be tried as war criminals and could be sentenced to death or to terms of imprisonment of at least ten years.[10] For the remainder of the conflict, the Japanese military either expressly or implicitly relied on this law, known to Allied prosecutors as the 'Enemy Airmen's Law', to execute other captured aviators, in many cases without a trial, contrary to Japanese military law.[11] The Japanese military's refusal to grant ordinary prisoner-of-war protections to flight crew had been foreshadowed before the outbreak of war with the Western Allies. At a meeting of the International Committee of the Red Cross in Tokyo in 1934, the Japanese government considered whether to ratify the 1929 Geneva Convention, which outlined the proper treatment of captured military personnel. Though the Japanese Foreign Ministry was amenable to the 1929 provisions, the navy and army were not. In submissions to the emperor, naval officials took the view that the expanded protections would greatly increase the chance of Japan being aerially bombed in any future conflict, as enemy aviators would know that they would be treated well even if they bailed out over Japan.[12] For the Japanese navy, opting out of the treaty served as a potential deterrent to aerial bombing, because it theoretically gave the Japanese military the authority to treat captured airmen as they saw fit.

Though the first Japanese executions of captured Allied fliers occurred early in the war, most took place from the latter half of 1944 onwards, and especially in 1945. The increase in executions can be attributed to two factors. First, Japanese resentment of Allied fliers increased, because Allied bombing of the Japanese home islands had become markedly more frequent and effective. Intensive attacks on the Japanese home islands did not begin until late 1944. Bombings at first were not particularly destructive. From early 1945, however, the US air force began to carpet-bomb Japanese cities with incendiaries, with the intent of burning entire city districts, instead of individual military targets.[13] These new tactics meant that large portions of Japanese cities were devastated, and

10. A translation of the document into English is available as the 'Enemy Airmen's Law', National Archives and Records Administration, College Park, MD (hereafter NARA), RG125, Supreme Commander of the Allied Powers, War Crimes Branch, Misc. 1944–49, Box 10, 'PACMIRS, War Crimes Info (2)'; Piccigallo, *The Japanese on Trial*, 69–74; Vance, 'Doolittle Raid', 109–10; United Nations War Crimes Commission, *Law Reports of Trials of War Criminals* (His Majesty's Stationery Office, 1948), vol. 5, 1–5.
11. Francis, 'To Dispose of the Prisoners', 480–81.
12. Sarah Kovner, *Prisoners of the Empire: Inside Japanese POW Camps* (Harvard University Press, 2020), 34–35.
13. See E. B. Kerr, *Flames Over Tokyo: The U.S. Army Air Force's Incendiary Campaign Against Japan, 1944–1945* (D. I. Fine, 1991).

the civilian death toll increased dramatically.[14] In the face of such destruction, both Japanese soldiers and civilians were probably less inclined to take captured aircrew as prisoners, and might instead kill them shortly after capture as revenge for the bombing campaign.[15] According to a post-war US report, 254 American air-crash survivors were confirmed to have been executed during raids against the military districts of Nagoya, Osaka, Fukuoka, and Tokyo. At least thirty-one of them were executed at some point after the Japanese had surrendered.[16]

The second reason for the increase in executions is that more Allied airmen fell into Japanese hands outside Japan in the later stages of the war. Allied militaries, especially the US military, began to blockade most Japanese-occupied islands from mid-1943 and to subject them to heavy air attack. Inevitably, some Allied aircraft crashed. In the Netherlands Indies in particular, the Japanese military executed many captured airmen.[17] Airmen were also executed in Burma. These killings, too, may have been a form of revenge for the destruction caused by the Allies in Japan, or retaliation for the blockade.

The Japanese military's explicit criminalisation of the bombing of civilian targets created a legal justification for sentencing captured aviators to death, provided that a legitimate trial was carried out. For the Allies, the Enemy Airmen's Law presented a major problem once the war was over. Allied attacks had killed approximately 330,000 civilians during the 1944–1945 strategic bombing campaign in Japan, including the atomic bombings of Hiroshima and Nagasaki in August 1945.[18] For the Allies, failure to prosecute those who had executed airmen might have implied that the Japanese military's law to criminalise strategic bombing had been valid and that the executions were lawful, and thus, that Allied airmen who had bombed Japan, and the commanders who had overseen the bombings, were war criminals. Failure to pursue responsibility for the executions would consequently also have undermined the credibility of all the Allied prosecutions. Soldiers from the same militaries that were judging Japanese personnel had themselves bombed the enemy. Indeed, some Japanese defendants argued that wartime Allied brutality meant that the Allies were in no position to

14. Thomas R. H. Havens, *Valley of Darkness: The Japanese People and World War Two* (University Press of America, 1986), 176–85.
15. E. B. Kerr, *Surrender and Survival: The Experience of American POWs in the Pacific 1941–1945* (New William Morrow and Company, 1985), 264–68; Moss and Fitzpatrick, 'Crimes Against Captured Airmen', 248–52.
16. NARA, RG331 Supreme Commander of the Allied Powers, Legal Section, War Crimes Files, 1945–49, Publications, Box 1350, Richard Rudisill, 'History of the Investigation Division', 27.
17. Moss and Fitzpatrick, 'Crimes Against Captured Airmen', 247–55.
18. Mark Clapson, *The Blitz Companion: Aerial Warfare, Civilians, and the City Since 1911* (University of Westminster Press, 2019), 117; William W. Ralph, 'Improvised Destruction: Arnold, LeMay, and the Firebombing of Japan', *War in History* 13 (2006): 517; United States Strategic Bombing Survey, *Summary Report—Pacific War* (Government Printing Office, 1946), 43.

judge Japanese actions.[19] For the Allies, prosecuting those who had participated in the execution of airmen was an essential part of maintaining not only the morality, but also the legality, of the bombing campaign and therefore of the Allied war effort.

Command responsibility was a major tool in Allied war crimes proceedings arising from the Japanese execution of aviators. It was probably natural for prosecutors in such cases to assume that the executions had been ordered by Japanese officers, even in cases where they had no evidence to substantiate such suspicions. Although the Japanese hatred for Allied pilots is well documented, aviators were high-value prisoners. Regardless of whether the captured aviator was a pilot or fulfilled some other role, he would likely have had important technical or strategic information that would be valuable to the Japanese military. Prosecutors would therefore have expected that a decision to execute such a potentially valuable prisoner would have been made by a relatively senior officer. The Japanese military did make serious efforts to exploit such prisoners. One camp in Japan was used expressly for captured aviators, submariners, and others thought to possess valuable information: the Ofuna POW Camp near Yokohama. The Imperial Japanese Navy ran this camp, in which prisoners were interrogated, sometimes harshly, for technical information.[20]

Nevertheless, the navy did execute some airmen.[21] When preparing cases based on charges for such executions, Allied prosecutors were unlikely to assume that an enlisted soldier, non-commissioned officer (NCO), or even a junior officer had issued an order to kill a high-value prisoner such as an aviator on his own initiative. Rather, they would conclude that an order to execute the prisoner had been issued from higher up the chain of command.[22] This presumption would be strengthened if there were no evidence that any Japanese military personnel had been punished under their own military law for carrying out the execution.

For post-war investigators and prosecutors, finding evidence of direct orders to execute prisoners illegally, whether soldiers or civilians, was almost impossible. When there had been no trial, it was improbable in the first place, for one of two reasons, that Japanese officers would have written down an order to execute an airman. First, if an officer had known that the execution without trial was illegal, he would be unlikely to leave evidence of an order. A second

19. Sandra Wilson, Robert Cribb, Beatrice Trefalt, and Dean Aszkielowicz, *Japanese War Criminals: The Politics of Justice After the Second World War* (Columbia University Press, 2017), 88.
20. NARA, Rudisill, 'History of the Investigation Division', 21; Michael Sturma, *Surface and Destroy: The Submarine Gun War in the Pacific* (University of Kentucky Press, 2011), 165–66.
21. NARA, RG125, Judge Advocate General (Navy), Case Files of Pacific Area War Crimes Trials, 1944–1949, Box 8, *USA v Tanaka Masaharu and Five Others* (hereafter *USA v Tanaka*).
22. NAA, War Crimes Trial of Endo Shinichi, Charge Sheet, 1–2, archived at [https://recordsearch.naa.gov.au/SearchNRetrieve/Interface/ViewImage.aspx?B=739446].

possibility was that the officer in question genuinely thought the Enemy Airmen Law to be sufficient grounds to execute an airman and may have believed that the law itself functioned as an order, and that nothing further was necessary. Written orders that were issued may also have been destroyed. Throughout the Asia-Pacific region, Japanese officers destroyed documents before surrendering to Allied forces, and many documents were also destroyed by the Allied bombing of the Japanese home islands.[23]

A lack of written orders was not the only impediment to Allied prosecutions for summary executions. Allied investigators believed that Japanese officers had covered up such crimes: in some war crimes trials, officers were charged not only with command responsibility for the offence itself, but also with the attempted cover-up. Japanese efforts to ensure that summary executions never came to trial appeared to continue after the war's end. In one trial involving command responsibility for the execution of eight airmen who were captured and killed in Singapore sometime between February and August 1945, the principal charge against several of the accused was not that they were responsible for the executions, but rather that they had been accomplices to the crime, as they had attempted to destroy evidence after Japan's surrender.[24] According to Allied investigators, such efforts were part of a wider problem concerning the post-war destruction of documents. During the Allied occupation of Japan of 1945–1952, investigators enlisted demobilised Japanese officers through the First and Second Demobilisation Bureaus to help find documents for trials.[25] Many of these former Japanese officers were believed to have falsified or hidden documents to help suspected war criminals avoid prosecution. Investigators thought that it was a bigger issue for summary executions, because they suspected that those executions had occurred under written orders, though whether this was actually the case is unclear.[26] Because of all these difficulties, in trials for the execution of aviators, the majority of evidence consisted not of written documentation, but of direct testimony from Japanese military personnel suspected of having some connection to the execution, through actually carrying out the killing, ordering it, or being in command of soldiers, including junior officers, who had carried out the execution.

Testimony from Japanese suspects and witnesses usually did not paint a clear picture for prosecutors. Those who were accused of carrying out the actual execution almost invariably claimed that they had acted under superior orders,

23. See Kazufumi Hamai and Peter Mauch, 'The Wartime Destruction of the Japanese Diplomatic Record in Historical Perspective', in *Defamiliarizing Japan's Asia-Pacific War*, ed. W. Puck Brecher and Michael W. Myers (University of Hawaii Press, 2019), 17–33.
24. TNA, WO 235/1102, *UK v Fukudome Shigeru and Five Others.*
25. Wilson, Cribb, Trefalt, and Aszkielowicz, *Japanese War Criminals*, 131, 320n4.
26. NARA, Rudisill, 'History of the Investigation Division', 3, 21.

either from a direct superior, or, more vaguely, 'from headquarters'.[27] Claiming that an order had come from headquarters might have been an attempt to avoid directly naming a superior officer. It may also have been the case, however, that the subordinate genuinely did not know who had given the order.[28] When officers were tried for killing a captive, they often claimed they had assumed that a trial had been carried out, and that a lawful order to execute the prisoner had been issued. Whether or not the accused knew the origin of the instruction on which he claimed to have acted, he attempted to mitigate his responsibility on the grounds of superior orders. More senior officers accused of ordering an execution would claim that they had instructed that a trial be carried out, or that the execution had occurred without their knowledge.[29] Some officers were more forthcoming, openly admitting that they had ordered the execution and taking full responsibility.[30]

Though the problem of witness reliability was far from exclusive to cases involving the execution of aviators, it was particularly likely to arise in such trials. The reason is that the summary execution of aviators usually took place at Japanese headquarters or barracks in the Japanese home islands or in occupied areas. In either case, it is likely that the only witnesses would have been from the Japanese army or navy. Thus, the witnesses would have reason to dissemble, in order to protect themselves or their colleagues. When POWs were executed, by contrast, the killing usually took place at or near a POW camp, and other prisoners knew what had happened to the victims, either because they witnessed it, it was made clear to them by their guards, or there was no alternative explanation for the victims' disappearance. The summary execution of civilians, which in many cases took place during reprisal or anti-guerrilla operations, would usually be witnessed by locals. Though former POWs and local civilians may have had their own motivation to falsify evidence in such cases, there was usually a greater variety of witnesses whom the court could question to determine what had happened.

If there were no direct evidence to support a case for command responsibility, prosecutors in trials for summary executions as well as other crimes would normally depend on circumstantial evidence to secure a conviction. Circumstantial evidence does not directly implicate someone in a crime but instead relies on

27. Wilson, Cribb, Trefalt, and Aszkielowicz, *Japanese War Criminals*, 812.
28. Peter Mauch, 'The Showa Political Crisis, July 1940: The Imperial Japanese Army Courts a Breach with its Sovereign', *War in History* 27, no. 4 (2020): 672–73.
29. For example, NAA, War Crimes Trial of Okada Tametsugu, archived at [https://recordsearch.naa.gov.au/SearchNRetrieve/Interface/ViewImage.aspx?B=739444].
30. Sharon W. Chamberlain, 'Justice and Reconciliation: Postwar Philippine Trials of Japanese War Criminals in History and Memory' (unpublished PhD thesis, George Washington University, 2010), 73–74; Wilson, Cribb, Trefalt, and Aszkielowicz, *Japanese War Criminals*, 84–85.

an inference that the accused carried out the crime. For example, if an accused officer had been on duty at the time that an execution was ordered by telephone, the prosecution could raise such evidence as implying that he had passed on the execution order. Such evidence, however, would not constitute irrefutable proof that the accused was guilty.[31]

In cases that relied on circumstantial evidence, command responsibility was an attractive tool. For prosecutors, arguing a case based on circumstantial evidence alone is hard work. Though the tribunals were not strictly bound to the criminal law maxim that guilt should be established beyond a reasonable doubt, the common knowledge of the phrase, and its frequent invocation by defence counsel, meant that judges probably still required a high standard of proof.[32] By using the doctrine of command responsibility, the prosecutor could avoid relying solely on circumstantial evidence about the actual situation at the time the crime was committed. Proof that the officer had been in command, unlike circumstantial evidence, was not a matter of inference. Rather, it constituted direct evidence that the officer was responsible for the offence. His duty to oversee the actions of his subordinates, coupled with circumstantial evidence indicating that he had likely ordered or at least known of the execution, potentially made the prosecutor's job significantly easier. For these reasons, US military lawyers claimed that use of the doctrine in prosecutions for executions of airmen was highly successful, from investigation through to trial, though they did not substantiate this claim with statistical evidence.[33]

Flexible Use of the Doctrine: The Trial of Lieutenant-Colonel Ichinoe Kimiya

The relative ease with which command responsibility could be used to convict commanding officers can be seen in the trial of Lieutenant-Colonel Ichinoe Kimiya. Before a US military tribunal in Yokohama, between 22 December 1947 and 16 January 1948, Ichinoe and six other Japanese military personnel were tried for the execution of a downed US pilot at Tokyo on the night of 9/10 March 1945. At the trial, Ichinoe was found guilty of permitting members of the army under his control to execute the airman and was sentenced to death.[34]

31. Allison Marston Danner and Jenny S. Martinez, 'Guilty Associations: Joint Criminal Enterprise, Command Responsibility, and the Development of International Criminal Law', *California Law Review* 93 (2005): 123–25.
32. Alan B. Lyon, *Japanese War Crimes: The Trials of the Naoetsu Camp Guards* (Australian Military History Publications, 2000), 45.
33. NARA, Rudisill, 'History of the Investigation Division', 24–25.
34. NARA, RG153, Records of the Office of the Judge Advocate General (Army), War Crimes Branch, Case Files 1944–49, Box 881, *USA v Ichinoe Kimiya and Six Others* (hereafter *USA v Ichinoe*), Review of the Staff Judge Advocate, 1–5.

After the post-trial review, Ichinoe's sentence was commuted to twenty-five years' imprisonment. The trial itself shows how prosecutors could use command responsibility opportunistically to secure convictions when a case appeared to be falling apart and highlights the strong desire amongst Allied tribunal staff to convict Japanese officers. Combined, the trial and the post-trial review provide a prime example of competing understandings of what was expected and what was required of command.

Ichinoe's case concerned Lieutenant Leland Fishback, a survivor of a US B-29 bomber that crashed in the village of Itabashi, on the outskirts of Tokyo, on the night of 9 March 1945.[35] Fishback had been shot down while bombing Tokyo in what became known as the Great Tokyo Air Raid. Over 90,000 civilians died during the raid, and approximately forty square kilometres of Tokyo were destroyed.[36] Imperial Japanese Army (IJA) soldiers captured and killed Fishback after his plane crashed. At the post-war American trial for this offence, the defence attempted to use the destruction caused by the raid as mitigation for the crime of killing Fishback. Ichinoe, who at the time was administratively responsible for the imprisonment, and most likely the interrogation, of captured aircrew in the Tokyo region, apparently ordered via messenger that the injured airman be taken to hospital. The destruction caused by the raid, however, meant that the hospitals that had not been razed were beyond capacity, and Fishback was not taken to medical care.[37] Two days after the aviator had been captured, members of the Kenpeitai executed Fishback in an abandoned lot outside Tokyo.

The prosecution initially argued that Ichinoe had directly ordered the flier's execution, relying on confessions from members of the execution party, who claimed that they had acted under Ichinoe's orders.[38] Affidavit testimony from other subordinates of Ichinoe, however, then claimed that Ichinoe had ordered that the aviator be taken to hospital.[39] With this new evidence, the prosecution changed its argument to allege that Ichinoe had failed to control and restrain military personnel under his command to prevent them from killing the POW. The prosecution argued that despite the fact that Ichinoe had sent an order that Fishback was to be taken to hospital, he was nonetheless responsible for the execution. According to the prosecution, because Ichinoe was in charge of captured

35. Robert F. Dorr, *Mission to Tokyo: The American Airmen Who Took the War to Japan* (Voyageur Press, 2012), 46, 190.
36. Thomas R. Searle, 'It Made a Lot of Sense to Kill Skilled Workers: The Firebombing of Tokyo in March 1945', *The Journal of Military History* 66 (2002): 103; Gordon Daniels, 'The Great Tokyo Air Raid, 9–10 March 1945', in *Modern Japan: Aspects of History, Literature and Society*, ed. W. G. Beasley (Charles E. Tuttle Company, 1976), 124–29.
37. *USA v Ichinoe*, Trial Transcript, 118–26; *USA v Ichinoe*, Prosecution Exhibit 36, 'Interrogation of Sonobe Rokuro', 1–3.
38. *USA v Ichinoe*, Trial Transcript, 118–26.
39. *USA v Ichinoe*, Defence Exhibit A, 'Affidavit of Akisada Matsumura', 1–3.

aviators in the Tokyo region, the Kenpeitai party which executed Fishback had by definition acted under his command and control.[40]

That the prosecution changed the argument from direct order, or foundational command responsibility, to a broader command responsibility as used at the Yamashita trial, suggests two possibilities. The first is that the prosecution may have accepted that Ichinoe had ordered that Fishback be taken to hospital. The second possibility is that the prosecution did not believe the new evidence but did not have enough grounds to refute it. After all, the most damning evidence against Ichinoe came from Japanese soldiers who had a clear incentive to claim that he had ordered the execution: acting under superior orders usually led to lighter punishment for direct participants in a crime in the post-war trials, so there was every reason for those who had carried out the execution to blame Ichinoe. For the prosecutors, pursuing Ichinoe under a broader version of command responsibility was a safer bet in case the bench found the evidence favouring Ichinoe to be the more reliable. It also meant that the direct perpetrators would not be able to claim mitigation through superior orders, because the prosecutor was no longer arguing that Ichinoe had ordered the killing.

The tribunal's decision to pass the death sentence on Ichinoe, despite evidence that he had not ordered the crime, and in the face of evidence showing that he had taken steps to get Fishback to hospital, points towards an interpretation of command responsibility as a strict liability. In short, because of Ichinoe's position as a commander, he was considered automatically liable for crimes committed in his area of command. Acting on the principle of strict liability in this case would have been attractive to the judges, not only because it secured a conviction, but also because it potentially met one of the trials' key goals, that is, as acting as a deterrent.

The post-trial review of Ichinoe's case recommended mercy, indicating that Ichinoe's sentence should be commuted to fifteen years' imprisonment, a recommendation that was accepted by the confirming officer. The review lawyers argued that since Ichinoe had taken steps to prevent Fishback from being executed, there should be some degree of mitigation of sentence. The extent of mitigation should be limited, however, because the messenger whom Ichinoe had dispatched to ensure Fishback was sent to hospital was only a sergeant, rather than a commissioned officer. The review lawyers argued, on two grounds, that a more senior messenger ought to have been sent to ensure that Ichinoe's order was carried out. The first was that the firebombing of Tokyo on 9/10 March 1945 had caused a huge amount of damage, and so would have exacerbated Japanese hostility to aviators, increasing the risk that any captured airmen would be executed. The second ground was that the capturing party included officers from the

40. *USA v Ichinoe*, Trial Transcript, 252–54.

Kenpeitai.[41] What relevance the review lawyers attached to the Kenpeitai officers is unclear. The most likely explanation is that they expected the Kenpeitai to be more brutal, or that, because of their role as military police, they were more likely to act under their own direction. This argument corresponds with an interpretation of command responsibility as a separate offence of the superior, not as a strict liability: in this version, the commander's actions, rather than his formal position, are the key issues determining culpability.

Ichinoe's petition against his sentence and verdict may also have influenced the review lawyers. The great majority of petitions by convicted Japanese military personnel against their sentences followed a standard pattern and had little effect. Petitions typically contained positive character statements from the family of the convicted, as well as from members of his community, and emphasised that the accused's family and community were dependent on him in various ways. While Ichinoe's petition did include such material, it also incorporated a petition from Prince Chichibu, Emperor Hirohito's younger brother. Ichinoe had been Chichibu's staff officer in China. The Japanese government's loss of sovereignty under the Allied occupation, together with the provisions of the new constitution that came into force in 1946, meant that the Japanese imperial family had almost no formal power. Allied authorities nevertheless wanted to preserve the imperial institution in some form, in the belief that it could be used to bolster democracy in Japan.[42] It is thus possible that Chichibu's petition had some effect on Ichinoe's sentence.

The Ichinoe case shows how command responsibility could be used to hold officers responsible for single crimes that had occurred under their command. In most cases, using command responsibility for a single crime meant taking the view that the doctrine created a strict liability, in which commanders are held responsible because of their position of command and control, regardless of their personal conduct. This interpretation was eventually used to convict Ichinoe. If strict liability applies, it is irrelevant that the commander did not know that a crime had occurred, or that he took reasonable steps to prevent a crime from occurring.[43] The rationale behind strict liability is that a crime took place of such a serious nature that there must be legal consequences for those who, by virtue of their position, had the power to stop the crime from occurring, or to punish it if it did occur.[44]

41. *USA v Ichinoe*, JAG Review, 12–16.
42. Stephen S. Large, *Emperor Hirohito and Showa Japan: A Political Biography* (Routledge, 1992), 135–38.
43. Danner and Martinez, 'Guilty Associations', 120–26.
44. Chantal Meloni, 'Command Responsibility: Mode of Liability for the Crimes of Subordinates or Separate Offence of the Superior?', *Journal of International Criminal Justice* 5 (2007): 622–23.

In the prosecution of war crimes, strict liability had a controversial start, because findings of guilt on this basis often produced harsh punishments. A. Frank Reel, one of General Yamashita Tomoyuki's defence lawyers, wrote a scathing critique of the doctrine of command responsibility in 1949, which heavily influenced subsequent discussion.[45] Yamashita was found guilty partially through an interpretation of command responsibility that used strict liability, and had been sentenced to death and executed. Many other officers were also sentenced to death or to lengthy prison sentences by means of this interpretation of the doctrine. For prosecutors who were aware that Japanese military personnel had executed hundreds of aviators and other victims, strict liability would probably have appeared to be the appropriate way of pursuing commanding officers. From their point of view, commanding officers like Ichinoe were part of a wider disregard within the Japanese military for international standards, a disregard that resulted in the mistreatment of prisoners, torture of civilians, and execution of surrendered soldiers. Strict liability thus offered a convenient way of ensuring that officers like Ichinoe were held criminally responsible for what the Allies considered to be a widespread problem.[46]

If command responsibility was interpreted as a separate offence of the superior officer, by contrast, accused officers were held liable for failing to prevent a war crime, halt the crime, or punish their subordinates for committing the crime.[47] When a war crime was prosecuted as a separate offence, the commander's specific, personal action or inaction in response to a potential, ongoing, or already committed war crime was on trial. Interpreting command responsibility as a separate offence of the superior meant that the accused persons had the opportunity in court to show that they had taken reasonable steps to prevent, halt, or punish war crimes, and that they ought to be found not guilty.[48] The prosecution of Ichinoe initially rested on this interpretation of command responsibility, but the prospects of conviction were threatened by evidence that he had taken action to prevent a war crime from occurring when he ordered that Fishback be sent to hospital.

The two applications of command responsibility are not mutually exclusive, and the Ichinoe case provides an excellent example of the combination of the two interpretations within the trial process. Applying the doctrine as a strict liability, which means that a commander is automatically guilty, does not necessarily mean

45. A. Frank Reel, *The Case of General Yamashita* (University of Chicago Press, 1949).
46. Arthur T. O'Reilly, 'Command Responsibility: A Call to Realign the Doctrine with Principles of Individual Accountability and Retributive Justice', *Gonzaga Law Review* 40 (2004): 128.
47. W. H. Parks, 'Command Responsibility for War Crimes', *Military Law Review* 62 (1973): 30–35.
48. O'Reilly, 'Command Responsibility: A Call to Realign the Doctrine', 144–51; Anne-Marie Prévost, 'Race and War Crimes: The 1945 War Crimes Trial of General Tomoyuki Yamashita', *Human Rights Quarterly* 14 (1992): 327.

that the punishment will be the same as it would have been if the commander had committed the actual crime. That is, the court can hold officers strictly liable for the crime and then use the framework of the separate offence interpretation to measure the extent of their guilt. This is what happened in the Ichinoe case.

Ichinoe was found guilty of failing to prevent the execution of a captured aviator. He had had formal jurisdiction over the prisoner, but the execution was carried out by members of the Kenpeitai, who were not under Ichinoe's control. The mere fact that the prisoner himself was under Ichinoe's control meant that Ichinoe was strictly liable for any harm done to him. This explains why Ichinoe was found guilty. The court, as opposed to the legal reviewer, does not appear to have given much weight to Ichinoe's apparent attempt to ensure that the prisoner was taken to hospital. Here, the problem of applying the principle of strict liability is clear: relying solely on strict liability creates unacceptable judgments. By contrast, the reviewing authority challenged the judgment by analysing what steps Ichinoe had taken to prevent or halt the crime or to punish the perpetrators. For the reviewing authority, it was clear that Ichinoe had taken steps that had a reasonable prospect of preventing the crime from occurring. Nonetheless, as the reviewing authority also noted, the crime did occur, and he failed to punish the offenders.[49]

In effect, the trial and review stages of the legal process operated together to reconcile the two different interpretations of command responsibility. This process had significant procedural flaws. In the absence of a reasoned legal decision from the tribunal bench, the review lawyers did not have a clear record of the thinking of the bench to inform their own decision-making. The trial transcript and associated evidence provide a fair understanding of how the tribunal reached its decision; but in the interests of consistency and accuracy, there is no substitute for a reasoned decision. Furthermore, in all jurisdictions, the decision of the post-trial review was non-binding, and the confirming authority could reject it – and often did.

The Ichinoe trial shows perhaps the best version of the post-war trials, where unacceptable outcomes could be adjusted during review to provide a more reasonable result. Holding Ichinoe strictly liable for the aviator's execution – and then assessing the extent of his criminal liability by applying the separate offence test – resulted in the best of both worlds: a commander was held to a standard where he was responsible for his subordinates' acts, but this responsibility was measured by reference to his own actions. This two-stage approach to command responsibility, however, was rarely used. In this sense, the Ichinoe trial highlights one of the most pressing flaws with the command responsibility trials. Allied legal authorities, like the review lawyers who changed Ichinoe's sentence, never

49. *USA v Ichinoe*, JAG Review, 8–10.

made it clear to prosecutors or tribunals that holding commanders strictly liable and strictly guilty for war crimes was a flawed approach. Those who were best equipped to do so never cautioned against the potential long-term ramifications of opportunistically securing convictions and the harshest punishment.

Creating Criminal Liability for Failure to Prevent Executions: The Truk Airmen Case

Though some subordinate military personnel killed Allied captives on their own initiative, others asked their commander, or attempted to convince them, to kill captives. In typical cases, either the subordinate, usually an NCO or junior officer, would eventually take matters into his own hands without further reference to his commander, or the commander would give a non-committal answer on whether the execution should go ahead.[50] In both cases, the superior officer could be held responsible for the crime.

In these situations, there was a clear rationale in applying command responsibility, because the commander had known there was an increased likelihood that his subordinates would commit a war crime. The fact that the subordinate had suggested an execution put the commander on notice that a crime was probably going to occur. It then became his duty to prevent the execution from being carried out. To the prosecutors and judges in post-war trials, it seemed particularly unlikely that a superior officer who genuinely did not want a prisoner to be executed would fail to stop an execution from happening, especially if the commanding officer then failed to punish the subordinates who had instigated the execution. The reasoning was that if the officer really had ordered that the execution should not take place, only to find out later that his subordinates had disobeyed him, there ought to have been repercussions in the interests of maintaining discipline. For the prosecution, the fact that the commander failed to prevent the execution and then failed to punish his subordinates did not point to a genuine failure of command, either by negligence or incompetence. Rather, prosecutors assumed that the commanding officer had directly ordered the execution, and that his subordinates later covered for him. Without any supporting evidence, however, it was very difficult to prove that this was what had happened. In this situation, the doctrine of command responsibility provided a much easier method of holding officers to account in court than relying on circumstantial arguments.

50. NARA, RG153, Office of the Judge Advocate General, Case Files, 1944–1949, Box 1385, *USA v Toyama Minoru and Two Others*; NAA, War Crimes Trial of Odamura Toshitake, archived at [https://recordsearch.naa.gov.au/SearchNRetrieve/Interface/ViewImage.aspx?B=693091]; TNA, WO 235/883, *UK v Abe Keiichi and Three Others*.

One recurring problem for Allied investigators and prosecutors was ascertaining exactly who had been in command when a crime was committed. Though there were organisational charts that seemed to indicate clear reporting lines in the Japanese military, the actual chain of command in the field was usually more complicated. Colin Sleeman, a UK defence lawyer at the trials of Japanese war crimes suspects, noted that the roles of formal commanders were often virtually ceremonial, especially in garrison units. NCOs and junior officers made the majority of decisions, which would then be communicated upwards.[51] Indeed, throughout the Asia-Pacific war, Japanese NCOs and junior officers frequently took decisions independently of the chain of command.[52] Thus, actual command did not always lie where it ought to have, and inexperienced senior officers might be incapable of exercising their authority over more experienced junior officers and NCOs. In other cases, the superior officer was uninterested in the day-to-day running of his unit, and essentially delegated command to his subordinates. Such circumstances allowed junior personnel to instigate executions.

The US trial of Naval Captain Tanaka Masaharu and two of his subordinates, held on 5 November 1946 at Guam, is a clear example of how command could be interpreted as a duty to act, and shows how evidence of a superior officer's prior knowledge of his subordinate's intent to execute a prisoner could be used to establish criminal responsibility. The trial also highlights an interpretation of command responsibility that focussed primarily on the duty to prevent war crimes.[53]

Tanaka and his subordinates Ensign Yoshinuma Yoshiharu and Lieutenant Danzaki Tomeroku were prosecuted for the execution of seven unidentified US prisoners on Truk Atoll, in the Caroline Islands. How the prisoners came to be on the island and how long they had been there was never made clear in the trial. There is some evidence that Truk, as well as operating as a major base for the Japanese navy, was a waypoint for high-value prisoners captured on the front lines who were to be transported to Ofuna POW Camp in Japan for interrogation.[54] On 17 February 1944, Yoshinuma had asked his superior officer, Danzaki, to execute the seven prisoners who were in custody in a Japanese compound on the atoll. The request was transmitted to Captain Tanaka, who was Danzaki's superior. In court, Tanaka testified that he had verbally opposed the execution, but had nonetheless informed Yoshinuma that he, Yoshinuma, needed to

51. Colin Sleeman, 'Introduction', in *Trial of Gozawa Sadaichi and Nine Others*, ed. Colin Sleeman (William Hodge and Company, 1948), xxiv–xxviii.

52. On disobedience in the Japanese military up to 1936, see Danny Orbach, *Curse on This Country: The Rebellious Army of Imperial Japan* (Cornell University Press, 2017).

53. *USA v Tanaka*.

54. Louis Zamperini and David Rensin, *Devil at My Heels: A Heroic Olympian's Astonishing Story of Survival as a Japanese POW in World War II* (HarperCollins, 2003), 122–28, 139.

get permission from the area commander, Vice Admiral Kobayashi Masashi.[55] Later that day, Danzaki and Yoshinuma executed the seven POWs by varying methods, including bayoneting, shooting, and beheading, without permission. Japanese military personnel had held no trial for the prisoners, and indeed, it was unclear whether Vice Admiral Kobayashi's headquarters ever received a request for permission to execute them.[56] Tanaka was found guilty under command responsibility for the killing of the American prisoners and sentenced to death. He was executed on 24 September 1946. Tanaka's subordinates were sentenced to life imprisonment.[57]

The prosecution's case against Tanaka was relatively unconcerned with the exact nature of his involvement in the executions. For the prosecutor, it did not matter whether Tanaka had ordered the execution himself or had passed on an order from a superior. The fact that Tanaka had been aware of his subordinate's intention to execute the prisoners meant that he had failed to prevent the unlawful killings. The prosecution argued that Tanaka could have stopped the executions by virtue of his position of command.[58] Central to the prosecution's argument, though never made explicit in the trial, was that Tanaka not only could have prevented the execution, but, furthermore, should have done so. It was not enough to defer to the judgment of a superior; rather, he should have exercised the powers of his own office to prevent war crimes.

As in many trials for summary executions, the defendants gave no clear explanation of why the prisoners had been killed. At no point did any of the defendants allege that the prisoners had attempted to escape. The most likely reason for the executions is that Japanese personnel had wanted retribution for a large-scale attack by the US navy on Truk that had occurred on the same day. The US Operation Hailstone had effectively destroyed the Japanese base on Truk and had caused high casualties amongst the garrison troops.[59] Alternatively, the prisoners may have been killed to prevent them falling back into Allied hands; the garrison may have interpreted the Allied attack as the beginning of an invasion. The fact that the defendants did not explain clearly why the prisoners had been executed was likely an attempt to limit the scope of prosecutions. If motive had been determined, it would have contributed significantly to identifying who had been ultimately responsible for the killings.

55. *USA v Tanaka*, Trial Transcript, 82; *USA v Tanaka*, Certificate of Execution, Tanaka Masaharu.
56. *USA v Tanaka*, Trial Transcript, 62.
57. *USA v Tanaka*, Warrant of Execution; *USA v Tanaka*, Trial Transcript, 106–7.
58. *USA v Tanaka*, Prosecution's Opening Statement, 1–2, 7–12.
59. United States Strategic Bombing Survey (Pacific), *The Campaigns of the Pacific War* (United States Printing Office, 1946), archived at [https://www.ibiblio.org/hyperwar/AAF/USSBS/PTO-Campaigns/USSBS-PTO-9.html], 194–5.

The US investigation into the execution of the airmen on Truk extended beyond Tanaka and the execution party. Vice Admiral Kobayashi Masashi, the overall commander of the Truk forces, was interrogated in Sugamo Prison in Tokyo in April 1946 about the executions. To the American investigators, it seemed implausible that US airmen would be executed without approval from higher up the chain of command. Kobayashi denied knowing at the time that the executions had been carried out, which seemed improbable. In what appears to have been an attempt to force Kobayashi to talk about the executions, the interrogators explained how command responsibility would be used in forthcoming trials for the killings. They claimed that unless they could identify one individual who had directly ordered the executions, everyone would be held responsible: 'Captain Tanaka, Admiral Wakabayashi [Kobayashi's staff officer], yourself, the Navy ministery [*sic*] and the Navy General Staff officials concerned' would all be tried for any connection they might have had to the crime.[60]

The interrogators' threat to use command responsibility against the staff officer Kobayashi, alongside a multitude of other officers, may well have been an effort to force Kobayashi to name the person who had ordered the crime. Unsurprisingly, interrogators often struggled to determine who was ultimately responsible, as Japanese military personnel, especially officers, were unlikely to discuss war crimes during interrogations. Using the doctrine of command responsibility might become an easy way to break open a case, as the threat of prosecutions, starting with direct perpetrators and running all the way up the chain of command, meant there was a genuine inducement for senior officers to talk about crimes with the prosecution team in order to protect subordinates or to protect themselves.

The interrogators' statement to Kobayashi about how command responsibility prosecutions would be carried out was unrealistic. Rather than establishing multiple trials for the same crime, in which suspects from each 'level' of the chain of command would be prosecuted in individual trials, it was far more common for all suspects from a unit to be tried in one proceeding. When there was a large number of suspects, it would have been overly burdensome for the Allied military authorities to hold multiple trials for the same crime. Nonetheless, the idea that individual trials had in fact been routinely held across the chain of command persisted after the tribunals ended. Earl Mountbatten of Burma, Supreme Allied Commander of South East Asia Command, claimed that command responsibility trials had relied on foundational trials, in which the direct perpetrators had been tried, before further trials of higher-ranking commanders were opened,

60. NARA, RG125, Judge Advocate General (Navy), Records Re Interrogations of Japanese Witnesses and Defendants in War Crimes Cases, 1945–1949, Box 3, Folder Kobayashi, Masashi, 'Interview with Kobayashi Masashi, Retired Vice Admiral, IJN, at Sugamo Prison, 11 April 1946', 11–12.

according to the outcome of the earlier trials.[61] Though this procedure was occasionally followed, it was far more common in British, American, Australian, and Philippines trials for all suspects, regardless of rank, to be indicted before the same tribunal.

The proceedings of the trial of Tanaka and his subordinates for the Truk killings show how the doctrine of command responsibility could be used in defining the duties of commanding officers. By all accounts, Tanaka knew that his subordinates were likely to execute the prisoners. His failure to follow up afterwards on how the executions had been authorised, and by whom, showed an apparently casual lack of interest in the actions of his subordinates and in the fate of the prisoners. In other words, Tanaka had abrogated his duty as an officer to protect POWs, and to ensure that the actions of his subordinates were carried out lawfully. Whether or not Tanaka's subordinates had gained permission to kill the prisoners, Tanaka had been in a position of command to prevent the crime. The severe sentence that Tanaka received also indicates that tribunals, or at least this tribunal, believed that failing to act in the face of clear evidence of a potential war crime made an officer as culpable as direct participants. In this case, command responsibility was an important tool in prosecuting an officer who had refused to exercise control in circumstances where he ought to have done so.

Trying to Locate Command: Prosecuting Staff Officers for Summary Executions

In summary execution trials and in other proceedings, prosecutors sometimes targeted staff officers in their attempts to locate where command lay, and, thus, where ultimate responsibility for the crimes lay. Military staff officers hold an administrative role. They are usually responsible for filtering information to and from the commanding officer, drafting orders, and supplying the logistical needs of a unit. The only orders that they give are to carry out the directions of their commanding officers. Allied authorities' decision to pursue staff officers was thus a surprising choice, and one which dramatically illustrates the problems that prosecutors had in locating the source of command in the Japanese military.

Because of the administrative position they had occupied, staff officers could often avoid prosecution, because they had held no official authority to command. When prosecutions did occur, they usually resulted from situations in which a staff officer had exercised some degree of actual command over lower-ranking soldiers. In the case of summary executions, two arguments were generally made against a staff officer. First, if a staff officer had passed on an order to execute someone, he was responsible for that order, and he should have taken steps to

61. Earl Mountbatten of Burma, 'Foreword', *Trial of Gozawa Sadaichi*, xiii–xiv.

find out whether it was lawful: that is, whether there had been a trial. Here, the prosecution asserted the same duty that was encapsulated in the doctrine of command responsibility, even though the staff officer was not a commander. It was not enough for a staff officer to have relied on the orders given by a superior officer. Second, the staff officer had actually held a position of command, and the ordinary protection granted to a staff officer by virtue of his intermediary position was therefore removed.

The Australian trial of Navy Captain Kawasaki Matsuhei shows how the underlying theory of command responsibility could be used to prosecute staff officers for passing on summary execution orders. It also demonstrates the difficulties that prosecutors had in determining where orders had come from and what the exact role of staff officers was within the Japanese military. In court, defendants often seized upon these ambiguities to minimise their presumed responsibility. The trial also highlights the point that Allied legal planners, and to a lesser extent tribunals, never established clear parameters on when, and in what situations, command responsibility could be used to indict an officer.

Kawasaki, a staff officer, was charged with the murder of an Australian POW who had been summarily executed on Ambon Island in the Netherlands Indies on 30 April 1945. Tried in Rabaul on 17 and 18 June 1947, Kawasaki was found guilty and sentenced to ten years' imprisonment.[62] The executed Australian prisoner, Private Frederick Schaefer, had stolen food supplies and had escaped from a POW camp on Ambon. In the post-war trial, the camp is referred to as Galala POW Camp, but it is more commonly known as Tan Toey POW Camp. Two weeks after Schaefer was recaptured, a Japanese officer from Tan Toey Camp gave Kawasaki a verbal report of his escape, and of the theft of the food. In court, Kawasaki alleged that he had forwarded the information to Rear Admiral Okada Tametsugu, who was responsible for courts-martial within Kawasaki's chain of command.[63] According to Kawasaki, Okada had authorised the execution of Schaefer. Kawasaki said that he passed the order back to the commander of the POW camp, and the prisoner was beheaded. In court as a witness, Okada denied that he had had any knowledge of the execution and stated that Kawasaki had ordered the execution himself.[64] At no point in the investigation or trial did anyone claim that a trial had taken place.

The prosecution's evidence was inconclusive. Kawasaki and Okada each had a clear motive to assign blame to the other for authorising the execution, to avoid what would almost certainly be a death sentence. Another Japanese witness, Vice

62. NAA, War Crimes Trial of Kawasaki Matsuhei (hereafter Kawasaki trial), Judge Advocate's Summary, 1–2, archived at [https://recordsearch.naa.gov.au/SearchNRetrieve/Interface/ViewImage.aspx?B=739442].
63. Kawasaki Trial, Judge Advocate's Summary, 1–2, Trial Transcript, 16–18.
64. Kawasaki Trial, Judge Advocate's Summary, 1–2, Trial Transcript, 16–18.

Admiral Ichise Shinichi, superior to both Kawasaki and Okada, had previously given a report to Australian investigators stating that Kawasaki had personally authorised the execution.[65] During the trial, however, Ichise claimed that he had not personally compiled the report, which had actually been produced by Lieutenant Commander Kobayashi Akira, a legal officer, and that Ichise had signed off on the report without reading it; in reality, he could not say whether Kawasaki or Okada had authorised the execution.[66]

Kobayashi's role or presumed role caused confusion in other trials as well. The Kawasaki case was only one of several Australian trials for summary executions on Ambon. Throughout the investigations and trials for these crimes, Japanese officers gave confusing and conflicting evidence about where, and from whom, orders had come. Kobayashi, along with several other officers, appears to have confused Australian investigators on purpose, and to have adapted his evidence in an attempt to bring about the acquittal of certain members of his own unit while implicating members of other units.[67]

In Kawasaki's trial, the only conclusive evidence given indicated that Kawasaki had at least passed on orders to execute the prisoner. In these circumstances, the prosecution adopted elements of the doctrine of command responsibility. The argument was twofold. On the one hand, according to the prosecution case, Kawasaki had neglected to ensure that the execution was carried out lawfully, which was his duty as a staff officer: that is, he had failed to confirm that a trial had taken place. On the other hand, Kawasaki had had a legal duty to disobey an order that was clearly illegal, in this case, an order to carry out the summary execution of the prisoner.[68]

The prosecution's argument that Kawasaki should have taken more steps to ensure that the execution of Schaefer was legal shows that Allied prosecutors held Japanese officers to high standards. The prosecution accepted that Kawasaki had relayed a superior's order, and that to some extent he was what David Cohen has identified as a 'mere conduit' in the chain of command.[69] Since Kawasaki was passing the orders down the chain of command, however, prosecutors maintained that he still had some discretion, and that this discretion meant he had a degree of command responsibility. At the same time, prosecutors accepted that Kawasaki had acted under superior orders, presumably from Okada, a factor that mitigated the extent of his responsibility for the execution. Presumably

65. Kawasaki Trial, Trial Transcript, 26–30.
66. Kawasaki Trial, Trial Transcript, 26–30.
67. Paul Taucher, 'Escape from Justice: The Failed Prosecutions of Baron Takasaki Masamitsu', *War in History* 28 no. 1 (2021): 190–93.
68. Kawasaki Trial, Trial Transcript, 32–33.
69. David Cohen, 'The Singapore War Crimes Trials and their Relevance Today', *Singapore Law Review* 31 (2013): 15–16.

because of this consideration, he received the relatively light sentence of ten years' imprisonment.

The Kawasaki trial shows how difficult it was for post-war tribunals to determine not only what command was and what it meant, but also how it translated into legal responsibility. Militaries rely on large numbers of personnel to carry out day-to-day functions. When a war crime occurs within this system, determining who was criminally responsible, and how, is a complicated process. Apportioning blame for Japanese war crimes was not a simple task of determining who had *de jure* authority, or where exactly an order had come from. At times, an entire command apparatus needed to be investigated and prosecuted because multiple individuals had had the opportunity to exercise discretion at various stages. In turn, many Allied tribunals saw the ability to exercise discretion, no matter how limited, as a hallmark of command, making staff officers legitimate targets of prosecution under command responsibility.

Trials for the Execution of Guerrillas and Civilians

Guerrilla attacks were a significant problem for the Japanese military during its occupation of the Asia-Pacific region. Such attacks not only killed Japanese military personnel, but also destroyed supplies and encampments, and destabilised the occupied region more generally. As a result, the Japanese military, like many other occupying militaries in other conflicts, deemed it necessary to deal with captured guerrillas harshly. Surrendered or wounded guerrillas were often killed out of hand. Civilians suspected of supporting local guerrillas potentially faced the same fate, especially in the final months of the war, when attacks against Japanese forces increased in occupied areas.[70]

No formal protections were afforded to guerrillas during the Second World War, and all militaries executed captured guerrillas. The rationale was that since guerrillas were not part of any organised armed force, they had acted outside of the laws and customs of war. Accordingly, guerrillas were treated as common bandits, or as other actors who violated the laws of the occupying power or the laws and customs of war.[71] Despite the fact that both the Allies and the Axis considered that protections granted to soldiers during wartime did not extend to

70. On anti-Japanese guerrilla warfare, see Ben Shephard, 'Guerrillas and Counter-Insurgency', in *The Cambridge History of the Second World War Volume One: Fighting the War*, ed. John Ferris and Evan Mawdsley (Cambridge University Press, 2015), 711–13; Charles A. Willoughby, *The Guerrilla Resistance Movement in the Philippines 1941–1945* (Vantage Press, 1972); Kelly Maddox, 'An Island of Killing and Slaughter: Anti-Guerrilla Warfare in Panay, 1943', *Journal of Contemporary History* 55, no. 3 (2020): 535–56; David W. Hogan, *U.S. Army Special Operations in World War II* (Center of Military History, Department of the Army, 1992), Chapter 4.

71. R. Baxter, 'So Called "Unprivileged Belligerents": Spies, Guerrillas, and Saboteurs', *British Yearbook of International Law* 28 (1951): 327.

guerrillas during the war, several post-war trials held that summarily executing guerrillas was a war crime: military tribunals needed to have been convened before a sentence could be carried out.[72]

Though guerrilla attacks had occurred across Japanese-occupied areas, the Philippines saw a particularly high number of attacks. As the war swung in the Allies' favour in 1944–1945, guerrilla attacks increased in both number and severity, especially in the lead-up to the US invasion of the Philippines in October 1944. Guerrillas were particularly effective in disrupting Japanese supply routes, and in creating enough trouble to make it necessary for the Japanese military to divert troops to occupation duties and away from fighting the regular Allied forces.[73] Thus, it was necessary for Japanese forces to take swift action against guerrillas in order to maintain an effective occupation and viable fighting force. Accordingly, the IJA, often through the Kenpeitai, carried out large numbers of anti-guerrilla raids. Summary executions often followed.[74]

In the urgent circumstances in which Japanese forces captured Philippine guerrillas, many Japanese officers probably believed that a cursory hearing of the facts about their activities would have fulfilled the requirements of a trial and would be enough to condemn the guerrillas to death.[75] Moreover, since there was no easy way to distinguish guerrillas from other civilians, in many cases civilians were summarily executed alongside actual guerrillas. In other cases, Japanese soldiers would impulsively kill any civilians they encountered immediately after a guerrilla attack.[76] Even when Japanese military courts had been constituted to try a suspected guerrilla, Allied war crimes trials were convened after the conflict ended if the Japanese trial was not considered to have been a legitimate exercise of judicial authority, because of deficiencies in court procedure.[77]

During the war in the Philippines, the Japanese military established no standardised trial procedure for suspected guerrillas. In some instances, those believed to be guerrillas or to have supported guerrillas were simply shot out of hand. In other cases, civilians would be paraded before a concealed informant,

72. Baxter, 'So Called "Unprivileged Belligerents"', 324–35; Lester Nurick and Roger W. Barrett, 'Legality of Guerrilla Forces Under the Laws of War', *The American Journal of International Law* 40 (1946): 563–70.
73. Satoshi Ara, 'Food Supply Problem in Leyte, Philippines, during the Japanese Occupation (1942–44)', *Journal of Southeast Asian Studies* 39 (2008): 64–65.
74. Maria Felisa A. Syjuco, *The Kempei Tai in the Philippines: 1941–1945* (New Day Publishers, 1988), 6–10.
75. Chamberlain, 'Justice and Reconciliation', 86.
76. Chamberlain, 'Justice and Reconciliation', 29–35.
77. For a similar case in New Guinea see NAA, War Crimes Trial of Shinohara Eitaro and Two Others, archived at [https://recordsearch.naa.gov.au/SearchNRetrieve/Interface/ViewImage.aspx?B=693056].

who would point out guerrillas.[78] The use of informants shows some attempt, albeit an extremely limited one, at identifying proper suspects, but there were significant problems with this method. The most glaring is that informants could use the process to seek retaliation against personal enemies. There was also a clear benefit for informants, who would presumably receive preferential treatment from the Japanese occupation force if they identified guerrillas.

The newly independent Philippines government conducted a significant number of trials between 1947 and 1949 for the summary execution of civilians. Command responsibility featured heavily in these trials, fundamentally because of how the crimes had been committed. In many cases, enlisted Japanese soldiers had gone beyond the official scope of an operation, and appear to have begun to kill civilians wantonly, rather than actively targeting guerrillas. To the Philippine prosecutors, it was clear that the Japanese army's atrocities were the result of a lack of control and leadership. Accordingly, Philippine prosecutors were even more likely than their counterparts elsewhere to resort to the doctrine of command responsibility, and, unlike in other jurisdictions, such trials were explicitly identified as command responsibility trials.

In many trials run by Philippine authorities, civilians who had witnessed summary executions, often family members of the victims, identified officers who had been present or had been in command of the soldiers who had carried out the killing. Many witnesses placed the blame for atrocities at the feet of such officers. For these victims and for Philippines tribunals, it was not enough that the highest-level commanders should be prosecuted; less senior commanders who had been visible, had come into contact with Philippine civilians, and had had more direct control over their soldiers also needed to be punished. In such cases, the fact that the crimes were committed in front of so many witnesses, who were then able to testify in court, encouraged the prosecution to use command responsibility for mid-level officers. Not only did it mean that the trial would almost certainly result in a conviction; it also allowed the newly independent government to demonstrate to Philippine civilians that justice was being meted out to those who were considered to be truly responsible.

The prosecution's confidence that the doctrine would secure convictions, and the strong desire to convict commanders, can be seen in the trial of Captain Shimamura Katsuji and Lieutenant Shimada Yasukasu, both members of the Imperial Japanese Navy. Tried in Manila from 23 August to 9 October 1948, the two officers faced command responsibility charges for the summary execution

78. NARA, RG331, Supreme Commander of the Allied Powers, Legal Section, Prosecution Division, *Philippines v Various Japanese War Criminals 1947–49*, Box 1728, *Philippines v Fujita Takefumi*, Trial Transcript, 71–83; NARA, RG331, Supreme Commander for the Allied Powers, Legal Section, Prosecution Division, *Philippines versus Various Japanese War Criminals*, 1947–49, Box 1728, *Philippines v Fujisaki Saburo*, Trial Transcript, 75–88.

of Philippine civilians in May 1945, in Japanese defensive positions just outside Manila.[79] During the first two weeks of that month, members of Shimada's unit had summarily executed an unknown number of Philippine civilians. Shimada pleaded guilty to ordering the executions and was sentenced to the comparatively light penalty of ten years' imprisonment.[80] Shimamura, who had had nominal command over Shimada because of his rank, pleaded not guilty to the charges and was acquitted, a relatively unusual outcome for an officer facing command responsibility charges. The acquittal was likely a result of the particularly dubious evidence that the prosecution raised against Shimamura, and the failure of the prosecution to show that Shimamura had a clear position of control and authority over Shimada.

Shimada's decision to plead guilty to the charges was unusual, as most defendants pleaded not guilty and attempted to counter all the evidence brought against them. The procedure used at Shimada's trial, however, shows that pleading guilty might have worked well for him, because the tribunal then ruled that the prosecution would not be permitted to produce evidence against Shimada. The rationale was that as Shimada had already pleaded guilty, any evidence against him would necessarily aggravate his guilt, given that the presumption of innocence had been removed. The defence, however, was entitled to present evidence in mitigation of criminal liability.[81]

Shimada claimed that on 1 May 1945, his superior officer, identified only as Lieutenant S. Sato, had ordered that all civilians in Shimada's area of command were to be evacuated.[82] According to Shimada, a second order was given the next day, stating that any civilians remaining in the area were to be considered guerrillas and were to be executed.[83] Because of this instruction, Shimada argued that he was acting under superior orders, but he admitted that nonetheless he had executed civilians without a trial and so was guilty of the charges against him. The tribunal's acceptance of Shimada's testimony, without any clear evidence of a superior order, was likely attributable to Shimada's early guilty plea: because of his readiness to accept personal responsibility and guilt, Shimada had established himself as a reliable witness.

79. NARA, RG331, Supreme Command for the Allied Powers, Legal Section, Prosecution Division, *Philippines versus Various Japanese War Criminals*, Case File, 1947–1949, Box 1694, Folder 2, *Philippines v Shimamura Katsuji and One Other* (hereafter *Philippines v Shimamura*), Trial Transcript, 6–9.
80. *Philippines v Shimamura*, Trial Transcript, 387–94.
81. *Philippines v Shimamura*, Trial Transcript, 22–27.
82. Chapter 4 closely examines the trial of accused Japanese war criminal Lieutenant-Colonel Sato So, who was charged with responsibility for two massacres in the Philippines. It is unclear from either record if Shimada's superior was the same Sato in the massacre trial.
83. *Philippines v Shimamura*, Trial Transcript, 33–37.

The tribunal's decision to imprison Shimada for ten years, rather than to impose a harsher penalty, probably represented an acknowledgement that he had operated under orders to execute the civilians. If this is the case, the defence of superior orders partially mitigated his sentence. Other factors, however, may also have played a part. Shimada had not received direct orders to execute those particular civilians, and he was to some extent operating under his own command. His relatively lenient sentence was probably not, therefore, based solely on the defence of superior orders. It is highly likely that the tribunal considered Shimada's early guilty plea to be a further mitigating factor: unlike many other junior officers, Shimada had readily accepted responsibility for his actions.

The prosecution's case against the other defendant, Shimamura, was that he had been in command at the time of the executions, though he had not explicitly ordered the killings. The evidence against him, however, was particularly poor. The main prosecution witness who gave evidence on Shimamura's role claimed that Shimamura had been present at one of the executions and had openly gloated over the killings. The witness also revealed that he himself had previously been tortured by Japanese military personnel, and that he suspected Shimamura of being in command when he was tortured.[84] Unsurprisingly, the defence counsel seized upon this point, arguing that Shimamura was on trial solely because of a witness' personal grudge against him, and that the evidence was unreliable. The defence also maintained that although Shimamura had had nominal command over Shimada, this was merely because of Shimamura's higher rank and did not reflect any actual command structure. The defence conceded that Shimamura may have been in command at the earlier time at which the witness had been tortured, and that there was a chance that he had been responsible for other war crimes as well, but argued that there was simply not enough evidence to convict Shimamura of the charges he actually faced.[85] The dubious nature of the evidence presented against Shimamura was not unusual for trials in the Philippines, whether they were conducted by the American or the Philippine authorities.[86] In the Yamashita trial, held by the Americans in Manila, several civilian witnesses had given evidence that was at best rumour, and, at worst, clearly fabricated.[87] While victims certainly exaggerated or fabricated evidence to secure a conviction at trials in other locations too,[88] the practice appears to have occurred more

84. *Philippines v Shimamura*, Trial Transcript, 73–82.
85. *Philippines v Shimamura*, Trial Transcript, 376–82.
86. Chamberlain, 'Justice and Reconciliation', 95–97.
87. George F. Guy, 'The Defense of General Yamashita', *United States Air Force Academy Journal of Legal Studies* 215 (1995): 221–23.
88. 'VC Award Would be a Mockery, Historian Warns Tribunal', *The Sydney Morning Herald*, 13 March 2012, 1.

frequently in the Philippines, probably because of the greater reliance on the testimony of civilian victims.

The prosecution's decision to try Shimamura on such poor evidence likely stemmed from two reasons. First, as we have seen, many tribunals held officers to high standards of responsibility and allowed limited opportunities for defendants to mitigate their liability for the crimes of their subordinates. In Shimamura's case, the prosecution probably felt that the poor quality evidence was not a significant barrier to securing a conviction, given the potential offered by the doctrine of command responsibility. Second, the prosecutor probably thought that Shimamura was guilty of committing a war crime at some point. Shimamura had been a mid-level officer at the 1945 Battle of Manila, in which Japanese naval forces had committed widespread atrocities. It would have seemed almost impossible that Shimamura had neither personally committed a war crime, nor had been in direct command of subordinates who had committed a war crime. In other words, the decision to prosecute Shimamura may have reflected the belief among many Allied legal authorities that virtually all Japanese officers had committed war crimes during the conflict, and that they should be brought to account whenever possible.

Shimamura's acquittal is at odds with the results of many other command responsibility trials for summary execution. Other officers in similar circumstances to Shimamura would usually have been convicted: the only tangible difference in Shimamura's case was that evidence that placed him at the scene of the crime was so unreliable as to be almost inadmissible. In other trials, however, simply being a superior officer of those who had committed war crimes was enough to secure a conviction. In this case, the bench apparently considered that there was a difference between mere seniority and formal command: for liability to attach there needed to be something more than simply being a higher-ranking officer.

The fact that the prosecution charged Shimamura under command responsibility shows how some Allied legal personnel conceptualised what command meant in the Japanese military, and who was really responsible for the crimes that had occurred during the war. The case against Shimamura was based not only on dubious evidence, but also on a very broad understanding of what command meant. For the prosecutor, and indeed many other Allied legal and military personnel, the widespread commission of crimes during the war pointed towards something fundamentally wrong with the Japanese military, for which the fault rested at the feet of the officer corps. Thus, officers who had had no clear formal control over lower-ranking subordinates were still considered to be responsible for war crimes, because they had held some form of broad command over all lower-ranking soldiers.

Conclusions

For individual junior and mid-level Japanese officers, summary executions that occurred under their chain of command were usually isolated events. Though some units did carry out summary executions on a relatively regular basis in the late stages of the war – in the Philippines, for example – these units were outliers engaged directly in anti-guerrilla operations. To Allied investigators and prosecutors, however, summary executions, and indeed all categories of war crime, appeared to have been prevalent across the Japanese military, at all levels of command. A form of selection bias probably explains this misapprehension. The majority of Japanese units and personnel to whom Allied investigators and prosecutors were exposed were suspected of committing war crimes. Investigators and prosecutors were likely to draw the conclusion, therefore, that all or most Japanese units had committed war crimes.

When command responsibility was deployed against senior officers, it was used to address widespread failures in an entire command structure. In the Yamashita case and in other trials of high-ranking personnel, command responsibility was triggered because many war crimes had been perpetrated over a large area and over a prolonged period of time, and authorities argued that the crimes had formed a pattern of atrocity. Using command responsibility against mid- and junior-level officers had different implications for prosecutorial strategy. When such officers were accused of responsibility for summary executions they could be, and often were, held liable for individual crimes. Rarely were they held responsible for a string of executions. Most were indicted for the murder of a small number of Allied POWs, downed airmen, or suspected guerrillas. The fact that summary executions were usually one-off events necessitated an application of command responsibility that held commanders to a very high standard.

Comparatively few officers at the lower levels of command were directly responsible for summary executions, but it was not considered sufficient to pursue only senior officers who had overseen multiple summary executions and, at the other end of the scale, those who had directly committed the killings. The trials were also meant to set new standards in international law, and holding lower-level officers criminally responsible was a necessary step in enshrining these new standards. Lower-ranking officers had exercised day-to-day authority over enlisted soldiers and NCOs and so were believed to have had the most control over the immediate situation in which war crimes had occurred. Because of the immediacy of such officers' command, tribunals were willing to consider their duty to be far more wide-ranging than what was articulated in the Yamashita decision, which had relied on the fact that crimes had been widespread and numerous.

Lower-ranked officers held responsible for summary executions were in a difficult position. They often had had little authority, even within their own units, to prevent, halt, or punish war crimes. Lack of formal authority would have made it difficult for some officers to punish a subordinate for killing enemy personnel. Indeed, since so many of the executions were individual and isolated crimes, there was often no opportunity to exercise authority within units: the crime had already been committed, and the same crime was unlikely to happen again. Thus, in terms of deterrence, there was no real benefit for the officer in punishing his subordinates. In other cases, officers had acted under superior orders, or were relatively inexperienced and had been placed in a position where they had to make a decision with little support from superiors.

The difficulties that officers had faced were evident in the majority of cases, but these problems were not what the trials had been designed to address. The tribunals were concerned with holding Japanese military personnel responsible for crimes committed against Allied soldiers and civilians. The format of the post-war trials meant that no explanation of why a war crime had occurred was ever necessary. As a result, the broader difficulties that more junior officers faced were rarely factored into the decision-making process of a tribunal, and the trials could never fully address the components of what command entailed. This was particularly the case in trials for summary execution because the tribunals were examining what was usually a single incident of a commander failing in whatever the court deemed to be his duty. Accordingly, courts did not deliberate on what was truly required of a responsible commander, especially at the middle and lower levels of command, which meant that in many cases, the question of what the chain of command looked like in practice was never addressed directly.

In command responsibility trials, the authorities tried to do two things at once. First, the prosecutions were intended to determine who was ultimately responsible for a crime, which meant looking at what actions an individual had taken, or more often, had not taken. Second, these trials were designed to set a suitable standard for future officers. This aim often meant setting harsh examples, to discourage commanders from allowing their subordinates to commit crimes in the first place. Within this framework, there was room for prosecutors to apply the doctrine opportunistically to prosecute a class of suspects who were likely considered guilty of something simply because of their position within the military hierarchy, even in cases with particularly weak evidence. The desire for retribution almost certainly played a part in the pursuit of such officers, many of whom had had almost no genuine opportunity to prevent, halt, or punish crimes. A large number of junior and mid-level officers faced harsh punishments for what was, for them, an isolated event, but for the Allies, represented a widespread problem within the Japanese military.

Though punishment for summary executions was often severe, the variation in sentencing shown in this chapter indicates that there was no real consensus on what the exact duties of an officer were. In Ichinoe's trial over the death of the airman who crashed in the Great Tokyo Air Raid, there was significant disparity between the sentence that the judges handed down, and what was recommended by the legal review and was eventually adopted. The two views show separate understandings of what could reasonably be expected of a commander, rather than any clear disagreement over how to interpret broad legal principles. In the Truk case, Tanaka was sentenced to death for failing to refuse outright his subordinate's request to execute prisoners, and, instead, deferring to the command of his own superior. Kawasaki, a relatively experienced staff officer, was imprisoned for ten years for passing on an order to execute prisoners on Ambon, and, critically, for failing to ensure that the execution was lawful. Both the Tanaka and Kawasaki cases involved an experienced officer failing to ensure that prisoners were adequately protected and deferring his own command potential to other officers, but they resulted in very different sentences. The trial of Shimamura, however, for executions in the Philippines shows the limits of command responsibility. Merely having informal command because of rank was not enough to attract liability.

3
Torture

During their occupation of the Asia-Pacific region, Japanese military personnel carried out many brutal interrogations of local people who were suspected to be insurgents or spies. Interrogators questioned and sometimes tortured civilians, including Westerners, who were believed to have carried out acts of resistance through direct or indirect support of guerrilla forces, by spying for the Allies or by providing captives with supplies or intelligence. Prisoners of war (POWs) who had attempted to escape might be tortured for information on how they had escaped, and to find out whether anyone outside the camp had assisted them. Recently captured POWs might also face torture in attempts to extract military or technical intelligence about the enemy. In rare cases, torture was perpetrated for no clear reason. This chapter shows how command responsibility was used to prosecute Japanese officers whose subordinates had carried out torture.

The application of the doctrine of command responsibility to torture cases reflected the distinct nature of the crime. Torture perpetrated during an interrogation differed from the harsh beatings that POWs and civilian internees sometimes faced during their captivity. In interrogations, torture was primarily carried out to extract information, not as punishment, although the ill-treatment of individuals during interrogation would still have served as punishment for suspected activity in resistance groups, as well as acting as a deterrent to others contemplating acts of resistance. The difference between the torture carried out in interrogations and the ill-treatment that occurred at camps was acknowledged at the trials: officers accused of responsibility for crimes committed during interrogation were charged with torture, while officers charged with crimes against prisoners were, almost invariably, charged with ill-treatment.

In many cases, victims had been tortured repeatedly over multiple days, if not weeks, and a sustained pattern of torture had been used in interrogating victims. Because the crimes were committed over a prolonged period and were an intentional part of maintaining Japanese rule, tribunals had little difficulty in connecting the substantive crimes of the subordinate to the expected or required behaviour of the commander. Tribunals assumed a close connection between the crimes of the subordinate and the superior officer's role in enforcing Japanese rule. On this basis, some prosecutors attempted to expand an officer's liability for his subordinates' actions into a substantive crime: that is, they argued that the commander's failure to act was itself a part of the initial crime. Though this expanded version of command responsibility was theoretically valid, tribunals appeared cautious to accept it, likely because of the complexity of such arguments. In the end, no substantial refinement of the doctrine of command responsibility emerged from torture trials to give prosecutors, and perhaps more important, defence lawyers, a clear understanding of when a commander could be held liable for the crimes of his subordinates, or in what form that liability arose.

Torture and Torture Trials

Many of the defendants in torture trials were members of the Kenpeitai, the Japanese military police. The role of the Kenpeitai had been broad, ranging from maintaining discipline in the Japanese army to training local pro-Japanese armies and policing occupied areas. Kenpeitai members also carried out counter-espionage operations and questioned recently captured prisoners.[1] The Tokkeitai was the equivalent organisation within the Japanese navy. During the war, both organisations had low numbers of personnel relative to the size of territory they policed. As a result, regular army and navy personnel were occasionally seconded to the command of the military police, as seen in the *Sook Ching* massacre in Singapore in early 1942.[2] Because the Kenpeitai and Tokkeitai had such a prominent role in investigating and subduing guerrilla movements, policing civilians in occupied areas and interrogating POWs, Allied militaries after the end of the conflict had a general policy of arresting these personnel immediately, on suspicion they had committed war crimes, even if no specific evidence was yet available.[3]

1. Raymond Lamont-Brown, *Kempeitai: Japan's Dreaded Military Police* (Sutton Publishing, 2002), 40–43; Joyce C. Lebra, *Japanese-Trained Armies in Southeast Asia* (Heinemann Education Books, 1977), 71, 97, 123.
2. Lamont-Brown, *Kempeitai*, 35–37; Peter Post, 'Policing Society', in *The Encyclopedia of Indonesia in the Second World War*, ed. Peter Post (Brill, 2009), 148–60; 'Kenpeitai', in Post, *The Encyclopedia of Indonesia in the Second World War*, 529–30.
3. Sandra Wilson, Robert Cribb, Beatrice Trefalt, and Dean Aszkielowicz, *Japanese War Criminals: The Pursuit of Justice After the Second World War* (Columbia University Press, 2017), 48; Fred L. Borch, *Military Trials of War Criminals in the Netherlands East Indies 1946–1949* (Oxford University Press, 2017), 155.

The torture trials suggest that the Japanese military had been consistent in the methods of torture used against victims. Physical beating with sticks was common, as were punching and kicking. Victims were routinely bound with rope and suspended from ceilings and rafters. The so-called water cure was widely used, in which victims were forced to drink large amounts of water before having their stomachs stomped on to induce vomiting. Victims were also frequently waterboarded, a form of torture in which water is poured over a cloth covering the victim's face, causing the sensation of drowning. Less regular forms of torture included shocking victims with electricity and burning them with lit cigarettes or hot irons.[4]

The most likely reason for the consistency in how torture was carried out was that both Kenpeitai and Tokkeitai members had had some degree of training in interrogation techniques. A captured Japanese handbook on interrogating prisoners explicitly stated that torture was the least reliable method of gaining information and should only be used as a last resort. The fact that the handbook acknowledged the use of torture suggests that some Japanese military personnel had had instruction on how to carry it out.[5] To what extent the direction to use torture as a last resort was followed in practice is unclear from the trials: the evidence presented implies that torture was the first step, rather than the final measure. It would have been unnecessary, however, for witnesses, prosecutors, or defendants to point out that other methods of interrogation had been used first: simply questioning a prisoner is not a war crime, nor would evidence of it be considered to mitigate the act of torture. Similarly, interrogations where torture was not used would not have resulted in trials.

Due to the fearsome reputation of both the Kenpeitai and the Tokkeitai for carrying out torture and harshly treating suspected resistors, it was not difficult for the prosecution to argue that commanding officers had known their subordinates were perpetrating war crimes, or had openly permitted their subordinates to commit crimes.[6] Despite the reputation of the military police, however, prosecutors rarely argued that Kenpeitai commanding officers had directly ordered their subordinates to torture. Since any version of the doctrine of command responsibility could, and often did, result in severe punishment, there was probably little incentive to rely on an argument that would require more evidence, of a kind that might be difficult to find. There was ample evidence of crimes of torture, and the doctrine of command responsibility was vague enough that simply being

4. See for example The National Archives of the UK (hereafter TNA), WO 235/872, *UK v Toyoda Akiichi*; TNA, WO 235/953, *UK v Ogata Tsuyoshi*.
5. TNA, WO203/5620, Treatment of Prisoners of War by Japanese, General Information on POWs, Enclosure No. 1, 'Notes on Interrogation of POWs,' undated.
6. Sandra Wilson, 'War Crimes Trials and the Politics of Justice: The Case of Kinoshita Eiichi, 1945–57,' *Historical Research* 92 (2019), 637–38.

in command was sufficient for a prosecutor to show that a commander should have known that an offence had occurred. It would be much harder to prove that a commanding officer had actually ordered the torture. Conversely, in cases where commanding officers had directly taken part in torture, prosecutors were unlikely to add a charge of command responsibility. Prosecutors seem to have wanted to secure a conviction through the most obvious charge, rather than complicating and lengthening a trial so that the accused could be held liable for all the crimes committed under his command.

As we will see below, prosecutors sometimes attempted to frame command responsibility in torture trials as an offence resembling that committed by an accomplice to a crime, rather than as a separate crime of omission. The commander was thus accused of direct responsibility, albeit a lesser responsibility than that of the prime perpetrator. In other cases, in the absence of enough evidence to show that he had actually intended the crimes to occur, it seems that the prosecution's approach was simply to attribute as much liability as possible to the accused commander.

Due to the prominent role of the Kenpeitai in Japan's occupation of the Asia-Pacific region during the war, many Kenpeitai commanders were brought to trial quickly. The decision to begin the trials with prominent defendants who were alleged to have been part of especially brutal crimes was presumably important in validating the trial process as a whole.[7] As group trials were common, such a strategy would also situate defendants accused of 'lesser' war crimes alongside those accused of more shocking offences. Additionally, trying commanding officers early would help to confirm the precedent that had been first established in the Yamashita trial.

Reaffirming the Yamashita Decision in Manila Courts

The US trial of Colonel Nagahama Akira, the Commander-in-Chief of the Kenpeitai in the Philippines from 30 September 1942 until 8 January 1945, was the first command responsibility trial among the proceedings administered by Australia, the US, the UK, and the Philippines in which the doctrine was applied to an officer below the rank of general. The trial shows that the tribunal was aware of the lack of clarity in the Yamashita judgment and believed that further trials might be capable of refining the doctrine of command responsibility. Ultimately, however, the Nagahama trial did little to clarify the doctrine, instead only reaffirming the basic principles of command responsibility and leaving the connection between command and criminal liability largely unsettled.

7. Wilson, Cribb, Trefalt, and Aszkielowicz, *Japanese War Criminals*, 65.

Nagahama was indicted on 9 December 1945, just two days after Yamashita had been found guilty by another US military commission in Manila and sentenced to death.[8] The quick indictment of Nagahama was no doubt because of his prominent role in the Japanese occupation of the Philippines. As chief of the Manila Kenpeitai, Nagahama had been a key figure in maintaining Japanese rule in the city and in working with Philippine collaborators. US prosecutors were probably also keen to extend command responsibility to a commissioned officer who had not been a member of the general staff. The importance of Nagahama's trial was certainly not lost on the bench, which, unusually, published a reasoned decision for its judgment.

Nagahama's trial took place between 25 February and 11 March 1946, immediately after General Honma Masaharu had been convicted of responsibility for the indiscriminate bombing of Manila in 1941 and for the Bataan Death March in April 1942.[9] The delay of two and a half months between indictment and trial was unusual; the trial record provides no clear explanation for the gap. It is possible that prosecutors were simply unprepared, or that they did not want to divert either their own focus, or the public's attention away from the Honma trial.

Prosecuted in Manila, Nagahama faced eleven charges of either allowing or permitting his subordinates to torture, treat brutally and inhumanely, or beat both Philippine civilians and US soldiers during his command of the Kenpeitai. Nine of these charges were for crimes committed by Nagahama's subordinates at specific times and places during 1944 and 1945. The other two charges covered the duration of Nagahama's command.[10] Possibly, the two broad charges were included so that torture carried out against individuals in more isolated events could be included without overloading the charge sheet with a litany of single specifications. It is more likely, however, that the prosecution simply did not have concrete evidence of specific crimes of torture or mistreatment committed during the earlier period of Nagahama's command, either because there were no available witnesses, or because torture was chiefly used in 1944 and 1945 rather than earlier in the war. Indeed, during 1942 and 1943, Nagahama made several public announcements that guerrillas who surrendered would not be subject to torture or execution. He also told other Japanese personnel that treatment of Philippine civilians should be aimed at encouraging cooperation.[11] On top of the

8. 'Jap Conqueror of Philippines Indicted', *Tweed Daily* (NSW), 10 December 1945, 3.
9. Philip R. Piccigallo, *The Japanese on Trial: Allied War Crimes Operations in the East, 1945–1951* (University of Texas Press, 1979), 65–67.
10. National Archives and Records Administration, College Park MD (hereafter NARA), RG331, Supreme Commander of the Allied Powers, Legal Section, Prosecution Division, *USA versus Japanese War Criminals*, Case Files, 1945–48, Box 1579, *USA v Nagahama Akira* (hereafter *USA v Nagahama*), Charge Sheet, 1–2.
11. A. V. H. Hartendorp, *The Japanese Occupation of the Philippines, Vol. 1* (Bookmark, 1967), 516–19.

eleven torture charges, Nagahama was accused of directly ordering the execution of ten Philippine POWs in Manila on 7 January 1945. Found guilty of all charges and sentenced to death, he was hanged in Manila on 11 March 1947.[12]

Most of the evidence at Nagahama's trial concerned the torture of prisoners at Fort Santiago, the Kenpeitai headquarters in Manila. During the Japanese occupation, Fort Santiago became notorious as the site of torture perpetrated by the Kenpeitai on a massive scale: starved and visibly tortured civilians were commonly released, likely as a way of deterring other civilians from resisting Japanese rule.[13] US and Philippine military prisoners, as well as Philippine civilians, were allegedly tortured at Fort Santiago throughout the whole of the Japanese occupation of the Philippines, from April 1942 to January 1945. None of the victims who testified to the torture, however, had been held there before October 1944; information about torture at Fort Santiago prior to that time was submitted as hearsay evidence. Though hearsay evidence was readily accepted at the post-war trials, it was usually in the form of unsworn affidavits. In this case, it consisted of rumours, rather than testimony from those who had actually been subjected to torture at the complex between 1942 and 1944.

Torture had been carried out at Fort Santiago predominantly to gain information on anti-Japanese guerrillas and their activities. White civilian internees and POWs were occasionally tortured for information on illicit camp activities: the Kenpeitai was concerned that senior US officers were collaborating with guerrillas.[14] Many people suffered prolonged beatings with wooden sticks, sometimes while suspended from the ceiling. The 'water cure' and waterboarding were common, as was shocking people with electricity.[15]

Similar torture was carried out at other locations in Manila. On the southern side of the city, in what was known as the Cortabitarte Garrison, the Kenpeitai had taken over two civilian houses to accommodate Japanese troops. Cortabitarte was used for interrogations when Fort Santiago had too many suspected guerrillas. The campus of the Far Eastern University in downtown Manila was also used as a Kenpeitai interrogation centre. In the final months of the Japanese occupation of the Philippines, the Wack Wack Country Club was the site of mass interrogations during which large numbers of captives were heavily beaten.[16] Unsurprisingly, the connection of the country club's name with these mass beatings was ignored at trial, at least in public.

12. Hartendorp, *The Japanese Occupation*, 516–19.
13. James M. Scott, *Rampage: MacArthur, Yamashita, and the Battle of Manila* (W. W. Norton & Company, 2018), 210–15.
14. Scott, *Rampage*, 212; Hartendorp, *The Japanese Occupation*, 401–2, 407–12, 603–4.
15. *USA v Nagahama*, Trial Transcript, 736.
16. *USA v Nagahama*, Trial Transcript, 442–44, 454–59, 500, 579.

As well as facing brutal torture, prisoners at Fort Santiago were held in over-crowded and unsanitary conditions and had insufficient food, water, and ventilation. Former storerooms were repurposed into cells and jammed with prisoners. Though the prosecution did not make the argument explicit, it was implied that poor treatment in the cells had been part of the interrogation process: those who cooperated with their captors were given water and food and were set free from the jail. According to the prosecution, between September and November 1944 approximately 450 prisoners died in the Fort Santiago cells due to suffocation.[17] The exact number, however, was never determined at the trial, partly because of complications arising from the large number of civilians who had been killed in fighting in the city itself during the final months of the Japanese occupation of Manila, especially during the Battle of Manila (3 February–3 March 1945). Approximately 100,000 civilians had died,[18] and as a result, there were several mass graves in the city. When bodies were recovered, it was impossible to determine whether the victims had died at Fort Santiago or elsewhere.[19] In court, the prosecution admitted that 450 was the upper limit of possible victims at Fort Santiago, and that it was likely that fewer had died there.[20]

One of the more unusual elements of the Nagahama trial was that the bench, along with the defence and prosecution, visited Fort Santiago, the site of the crimes. The prosecution had contended that Nagahama would have been able to hear prisoners screaming from his office within the fort. To test this claim, the tribunal judges sat in Nagahama's office while the prosecution made as much noise as possible in the Fort Santiago cells. The judges were unable to hear anything; the prosecution argued that traffic noise was responsible.[21]

This testing of evidence in the field at Fort Santiago is an important aspect in assessing how the prosecution understood command responsibility in this case. In attempting to demonstrate that Nagahama could have heard screaming in the cells, the prosecution tried to show that he must have had knowledge that something was wrong and ought to be investigated. This means that prosecutors were not trying to hold Nagahama responsible simply because he was the commander, but because they thought that he had known, or should have known, that his subordinates were committing crimes. In other words, they implied a separate offence of the superior officer.

17. *USA v Nagahama*, Trial Transcript, 514–23.
18. Miguel Miranda, *Battle of Manila: Nadir of Japanese Barbarism, 3 February 1945–3 March 1945* (Pen and Sword Military, 2019), 104; Richard Connaughton, John Pimlott, and Duncan Anderson, *The Battle for Manila: The Most Devastating Untold Story of World War II* (Bloomsbury, 1995), 13.
19. *USA v Nagahama*, Trial Transcript, 881.
20. *USA v Nagahama*, Trial Transcript, 825.
21. *USA v Nagahama*, Trial Transcript, 706–11.

The defence contended that Nagahama had been unaware of the torture carried out at his headquarters, but this claim was at odds with evidence that he had visited the cells. Furthermore, Nagahama admitted that he became aware, after the fact, of the mass suffocation of prisoners.[22] For the Judge Advocate General (JAG), in reviewing the trial, the fact that Nagahama knew that the prisoners had suffocated while under the control of Warrant Officer Saito Takao, one of his subordinates, together with the fact that that subordinate had not been punished, and had even been allowed to maintain control over the surviving prisoners, was clear evidence of Nagahama's failure of command.[23]

Nagahama's lawyers offered a limited defence, presenting no evidence or witnesses. The defence lawyers' cross-examination of both Japanese witnesses and Philippine civilians raised only the point that Nagahama had apparently never given a direct order to carry out torture and was not present during any of the alleged crimes. Nagahama himself offered some defence of his own conduct in a short statement he read at the end of the trial. He claimed that he had arrived in the Philippines with a policy of 'education and rehabilitation' of Philippine civilians and guerrillas to enable them to become full participants in the Japanese Greater East Asia Co-Prosperity Sphere. He stated that many of his subordinates, on the other hand, were veterans of the war in China, where harsh tactics were expected: according to Nagahama, it was impossible to eradicate the use of torture by those subordinates.[24] In taking this line, Nagahama was one of the few officers who attempted to rationalise his subordinates' crimes on the basis of their past military experience. The Japanese war and occupation in China had been extremely harsh. In this undeclared war, the Japanese military appears to have made little attempt to comply with international laws and norms, unlike in the rest of the Asia-Pacific region.[25] Nagahama argued that his subordinates had arrived in the Philippines with expectations of how they would carry out their duty, and that they treated the occupation of the Philippines no differently from that of China.

In the same statement, despite his attempt to deflect liability, Nagahama accepted that as the commanding officer, he bore some degree of responsibility for the crimes committed.[26] Though his partial admission of responsibility may have contributed to the court's finding that he was guilty, it is likely that

22. *USA v Nagahama*, Trial Transcript, 911–13.
23. *USA v Nagahama*, JAG Report, 2–3.
24. *USA v Nagahama*, Trial Transcript, 907–8.
25. Edward J. Drea and Hans van de Ven, 'An Overview of Major Military Campaigns during the Sino-Japanese War, 1937–1945', in *The Battle for China: Essays on the Military History of the Sino-Japanese War of 1937–1945*, ed. Mark Peattie, Edward J. Drea, and Hans van de Ven (Stanford University Press, 2012), 37–40.
26. *USA v Nagahama*, Trial Transcript, 907–8.

by this point in the trial, a decision had already been reached: there was simply too much evidence against members of Nagahama's command. Perhaps most damning was that Nagahama's argument about his subordinates' experience in China could have been construed as an admission that he had known the torture and ill-treatment were taking place, or were likely to take place, and had done nothing to prevent or halt the abuses.

In his petition against his conviction, Nagahama requested a retrial. He argued that during the proceedings that had just ended, he had not been aware of the gravity of the charges.[27] This may have been true, as the result of the Yamashita trial had only recently been finalised in the US Supreme Court, where the legality of the US war crimes trials, and by default the doctrine of command responsibility, were affirmed. Nagahama may indeed have been unaware that command responsibility created a criminal liability for crimes committed by his subordinates.

Nagahama's petition implied that he had not been adequately defended, which was probably also true, and may help to explain why he did not understand the gravity of the charges. Both of the two American defence counsel originally allocated to Nagahama had been reassigned to other duties prior to his trial, though it is unclear from the trial documents exactly when this occurred.[28] Being assigned new counsel after preparations for the proceedings had begun almost certainly would have disadvantaged Nagahama, because the new counsel would have had less time to work on the case before proceedings began. Considering that the two replacement defence lawyers, who were again American, made limited attempts to cross-examine prosecution witnesses or rebut prosecution evidence, and offered no evidence or witnesses of their own, it is questionable whether Nagahama did receive a fair trial. Several US military lawyers working in the Philippines, moreover, garnered a reputation for heavy drinking and poor representation of their clients.[29]

Even if Nagahama's defence was inadequate, however, this defect probably had limited impact on the outcome of the trial. Nagahama himself had admitted some degree of responsibility for crimes of torture in his statement to the court. In view of his position, it is likely that he would have received the same sentence, even with a more spirited defence: not only was he a colonel commanding subordinates who had committed war crimes, but he was also the ranking member of the Kenpeitai in the Philippines.

In a rare example among the US trials, the tribunal presented a reasoned decision in Nagahama's case. The tribunal stated that the crimes that had

27. *USA v Nagahama*, Petition of the Accused, 1–3.
28. *USA v Nagahama*, Judge Advocate Review, 5.
29. Piccigallo, *The Japanese on Trial*, 93. Piccigallo does not name these lawyers.

occurred under Nagahama's command had not been committed by a disorganised body of ordinary soldiers, but rather by officers of high rank. Furthermore, in the tribunal's view, the fact that the crimes had been committed over a two-year period was proof that they had been part of an organised plan.[30] Both these factors were important in finding Nagahama guilty. Using wording from the Yamashita decision, the Nagahama tribunal stated, somewhat surprisingly, that it was impossible for a commander to be held responsible for a single crime. On the other hand, '[where] a series of repeated criminal acts are committed by a military unit following a method or pattern . . . a commander cannot argue that they did not intend, or did not know, that the crimes were occurring', because the position of a commander comes with 'broad and heavy responsibilities . . . to search out and detect failure on the part of his subordinates'.[31]

The Nagahama tribunal's rejection of the idea that command responsibility could be applied to single crimes mirrored the Yamashita trial judgment. Neither the Yamashita nor the Nagahama decisions, however, proved durable: as seen in the previous chapter, commanders were held liable for single crimes that they had not directly perpetrated. It is highly likely that consciousness of inconsistencies such as this was a key reason for the fact that later tribunals did not explain their judgments but restricted themselves to pronouncing findings on guilt and applying sentences. The trials were not meant to establish precedents on specific points of law, and there was no expectation that tribunals would adopt specific points of precedent. Nonetheless, conspicuous failure to conform to previous decisions would have affected the credibility of the trials, because in a legal system that purports to mete out justice, laws are interpreted and applied consistently.

Though the Nagahama tribunal relied heavily in its decision on wording from the Yamashita judgment, it also used additional, more precise reasoning to hold Nagahama liable for the crimes of his subordinates. By this means the tribunal attempted to clarify and refine how the doctrine of command responsibility should operate. Rather than focussing on the sheer number and geographical distribution of crimes, as the Yamashita decision had done, the Nagahama tribunal instead placed more emphasis on the pattern of criminality that had occurred under Nagahama's command, emphasising the fact that the multiple crimes that had been perpetrated over a prolonged period were similar in nature.

---

30. *USA v Nagahama*, Trial Transcript, 925. A similar argument would be applied at the International Military Tribunal for the Far East. See Robert Cribb, '"Conventional War Crimes": The International Military Tribunal for the Far East and the Ill-Treatment of Prisoners of War and Civilian Internees', in *The Tokyo Tribunal: Perspectives on Law, History, and Memory*, ed. Viviane E. Dittrich, Kerstin von Lingen, Philipp Osten, and Jolana Makraiová (Torkal Opsahl Academic EPublisher, 2020), 177–200.
31. *USA v Nagahama*, Trial Transcript, 925–26.

Despite this relatively precise wording, the explanation of the decision on Nagahama remained somewhat ambiguous. Much like the Yamashita judgment, the Nagahama gave no clear example of the ways in which the commander's conduct had been criminal: in other words, the tribunal did not provide a legal formula that connected specific actions or inactions to specific crimes. The failure of the early tribunals to elucidate their reasoning goes a long way towards explaining why command responsibility proved to be so malleable during the trials.

The bench did not make clear whether it held that Nagahama had known that the crimes were occurring and negligently did nothing to stop them, or whether he had intended the crimes to occur. Thus, it did little to establish a clear legal process or argument for subsequent tribunals to follow. The failure to distinguish between mere omission and intent was common in prosecution arguments in war crimes trials in the Pacific Theatre. Indeed, as we will see below, the prosecution in some trials attempted to frame omission as evidence of intent: to argue that a commander's failure to prevent, halt, or punish the crimes of his subordinates should be taken as evidence that the commander had intended that the crimes would occur. The failure of the bench to separate negligence and intent shows how difficult it was for Allied military tribunals to apply the new doctrine.

Commanders as Accomplices: Joint Criminal Enterprise in Torture Cases

Attributing intent through evidence of omission appears to have been an attempt by prosecutors to apply an early form of what would now be called the doctrine of joint criminal enterprise. Though joint criminal enterprise was well-established in some domestic criminal systems, including those of the UK and Australia, applying the doctrine to a military hierarchy proved to be a complex and uncertain exercise. The legal doctrine of joint criminal enterprise makes it possible for an entire group – in this case a military unit – to be prosecuted, when all the accused members of the group are held to have taken steps to carry out a common plan.[32]

The use of the principle of joint criminal enterprise differs from jointly trying members of a unit. Prosecutions using joint criminal enterprise hold all members of a group liable for all the criminal actions that occurred when members carried out a common plan. Running a joint trial, in most instances,

32. Nina H. B. Jørgensen, 'On Being "Concerned" in a Crime: Embryonic Joint Criminal Enterprise?', in *Hong Kong's War Crimes Trials*, ed. Suzannah Linton (Oxford University Press, 2013), 146–57; Lachezar D. Yanev, *Theories of Co-Perpetration in International Criminal Law* (Brill-Nijhoff), 131–40, 174–81.

simply means that all the accused are believed to have separately committed the same or similar crimes against the same victims during the same period. Though there is now a relatively clear legal difference between joint criminal enterprise and command responsibility, at the post-conflict war crimes trials, the difference was not fully fleshed out.[33] Torture trials provide some prominent examples of prosecutors applying arguments that primarily relied on the idea of joint criminal enterprise to convict commanders, in a confusing mixture of that doctrine with the principle of command responsibility.

In the Allied trials that followed the Second World War, the doctrine of joint criminal enterprise was aimed primarily at suspected Nazi war criminals. The SS had been designated as a criminal organisation, and the principle of joint criminal enterprise proved to be a valuable tool in prosecuting members.[34] War crimes legislation in the UK and Australia, as well as the Netherlands, enabled the use of the doctrine in trials of Japanese suspects as well.[35] Since the Allies labelled no specific elements of the Japanese military or government as criminal organisations, however, joint criminal enterprise was not deployed in the same form, or as frequently, at the trials of Japanese suspects. Command responsibility was much more extensively used.

Nevertheless, an embryonic form of the doctrine of joint criminal enterprise is visible in the trials of Japanese military personnel, especially in torture cases. Fundamentally, it was useful because it seemed to allow prosecutors to expand the notion of command responsibility. The two doctrines tended to be confused with each other, which is not surprising at this early stage in the evolution of both. Joint criminal enterprise and command responsibility can both result in an individual being held liable for the actions of another. The key difference is in how that liability arises.[36] Under command responsibility, it is the commander's position that creates a positive duty to ensure that subordinates act within the law. Liability under joint criminal enterprise, by contrast, arises when members of a group, regardless of rank, all take part in a criminal act; hierarchy is not the issue. Though trials of officers that relied solely on command responsibility far outnumbered those that implied the use of joint criminal enterprise, a consciousness of both doctrines is evident in most trials of commanding officers.

33. Alison Marston Danner and Jenny S. Martinez, 'Guilty Associations: Joint Criminal Enterprise, Command Responsibility and the Development of International Criminal Law', *California Law Review* 93 (2005): 151–52.
34. Yanev, *Theories of Co-Perpetration*, 75–81.
35. Nina H. B. Jørgensen, 'Theories of Joint Criminal Responsibility at the Asian Tribunals: Hong Kong, East Timor and Cambodia', in *Trials for International Crimes in Asia*, ed. Kirsten Sellars (Cambridge University Press, 2016), 318–22; Borch, *Military Trials of War Criminals in the Netherlands East Indies*, 32–33, 154–57.
36. Danner and Martinez, 'Guilty Associations', 108–12, 148–50.

Trials of Kenpeitai members evidently presented the best opportunity to expand the practical application of command responsibility, potentially into the territory of joint criminal enterprise. The use of torture by Kenpeitai officers had been directly connected to their role in maintaining Japanese rule in occupied Asia and the Pacific. In other trials, such as those for massacre and summary execution, junior and mid-level officers rarely oversaw multiple separate crimes. At prison camps, many officers seemed to be simply uninterested in the day-to-day running of the camp, leaving such duties to non-commissioned officers and guards. Kenpeitai officers, however, had had a clear, formal mission to suppress opposition to Japanese rule. Such a mission implied a strong hierarchy and a coherent purpose. Thus, some prosecutors apparently saw an opportunity to interpret command responsibility as creating a form of participatory liability. What can now be identified as an early form of the doctrine of joint criminal enterprise was used to accuse some Kenpeitai commanders of actually taking part in a crime, rather than being passively responsible for it because of their failure to prevent, halt, or punish the commission of the crime.

The UK trial of Kenpeitai Captain Shibata Shigeo, who was prosecuted alongside his subordinate, Sergeant-Major Oba Takao, shows some of the similarities, and resulting confusion, between command responsibility and early versions of joint criminal enterprise. Tried between 10 February and 7 March 1947 in Hong Kong, the two were accused of being concerned in the ill-treatment of civilians during the Japanese occupation of Hong Kong.[37] Surviving victims testified that Oba had frequently tortured prisoners suspected of spying or insurgency by beating and waterboarding, and by setting an Alsatian guard dog to attack them.[38] Most of the evidence from surviving victims, however, was of general abuse, rather than specific incidents. Oba was found guilty and sentenced to three years' imprisonment. Surprisingly, Shibata was acquitted, even though he had been Oba's commanding officer when the crimes occurred.

The prosecutor's opening address outlined three possible ways of convicting Shibata, though, as it turned out, two of them remained unsubstantiated by evidence. In the first, the court could find that Shibata had personally ordered or directly participated in the ill-treatment of civilians. In the second, he could be found to have been a key component of a superior officer's policy to torture civilians, and thus to be jointly liable with that superior officer. In the third scenario, Shibata had furthered the crimes, because he had acquiesced when his subordinates carried out the torture, or had connived at the criminal acts because he had knowingly failed to stop them.[39] The third argument is unusual, because it

37. TNA, WO 235/1007, *UK v Shibata Shigeo and One Other*, Charge Sheet, 1.
38. WO 235/1007, Trial Transcript, 8–10, 20, 25, 29.
39. WO 235/1007, Trial Transcript, 5

implies that a failure to prevent his subordinates from committing war crimes was a necessary component of the substantive crimes. The accusation of furthering crimes through inaction, rather than simply allowing them to happen, was not normally a part of the doctrine of command responsibility. This argument adopts an aspect of command responsibility – the duty to prevent a crime – and then applies it to joint criminal enterprise by maintaining that Shibata had joined in the crime by acquiescing to it or conniving at it.

The prosecution produced no direct evidence against Shibata during the trial; thus, the first of the three possible routes to conviction was ruled out. The defence made no plea of superior orders, thereby ruling out the second. The prosecutor's closing address essentially restated the third argument.[40] Again, the prosecutor argued that Shibata's position as a commander meant that he had been responsible for the actions of his subordinates, and that if he had done nothing to prevent crimes from occurring, he had acted to further those crimes. The prosecutor's argument that Shibata's inaction was a necessary part of furthering the crimes was an unusual argument. The fact that Shibata was acquitted presumably means that the bench rejected this argument.

The reason for Shibata's acquittal is difficult to uncover. In his review of the trial, the JAG expressed surprise that Shibata was found not guilty. Even though Shibata had been acquitted, the JAG considered that the defence's case had been particularly weak and unconvincing. Furthermore, he noted that the tribunal had had more than enough scope to find Shibata guilty through command responsibility, presumably through strict liability, because his subordinates had committed the crime.[41] The fact that a fellow lawyer from the JAG's Office believed that the prosecutor could and perhaps should have used command responsibility to argue Shibata's guilt makes the approach taken in the trial even more puzzling. It may be relevant that two of the judges in Shibata's trial were from the UK Judge Advocate General's Office and had had a higher level of legal training than was normal for tribunal members, and so would likely have had some understanding of how joint criminal enterprise operated.[42] In many cases, tribunal members had had no legal training at all. Perhaps the prosecutor's blend of joint criminal enterprise and command responsibility was unconvincing, or simply too difficult to piece together: joint criminal enterprise has long been considered a contender for 'the most convoluted and opaque branch of criminal law'.[43]

Another possibility is that while tribunals could accept that commanding officers might be held liable for their subordinates' crimes, accusing them of

40. WO 235/1007, Prosecutor's Closing Address, 1–3.
41. WO 235/1007, JAG Review, 1–2.
42. WO 235/1007, Form for Assembly and Proceeding of a Military Court for the Trial of War Criminals, 1.
43. A. Reed and B. Fitzpatrick, *Criminal Law* (Sweet & Maxwell, 2009), 148.

actual intent to further the crimes of those subordinates was pushing the understanding of command too far. Holding officers responsible for the crimes of their subordinates acknowledges that the crimes on trial had occurred within a military hierarchy. But many judges may have struggled to find that an individual exhibited criminal intent because of the actions of his subordinates. In other words, the bench may have understood that while command came with broad and onerous responsibilities, command alone could not imply or construct criminal intent. Rather, intent needed to demonstrable and to be attached to an individual, rather than the position of commander.

The prosecutor from the Shibata trial, Major R. C. Lai, evidently learnt from his experience. At the trial some five months later of Kenpeitai Captain Ushiyama Yukio and three of his subordinates, Lai gave a much clearer explanation of how command responsibility and joint criminal enterprise could be merged. Tried in Hong Kong between 7 and 12 August 1947, Ushiyama and his subordinates were charged with the torture and mistreatment of civilians in Hong Kong between 30 December 1941 and 17 February 1945.[44] The specific crimes were remarkably similar to those prosecuted in other Kenpeitai trials, such as the proceedings for crimes committed at the infamous Shanghai Bridge House, and for the Double Tenth incident in Singapore, in which fifty-seven white civilians were arrested and tortured in 1943.[45] The Hong Kong victims had been routinely beaten, often while suspended from the ceiling, waterboarded, and held in unsanitary and overcrowded cells with little to eat or drink.[46] Ushiyama and two of his subordinates were found guilty of the crimes. Ushiyama was sentenced to death and hanged in Hong Kong on 22 October 1947. Sergeant-Major Ishiyama Kakue was sentenced to fifteen years' imprisonment, while Sergeant-Major Morino Sakuzo was sentenced to six years' imprisonment. The third subordinate, Sergeant-Major Matsuyama Hiroshi, was found not guilty of all charges.[47]

The prosecution did not raise evidence that Ushiyama had directly participated in any mistreatment of prisoners, nor that he had ordered any mistreatment, maintaining instead that he should be found guilty through either one of two separate legal arguments. In the first, Ushiyama had known that the crimes were occurring, and his refusal to stop them was equivalent to acquiescing. In

44. TNA, WO 235/1041, *UK v Ushiyama Yukio and Three Others*, Charge Sheet, 1.
45. See Peter Clague, *Bridge House: The True, Chilling Story of a Shanghai Chamber of Horrors* (South China Morning Post, 1983); H. F. Pringle, *Bridge House Survivor: Experiences of a Civilian Prisoner-of-War in Shanghai and Beijing, 1942–5* (Earnshaw Books, 2010); Wilson, 'War Crimes Trials and the Politics of Justice: The Case of Kinoshita Eiichi, 1945–57', 637–38; Joseph Kennedy, *British Civilians and the Japanese War in Malaya and Singapore, 1941–45* (W. Hodge, 1951), 147–51, 157–58; Bernice Archer, *The Internment of Western Civilians under the Japanese 1941–1945: A Patchwork of Internment* (Routledge-Curzon, 2004), 78–79.
46. WO 235/1041, Trial Transcript, 18, 34–36, 49–52, 61–63.
47. WO 235/1041 Trial Transcript, 290.

other words, he knew about, and failed to prevent, halt, or punish the commission of the crimes; therefore, he facilitated those crimes. In the second argument, Ushiyama had connived at committing the crimes 'to the extent that the Court can find beyond reasonable doubt that the accused was concerned in the crimes alleged'.[48] This second argument relies on the court finding that Ushiyama intended the crimes to happen, even without any evidence that he had ordered them to occur, and that this intent meant he had taken part in the torture as a participant, rather than merely failing to prevent the torture.

By the end of the trial, the prosecution had effectively merged aspects of the two arguments. In his closing address, the prosecutor claimed that because Ushiyama had been the commanding officer when the crimes were perpetrated, he was legally responsible for the actions of his subordinates. In using this argument, he invoked the strict liability version of command responsibility. Since the prosecutor also contended that the accused had known of the crimes, Ushiyama's failure to act also meant, in this view, that he was a party to those crimes. In other words, the prosecutor viewed Ushiyama as an accomplice to the crimes of his subordinates. According to the prosecutor, this accomplice form of liability had precedent in the Yamashita trial.[49]

The prosecutor's claim was questionable. On the one hand, the wording of the Yamashita judgment was vague enough to support this view. On the other hand, the more common understanding of the Yamashita judgment interpreted a commander's liability as some other form of responsibility, rather than a participatory offence in the substantive crime. In other appeals to the Yamashita trial, the prosecution insisted simply that commanders had a duty to prevent, halt, or punish the commission of war crimes. This prosecutor, by contrast, argued both that the commander had been strictly liable by virtue of his position, and that he had been a direct participant. His failure to act was seen not as a mere act of omission, but rather as an act of commission that had been necessary for the crime to occur.

The prosecution's mixed argument shows the difficult legal environment within which Japanese officers were tried for crimes committed by their subordinates. Ushiyama and his subordinates were brought to court in August 1947, which was relatively late in the trial process. Even at this stage, prosecutors could still struggle to articulate clearly how commanders should be held responsible for war crimes. As the prosecutors did not always present a consistent argument throughout the trial, defence counsel must also have had difficulty in clearly answering the charges against their clients. Rather than working from a well-defined doctrine and theory of criminal liability, prosecutors could essentially

48. WO 235/1041, Trial Transcript, 1–3.
49. WO 235/1041, Prosecutor's Closing Address, 1–2.

make their case on the run, leaving the defence little option but to do the same. In such an environment, there was limited opportunity to prepare an organised and comprehensive defence.

Though the prosecutor's argument in the Ushiyama trial differed from what had been proposed in the Shibata trial, both arguments were an attempt to frame the commanding officer as having intended the crimes to occur. That the two benches, dealing with relatively similar circumstances and arguments, could arrive at such different verdicts – the first acquitted and the second hanged – highlights not only the difficult legal questions that the trials raised, but also the variety of opinion about what command meant, and how liability was attached to it. The problem of whether omission could be interpreted as participation hovered over many of the torture trials, and, as we will see, trials for the mistreatment of prisoners.[50]

Strict Liability in the Face of Responsible Command

In late 1945 and throughout 1946, the war crimes trials did little to refine how command responsibility worked, or to distinguish the separate offence interpretation from the strict liability interpretation. In early 1947 a new national authority began to try suspected Japanese war criminals, a situation that offered the opportunity to clarify command responsibility. Following the declaration of Philippines independence on 4 July 1946, the US military handed over the trials for war crimes committed in the Philippines to the new Philippines government in March 1947.[51] Despite the fresh start, however, difficulties in interpreting command responsibility continued. The Philippine trial of Captain Fujita Takefumi shows the ongoing difficulty that tribunals had in articulating how command responsibility held an officer criminally liable for the actions of his subordinates, and what exactly was expected of a commanding officer.

Fujita had been the commander of a Kenpeitai detachment in North Manila during November and December 1944. As a member of the Philippines Kenpeitai, he operated within Colonel Nagahama Akira's chain of command. Fujita was prosecuted between 5 September and 10 November 1947, in the third of seventy-three trials run by Philippine authorities.[52] He faced three charges of

50. For other torture trials where joint criminal enterprise was applied successfully, see TNA, WO 235/993, *UK v Kishi Yasuo and Fourteen Others*; National Archives of Australia (hereafter NAA), War Crimes Trial of Yutani Yujiro and Two Others, archived at [https://recordsearch.naa.gov.au/SearchNRetrieve/Interface/ViewImage.aspx?B=722377].
51. Sharon W. Chamberlain, 'Justice and Reconciliation: Postwar Philippine Trials of Japanese War Criminals in History and Memory' (PhD thesis, George Washington University 2010), 55.
52. Sharon W. Chamberlain, *A Reckoning: Philippine Trials of Japanese War Criminals* (University of Wisconsin Press, 2019), 61.

permitting members of his command to torture civilians. He was also charged with contributing to the murder of two civilians at Fort Santiago by permitting his subordinates to torture them at a separate location; the prisoners died at Fort Santiago after being interrogated elsewhere.[53] Philippine guerrillas had increased attacks against Japanese forces following the US invasion of the Philippines in October 1944, and all the civilian victims in the Fujita case were suspected of either being or aiding guerrillas. Fujita was found guilty of the first three charges and of an amended version of the fourth charge of permitting members of his command to torture the two civilians, but he was found not guilty of contributing to their murder. Sentenced to life imprisonment, Fujita, along with all other surviving Japanese war criminals convicted of crimes committed in the Philippines, was pardoned in 1953.[54]

As in many other command responsibility trials of junior and mid-ranking officers, the charges against Fujita accused him of direct participation in the alleged crimes. Unlike in most other trials of such officers, however, the prosecution explicitly framed the Fujita proceedings as a command responsibility trial in its opening statement to the tribunal.[55] When trying junior and mid-level officers, prosecutors who intended to argue command responsibility often left open the option of pursuing the accused for direct responsibility, probably to hedge their bets: they could either show successfully that the accused had directly ordered the crimes to take place, or could adapt their strategy as the trial developed to focus on command responsibility. Though some junior and mid-level officers, like Fujita, were explicitly tried under command responsibility, it was far more common to apply the doctrine directly in trials of senior officers from the general staff. Considering that Fujita was one of the first accused war criminals to be tried by the Philippines, it is likely that the prosecution was keen to make it clear that command responsibility would be a central component of the Philippine trials, just as it had already been at the UK, US, and Australian trials.

The prosecution's case was relatively straightforward. The prosecutor showed that Fujita had commanded a Kenpeitai detachment, and that he had been in direct command in North Manila, where the crimes were committed.[56] Surviving victims claimed in their testimony that they had been tortured by

53. NARA, RG331, Supreme Commander of the Allied Powers, Legal Section, Prosecution Division, Philippines Verses [*sic*] Japanese War Criminals 1947–1949, Box 1728, *Philippines v Fujita Takefumi*, Charge Sheet, 1–2.
54. *Philippines v Fujita*, Trial Transcript, 775–76; Chamberlain, 'Justice and Reconciliation', 235; Wilson, Cribb, Trefalt, and Aszkielowicz, *Japanese War Criminals*, 214–20.
55. *Philippines v Fujita*, Trial Transcript, 2–4.
56. *Philippines v Fujita*, Trial Transcript, 760–64.

Kenpeitai personnel, or that they had seen civilians taken away for what they presumed to be torture.[57]

Despite the prosecution's statement at the start of the proceedings that Fujita was being tried under the doctrine of command responsibility, it appears that the defence lawyers only realised that he was being held responsible for the acts of his subordinates when the prosecution rested its case. After the prosecution had finished, the defence moved that the case against Fujita be dismissed, because none of the evidence showed that he had personally committed a crime, and because the evidence that members of his command had carried out the crimes was entirely circumstantial – the defence's case was that the prosecution's evidence connecting Fujita to the crimes, either personally or through his subordinates, was speculative.[58]

The prosecution argued that dismissing the trial on these grounds would violate the entire purpose of the war crimes trials. According to the prosecution, if the case were dismissed because no evidence directly indicated that Fujita had personally participated in or ordered the crimes, or even that he had known of the crimes, then there would be no point in holding command responsibility trials at all. In the prosecution's view, the military tribunals were the only appropriate courts for prosecuting officers for war crimes, because it would only be possible to understand the full picture of how an atrocity had occurred, and, therefore, how a commanding officer had contributed to the crime, in a tribunal with relaxed rules that allowed a broad range of circumstantial evidence, and especially hearsay evidence, to be presented.[59] Though most prosecutors merely stated that circumstantial and speculative evidence were admissible under the relevant regulations, the prosecutor in the Fujita trial then went one step further. In reply to the defence request that the case be dismissed, he argued that the relaxed rules of evidence were explicitly designed for officers like Fujita. In presenting this argument, the prosecutor was certainly attempting to convince the tribunal to continue the trial, but he also appears to have been trying to help the defence counsel understand the nature of the charges against Fujita.[60]

The defence's failure to understand the prosecution's case until twelve days after the trial had started is startling. For a fair trial to occur, the defendant, and more important, the defendant's lawyers, need to understand how criminal liability is alleged to have arisen. In Fujita's case, the misunderstanding may have occurred partly because of poor quality interpreting and translating between Japanese and English. The two defence lawyers were Japanese and relied on

57. *Philippines v Fujita*, Trial Transcript, 9–24, 71–83.
58. *Philippines v Fujita*, Trial Transcript, 211–14.
59. *Philippines v Fujita*, Trial Transcript 202–3.
60. *Philippines v Fujita*, Trial Transcript, 202–3, 229.

interpreters throughout the trial. Evidence of poor interpretation and, possibly, poor translation of documents, can be seen in the trial transcript. Though most of the defence examination and cross-examination of witnesses as interpreted into English was relatively clear, the defence's longer questions, and their opening and closing statements, often made little sense in English. The same interpreters rendered Japanese into English and English into Japanese. The poor English in some sections of the transcript, therefore, suggests that those interpreters may not have had a sufficient understanding of English to interpret the prosecution arguments adequately into Japanese, especially in the case of lengthier statements.

The imprecise wording of the charges was almost certainly another part of the problem. Defendants are notified of the charges that they will face in advance of a trial so that the defence can focus its efforts on relevant points of law. Not only in the case of Fujita, but indeed in most trials involving command responsibility, the charges failed to make clear that the accused would not be tried as a direct participant. Rather, the charges were worded openly enough to permit the prosecution to argue that liability arose because the defendant was either a direct perpetrator or a responsible superior. Prosecutors would have welcomed this flexibility and used it to mould their arguments as their cases unfolded in court, but it is also likely that broadly worded charges were used out of sheer necessity. The circumstances in which war crimes had taken place were often confusing: documentary evidence was usually limited, and many witnesses were dead, missing, or simply unavailable. These factors, combined with the expedited nature of the trials, made it likely that prosecutors themselves had insufficient time to familiarise themselves with the charges and the circumstances of the crime at the beginning of the process. Imprecise wording of the charges, moreover, reflected the fact that command responsibility was not itself a precise charge: the Yamashita verdict and the subsequent trials did not give a clear picture of how exactly a commander could and should be held liable.

Central to Fujita's defence was the unreliability of the prosecution witnesses. Two Filipino witnesses who had testified at the earlier US trial of Nagahama gave evidence at Fujita's trial that contradicted what they had said at Nagahama's. Arrested as suspected insurgents and imprisoned at the Wack Wack Country Club, they stated in the Nagahama trial that they had been beaten with baseball bats. At the Fujita trial, which was for the same set of incidents, the same witnesses claimed instead that they had been given electric shocks. Furthermore, at the Nagahama trial, these witnesses had been unable to identify the Japanese officers responsible for their mistreatment. At Fujita's trial, both witnesses positively identified Fujita, even though they stated that they had seen him only a few times within a thirty-minute window before being tortured.[61] Evidence from

61. *Philippines v Fujita*, Trial Transcript, 653–55, 185–93; *USA v Nagahama*, Trial Transcript, 442–50.

other witnesses about the amount of food and water provided to prisoners, as well as the number of soldiers present during their imprisonment, was also contradictory. Though the defence lawyers conceded that witness testimony would naturally change over time, they contended that the changes in evidence were so dramatic that the witnesses could not be believed.[62]

Witness testimony in the Kenpeitai trials was perhaps especially likely to be unreliable. In many cases, the Kenpeitai had worked closely with local police forces and civilians in carrying out their duties. Local residents had assisted in identifying and arresting suspected insurgents and spies, and in interpreting in interrogations. After the conflict ended, wartime collaboration with the Japanese became a major issue in the Philippines and elsewhere.[63] In the war crimes trials, therefore, Philippine civilians who had assisted the Japanese had a clear incentive to testify against their former masters, in order to demonstrate to Allied authorities and their own compatriots that during the conflict they had acted under duress in collaborating with the occupiers.[64]

In addition to attempting to discredit the prosecution witnesses as much as possible, the defence also claimed that in this case the wrong people were in the dock. Evidence was produced to show that Kenpeitai commanders in the Philippines had used regular army soldiers to increase their ranks for particular operations, especially in the later months of 1944, when the crimes in question took place, because increased guerrilla attacks in support of the US landings had become a serious threat to Japanese control of the Philippines. Philippine civilians, according to Fujita's defence lawyers, tended to attribute war crimes to the Kenpeitai, when, in fact, regular Japanese army units had committed most of the offences. The defence conceded that it was to some extent natural for Philippine civilians to assume that any Japanese soldier who interrogated them was a Kenpeitai member. After all, for most of the Japanese occupation of the Philippines, anti-guerrilla operations had been conducted by the Kenpeitai. The defence maintained, however, that as a result of the increased guerrilla attacks in 1944, many regular Japanese army units had begun to conduct their own anti-guerrilla roundups. According to the defence, none of the witnesses had definitively identified a single Kenpeitai member at the Wack Wack Country Club; they had simply assumed that those soldiers carrying out the torture were members of the Kenpeitai. Accordingly, the defence maintained that the prosecution had failed to show that Fujita, as the regional Kenpeitai commander, was ultimately responsible for the crimes with which he was charged.[65]

62. *Philippines v Fujita*, Trial Transcript, 702–15.
63. On collaboration in the Philippines, see Joel Steinberg, *Philippines Collaboration in World War II* (University of Michigan Press, 1967).
64. Chamberlain, 'Justice and Reconciliation', 90.
65. *Philippines v Fujita*, Trial Transcript, 668–70, 674–77.

As a separate part of Fujita's defence, two of his subordinates gave evidence that he had been a strict commander who had harshly punished subordinates for disobeying orders or failing to carry out their duty.[66] This aspect of the defence was a direct response to the accusation of command responsibility. In leading evidence that Fujita had ensured that his subordinates either followed his orders or faced consequences, the defence attempted to show that he had taken steps to prevent his subordinates from committing war crimes by trying to ensure that his orders were followed. Thus, even if Fujita's subordinates had committed the alleged crimes, a claim that Fujita rejected, he had nonetheless carried out his duty as a commanding officer, and therefore, in this view, should not be held liable under the doctrine of command responsibility.

The tribunal stated that due to the significance of the trial, it would produce a reasoned decision.[67] Whether the trial was especially significant because of the nature of the alleged crimes, or the fact that it was the first Philippine trial to use command responsibility, or for some other reason, was not made clear. In its judgment the tribunal explicitly rejected the defence's claim that Fujita had carried out his duties as a commander by enforcing or attempting to enforce strict discipline and thus ought not to be held responsible for the crimes. According to the tribunal, the defence's legal argument ran counter to the underlying theory of command responsibility, because Fujita's strict discipline did not 'totally preclude the possibility that some of his men may have committed unlawful acts'.[68] Thus, the judges found that the mere occurrence of war crimes within a chain of command meant that the accused officer was liable.

Somewhat puzzlingly, this reasoning relies on wording that suggests an understanding of command responsibility as a separate offence of the superior, rather than as a strict liability. The emphasis was on the fact that strict discipline was not enough to prevent war crimes, rather than on holding Fujita responsible simply because he was the commanding officer. The judgment is contradictory – it implies that responsible commanders discipline their troops, but that even where there is strict discipline, the commission of war crimes by the commanding officer's subordinates shows that the accused was irresponsible. This judgment highlights the difficulty that the post-war trials encountered in reconciling the desire to punish those in a position of command for war crimes with the fact that command was, in reality, rarely absolute.

There is a striking parallel between the Fujita trial and that of Yamashita Tomoyuki. Both Yamashita and Fujita were the first to be tried in their respective national jurisdictions under command responsibility. In both cases, the tribunal

66. *Philippines v Fujita*, Trial Transcript, 235–37; 373.
67. *Philippines v Fujita*, Trial Transcript, 771.
68. *Philippines v Fujita*, Trial Transcript, 773.

published an ambiguous judgment: it could be interpreted either as an assertion that a commander was strictly liable for the crimes of his subordinates, or as condemnation of the commander's personal failure to prevent and punish crimes. It is unclear whether the ongoing failure of the tribunals to give explicit direction on how they had used command responsibility should be attributed to factors such as limited legal training, unintentionally poor wording of charges, and a focus on the outcome of the trial rather than on the procedure. It is just as likely that tribunal members were aware that the value to them of the doctrine command responsibility lay partially in vagueness in the application of the doctrine.

Command Responsibility as Moral Responsibility

Like most suspects throughout the trials of Japanese military personnel, most officers accused of liability for war crimes under the doctrine of command responsibility pleaded not guilty. Judging from the content of post-trial petitions against conviction and sentence, it appears that the accused commanders believed they had done nothing wrong, and that there was no charge to answer, because they had not directly participated in the crimes. In a small number of cases, the accused initially pleaded not guilty but accepted responsibility during the proceedings.[69] This contradiction between what had been pleaded at the start of the trial and what was accepted in court likely arose from the fact that the charges almost invariably framed the offence as direct participation in a crime. Usually, it was not until the trial was well underway that it became clear that the accused officer was actually being charged with command responsibility.

In some cases, officers would accept responsibility for war crimes committed by their subordinates, in the hope of saving them from harsher punishment. Tribunals usually looked favourably upon commanders who did so, and, as we will see below, would sometimes reduce the sentence imposed. It is likely that a tribunal was willing to mitigate the severity of a sentence in such cases for two reasons. First, the officer had recognised that he had failed in his duty to control his subordinates and thus had demonstrated an acceptance of some level of guilt, even if he had not pleaded guilty. Second, accepting responsibility for the crimes of a subordinate may have been interpreted by the bench as a noble

69. See, for example, NAA, War Crimes Trial of Ichise Shinichi and Five Others, archived at [https://recordsearch.naa.gov.au/SearchNRetrieve/Interface/ViewImage.aspx?B=722845]. Though Vice-Admiral Ichise accepted moral responsibility for crimes that had occurred under his command, he was found not guilty.

attempt to protect subordinates. In other words, the officer appeared to be sacrificing himself to protect his subordinates, which was expected of responsible commanders.

The trial of Major Higashigawa Yoshinobu and Captain Terata Isamu, alongside thirty-four of their subordinates, offers an example in which the war crimes trial process mitigated the severity of a sentence when an officer accepted responsibility for the crimes of his subordinates and attempted to cover up his subordinates' crimes. In this sense, the trial's outcome provides some indication of how the tribunal expected a commander to behave, at least after a crime had been committed.

Between 30 August and 28 September 1946, Higashigawa, Terata, and their subordinates were tried in a British court for the torture and ill-treatment of civilians at the town of Butterworth and on Penang Island in Malaya. Major Higashigawa, who was a captain at the time, was the regional commanding officer of the Kenpeitai from November 1942 to April 1943. Terata had commanded the same detachment from April 1943 until the end of the war.[70] Higashigawa and Terata were the only officers charged in the joint trial, which included Kenpeitai staff of various ranks, plus civilian interpreters. Both officers were found guilty through the doctrine of command responsibility and were sentenced to death. Higashigawa was hanged in Penang on 17 December 1946, alongside nineteen of his subordinates. Terata was sentenced to death by firing squad rather than hanging. The choice of firing squad indicated that the tribunal had already acknowledged mitigating factors in his case – facing a firing squad was considered to be the more honourable way for a soldier to die.[71] The court reinforced its assessment by recommending mercy to the confirming authority. Terata's sentence was subsequently commuted to life imprisonment. The remaining eleven subordinates were sentenced to terms of imprisonment ranging from five to fifteen years.[72]

Most of the crimes had occurred at Penang Jail, which also served as the Kenpeitai garrison. Prosecution witnesses, most of whom were local civilians who had worked as clerks and warders at the jail, alleged that water torture, electrocution, and beatings were carried out by all the accused, except for the two officers.[73] Though none of these civilians admitted to beating prisoners themselves, a local interpreter openly admitted to torturing prisoners under the direct orders of Kenpeitai personnel.[74] This witness was not subject to prosecution as he was not Japanese, so his admission did not imperil him. According to witnesses,

70. TNA, WO 235/931, *UK v Higashigawa Yoshinobu and Thirty-Four Others*, Charge Sheet, 1–3.
71. A. Frank Reel, *The Case of General Yamashita* (Octagon Publishing, 1971), 175.
72. WO 235/931, JAG Report, 2.
73. WO235/931, JAG Report, 6.
74. WO 235/931, Trial Transcript., 135–38.

one of the accused interpreters burnt out a victim's eye with a cigarette. One prisoner attempted suicide by cutting his neck with the lid of a tin can; later this prisoner successfully suicided by hanging himself in his cell. Another interpreter allegedly cut off a female captive's breast with a sword before dragging her behind a motorcycle. She died from her injuries. Though no explicit claims were made in the trial, it is likely that some female prisoners were sexually assaulted. Evidence was submitted that one of the accused, Sergeant-Major Washio Koji, took female prisoners out of their cells and returned them in a 'frightened' state. A local doctor treated one prisoner for serious wounding to the vagina. The doctor did not ask how the injury had occurred, as he was afraid that the Kenpeitai would punish him for asking questions.[75]

Major Higashigawa's defence was limited and not particularly convincing. Higashigawa had been in command of the Penang Kenpeitai during a major roundup of suspected communists in early 1943. He maintained that though his unit had assisted in the arrest of suspected communists, and was present at Penang Jail, the Kenpeitai had had no independent authority to interrogate suspects. Higashigawa argued that his unit was instead under the command of the local garrison unit, and that he personally had had nothing to do with the mass arrests, nor the interrogation of suspects. When cross-examined about what exactly his role was at the time, he gave evasive answers that provided no substantial indication of why his unit had been in Penang. Higashigawa, who was based in Butterworth, also maintained that he had only visited Penang Jail four times, and that since he never knew, nor could have known, that his Kenpeitai subordinates were carrying out torture, allegedly under the direction of the local garrison commander, there was no need for him to monitor them or ensure that they were not committing crimes against civilians.[76]

Terata, by contrast, made no real effort to avoid culpability for the crimes committed by his subordinates during his period of command of the Penang Kenpeitai. Evidence was given to show that Terata had known that some of his subordinates were beating prisoners, and that he had taken some steps to prevent them from committing further crimes. Indeed, a prosecution witness stated that he saw Terata admonishing one of his subordinates for beating a prisoner. Terata claimed that as well as verbally reprimanding the subordinate, he had also beaten him as punishment. Terata acknowledged that as the commanding officer he had had some responsibility for the acts of his subordinates, even when he had had no personal knowledge that crimes were taking place.[77]

75. WO235/931, Trial Transcript, 30–33, 80, 84.
76. WO 235/931, Trial Transcript, 578–85.
77. WO 235/931, Trial Transcript, 425–26.

Terata also attempted to cover for his subordinates. He claimed that two corporals who oversaw an interrogation in which the victim died had neither beaten the prisoner, nor had had any actual command over the interrogation. In addition, he provided an alibi for Sergeant-Major Washio, who was regarded by prosecution witnesses as the most brutal of the Kenpeitai staff at Penang. Terata claimed that Washio could not have carried out several of the more violent acts against female prisoners because he was in hospital at the relevant time. He made this statement despite the fact that hospital records showed that Washio had only been admitted once, on a different occasion, and despite the copious prosecution evidence that was brought against Washio.[78]

It was not unusual for defendants to take the blame for war crimes, and to attempt to convince the court that they were more responsible than their fellow soldiers.[79] What sets this case apart is that the court was convinced that Terata was committing perjury for the benefit of others, rather than just accepting liability. At the end of Terata's testimony, the court president commended him for his attempt to cover for his subordinates:

> Captain Terata, you have made a very elaborate effort to save your subordinates at your own expense, and the Court wishes to say that your attitude appears very favourable compared with that of Major Higashigawa.[80]

Undoubtedly, the court decided that Terata's attempt to save his subordinates was the honourable thing for a military commander to do; thus, the tribunal recommended that the confirming authority grant mercy and commute his sentence.[81]

The decision of the court to recommend mercy in such circumstances was unusual. Terata had commanded a unit that had committed crimes for a significant portion of the war and had admitted that he knew that crimes were occurring under his command. The degree of mitigation of Terata's punishment – not only the comparison between his original sentence and his actual punishment, but also the comparison between his punishment and that of Higashigawa – raises questions about what kind of justice the tribunal, and indeed, the entire trial and review process, was handing down. The tribunal's apparent response to Terata's acceptance of responsibility and to his attempts to save his subordinates suggests that it was more interested in moral judgment, focussing on the defendant's own sense of culpability, responsibility, and duty, than in accountability for the substantive crimes that Terata had overseen.

78. WO 235/931, Trial Transcript, 424–27, 436–38.
79. For example, TNA, WO 235/890, *UK v Murakami Seisaku and Three Others.*
80. WO 235/931, Trial Transcript, 438.
81. WO 235/931, JAG Review, 2.

The tribunal's commendation of Terata at the end of his testimony, and before the testimony of other defendants, unwittingly revealed that it had already reached a decision on the guilt of several of the other accused. For Terata to be covering for his subordinates, those subordinates must have been guilty of the alleged crimes. At this stage the defence had presented only two of its witnesses, yet the tribunal had apparently already come to a decision on guilt. To have reached a decision before the defence had closed its case suggests that the tribunal was ignoring, or was planning to ignore, any further, potentially exculpating, evidence; or at least, that it did not expect to be convinced by any such evidence. The post-war trials were intended to display Allied justice as open and fair, even if they were not explicitly designed to achieve procedural justice. In this case, the tribunal's willingness to arrive so obviously at a decision so early in the trial seriously undermined the legitimacy of the proceedings.

The Higashigawa trial shows the breadth of material that tribunals could take into account when assessing commanders' guilt and responsibility. Terata's acceptance of responsibility appears virtually irrelevant to the overall goal of the post-war proceedings, which were intended to achieve justice for the crimes that had been committed. Terata's admission of responsibility, well after the crimes had occurred, did nothing to reduce the effect of the crimes of his subordinates, crimes for which he was held liable as a responsible officer. Nonetheless, the tribunal apparently considered that admitting responsibility went a considerable way to mitigating or alleviating liability.

The tribunal's sentencing of Terata, and the recommendation of mercy, also illuminate how tribunals understood command, and how the application of command responsibility interacted with this understanding. For the tribunal, command was tied to accountability: at some point, someone in the chain of command was accountable for what had happened. The doctrine of command responsibility was meant to determine with whom this accountability lay. In the eyes of the bench, Terata's acceptance of responsibility necessarily made him a more proper officer than his superior, Major Higashigawa, and he was therefore less culpable.

Sexual Violence and Command Responsibility

One way in which Japanese military personnel mistreated civilians in occupied territories was through the crime of rape. None of the trials considered in this chapter or in other parts of this book, however, featured the application of command responsibility in cases where a commanding officer's subordinates were alleged to have committed rape. In Higashigawa's trial, on the other hand, evidence appears to have the potential to support rape charges: several witnesses testified that one of the defendants, Washio, repeatedly took female civilians out of the cells by himself.[82]

Rape was explicitly prosecuted through command responsibility in a number of national trials of high-ranking officers, including those of Yamashita, Lieutenant-General Honma Masaharu, and Admiral Toyoda Soemu.[83] In these three trials, only Yamashita was held responsible for rape, likely because the crime was widespread during the Battle of Manila.[84] Honma, who was convicted of responsibility for the Bataan Death March, was acquitted of charges of rape during the Japanese invasion of the Philippines in 1942 for two reasons. First, the prosecution submitted thirteen cases of rape, which was a comparatively small number compared with the number of cases of other crimes with which he was charged. The defence successfully argued that incidences of rape had therefore not been sufficiently numerous to attract the attention of a commanding officer of Honma's high rank. Second, during the relevant time, Honma's command had held multiple courts-martial of Japanese personnel accused of rape. The defence argued that Homma had ensured the crime was punished.[85] Toyoda was acquitted of all charges on the grounds that he was not the commander at the relevant place and time.[86]

In trials of mid- and junior-level officers, which are the focus of this book, it appears that prosecutors were unwilling to use command responsibility to pursue defendants for rape committed by their subordinates. Instead, rape at the lower-level trials seems to have been prosecuted only as a crime of direct commission. It is not clear why prosecutors were reluctant to hold lower-level commanders responsible for rapes committed by their subordinates, but the most likely reason is that rape was seen as the perpetrator's direct and individual action. In the case of other crimes – massacring prisoners of war, civilians, or guerrillas; summarily executing prisoners; or torturing captives for information – prosecutors may have suspected that subordinates had acted under their superiors' orders partly on the grounds that such crimes appeared to have had some connection to military goals or objectives. Rape, by contrast, may have been considered so far

82. WO 237/931, Trial Transcript, 30–31.
83. See Gurgen Petrossian, 'Elements of Superior Responsibility for Sexual Violence by Subordinates', *Manitoba Law Review* 42, no. 3 (2019): 123–52. On the Australian national trials for crimes of sexual assault and rape, see Helen Durham and Narrelle Morris, 'Women's Bodies and International Criminal Law: From Tokyo to Rabaul', in *Beyond Victor's Justice? The Tokyo War Crimes Trial Revisited*, ed. Yuki Tanaka, Tim McCormack, and Gerry Simpson (Martinus Nijhoff Publishers, 2011), 283–90.
84. Connaughton, *The Battle for Manila*, 115–16, 119–21, 149, 154.
85. Yuma Totani, *Justice in Asia and the Pacific Region, 1945–1952: Allied War Crimes Prosecutions* (Cambridge University Press, 2015), 42–43.
86. W. H. Parks, 'Command Responsibility for War Crimes', *Military Law Review* 62 (1973): 69–73.

removed from military procedure that responsibility must have been individual and prosecutors would not even try to attach it to a low-level commander.

Yet, senior officers were held responsible for rapes committed by their subordinates. The decision not to prosecute lower-level officers for rape under command responsibility has significant implications: it suggests that prosecutors understood the purpose of the doctrine differently depending on the level of command on trial. Junior and mid-level officers were most often tried for crimes that prosecutors strongly suspected they had ordered, while senior officers were on trial for failing to control their subordinates.

Prosecuting Commanders Without Invoking Command Responsibility

Some Kenpeitai commanders were tried unambiguously as direct participants in torture, without recourse to the doctrine of command responsibility. Several Australian trials took this approach.[87] Australian authorities prosecuted relatively few Kenpeitai personnel, mostly because of the geographical jurisdiction for which the Australian military was responsible after the war.[88] Though Australian prisoners and civilians had certainly been tortured during interrogations, the resulting trials were usually conducted by either the UK or the US authorities, because those countries' militaries had jurisdiction over the major population centres in the Asia-Pacific region, where Kenpeitai headquarters were concentrated. Australian trials were held in Singapore and Hong Kong, but trials for crimes that had actually occurred in or near these cities were mainly carried out by the UK; many Australian trials there concerned crimes on the Burma–Thailand Railway. Similarly, the US took responsibility for crimes committed in Japan, including in the many POW camps situated there.

The separate trials of Captain Hoshijima Susumu and Colonel Obana Yoshimasa provide examples of proceedings in which prosecutors chose not to use command responsibility because charges of direct perpetration were available. Captain Hoshijima, commander of the infamous Sandakan POW camp in Borneo, explicitly ordered – and occasionally participated in – the torture of prisoners who had violated camp regulations. It was not necessary for prosecutors to invoke command responsibility to convict him. Evidence at Hoshijima's trial, which was conducted by the Australian military at Labuan in Borneo between 8 and 20 January 1946, showed that command responsibility could have been used to pursue him for other crimes of torture committed by his subordinates, which he had not ordered and in which he had not directly participated. With clear

87. Narrelle Morris, *Japanese War Crimes in the Pacific: Australia's Investigations and Prosecutions* (National Archives of Australia, 2019), 294–98, 309, 317, 328–33, 341–42, 351–52, 360.
88. Wilson, Cribb, Trefalt, and Aszkielowicz, *Japanese War Criminals*, 33.

evidence of his direct participation in multiple other incidents, however, the prosecutor did not pursue command responsibility charges for those crimes.[89] In another Australian trial, held in Singapore from 2 to 11 September 1946, Colonel Obana, too, escaped command responsibility charges for other offences, simply because it could be shown that he had directly ordered the torture of twelve captured Australian airmen.[90] In both cases, direct participation in brutal torture was enough to secure a death sentence for the accused officers.

The fact that in both cases the prosecution chose not to pursue command responsibility charges indicates that the authorities were focused on finding particular individuals guilty rather than on holding an accused person liable for every crime for which he was considered responsible. The initial Allied assertion that the post-war trials would secure comprehensive justice could take a back seat to practical considerations; if a commander was likely to receive a heavy sentence because of his own actions, there was limited point in extending a trial to pursue other charges that would cover the same substantive crime.[91] Examples like those of Hoshijima and Obana also show that prosecutors probably treated the doctrine of command responsibility as a second-best option, less preferable than conviction for direct commission of a crime.

Conclusions

Torture trials provided good opportunities for the exploration of command responsibility – in torture cases, more than for other crimes, it appeared obvious to the prosecution and probably to the bench that commanders must have known what was happening. While many prosecutors were suspicious that an officer had most probably ordered a summary execution, the kind of deliberate abuse that was the hallmark of the torture trials was different in character. At the torture trials, prosecutors were quick to notice that similar abuses had been meted out to victims across different localities. Victims were routinely suspended from the ceiling for hours while being beaten. Waterboarding and electrocution were common, as well as forcing victims to kneel over wooden blocks in extremely uncomfortable positions. The similarity in forms of torture in widely differing locations appears to have fuelled suspicion among prosecutors that commanding officers knew exactly what was going on under their command: since so many

89. Paul Taucher, 'Command Responsibility at the Sandakan-Ranau War Crimes Trials' (Honours Thesis, Murdoch University, 2016), 35–40; NAA, War Crimes Trial of Hoshijima Susumu, and Sixteen Others, archived at [https://recordsearch.naa.gov.au/SearchNRetrieve/Interface/ViewImage.aspx?B=1900164].
90. NAA, War Crimes Trial of Obana Yoshimasa and Seven Others, archived at [https://recordsearch.naa.gov.au/SearchNRetrieve/Interface/ViewImage.aspx?B=739024].
91. Wilson, Cribb, Trefalt, and Aszkielowicz, *Japanese War Criminals*, 25.

different units were using the same form of torture, the instructions, it might be assumed, must have come from higher up. Driven by such suspicion, some prosecutors went so far as to attempt to take advantage of the flexibility of command responsibility in order to accuse commanders of criminal intent, rather than of some form of criminal negligence.

That prosecutors attempted to expand command responsibility to imply criminal intent is somewhat surprising, because the torture trials offered such a clear path to conviction under a basic application of command responsibility. The doctrine was designed to prosecute and convict commanders without proof of intent, or even of direct knowledge. Many of the torture trials appear to have been relatively straightforward, especially in cases involving the Kenpeitai. Officers had frequently commanded units that had committed multiple crimes of torture over a prolonged period, and, furthermore, the role of the Kenpeitai in maintaining Japanese rule could be clearly linked to the crimes. Perhaps prosecutors were concerned that without intent, tribunal judges would be unlikely to hand down severe sentences. But if these concerns did exist, they were probably unfounded: in most cases where intent, or some form of accessory participation, was not argued, sentences were still severe.

In cases where intent was not a key component of the prosecution's case, the tribunals still struggled with what exactly officers who were found guilty under command responsibility were guilty of. In both US and Philippine tribunals, the courts tried to clarify how a commander could be held liable under command responsibility, relying on wording from the Yamashita judgment. Because the Yamashita judgment provided only a basic statement of the broad principles of command responsibility, however, using direct wording from that text as a foundation to refine the doctrine only served to maintain the initial ambiguity, and provided little direction to defence lawyers hoping to understand how exactly the doctrine operated. This ambiguity would have suited prosecutors, who could rely on the opaqueness of the doctrine to gain an advantage in court.

The different understandings of command responsibility were fundamentally the result of prosecutors, defence lawyers, tribunal judges, and review lawyers entering the trials with no unified theory of what command meant. Confusion about the exact duties and qualities of command meant that officers were sometimes found guilty under contradictory applications of the doctrine. Other officers escaped conviction because prosecutors attempted to take the doctrine too far. Some commanders received relatively light sentences because even though they oversaw the ongoing commission of war crimes at the hands of their subordinates, they could show that they still upheld some of the requirements of command, albeit in relation to their own soldiers rather than to victims.

4

Massacres of Soldiers and Civilians

During fighting in China and the Asia-Pacific region, Japanese forces massacred prisoners of war (POWs), civilians, and guerrillas. The number of massacres was comparatively small, but the crime loomed large over the war crimes trials. The first massacre by Japanese forces to receive international attention in this period was at the Chinese capital, Nanking (Nanjing), and was perpetrated in December 1937 and January 1938 during fighting between Japanese and Nationalist Chinese forces.[1] After the outbreak of war with the US and its allies, Japanese troops killed large numbers of civilians and POWs on specific occasions in Singapore, Wake Island, the Philippines, North Borneo, and elsewhere. After the war, crimes relating to massacres were prosecuted before national tribunals, as well as playing a major role in the prosecution's case at the International Military Tribunal for the Far East (IMTFE).[2]

Some Allied prosecutors, and some later scholars, have claimed that 'death marches' organised by the Japanese military effectively constituted massacres.[3] This assertion, however, is without foundation. The deaths of prisoners in those situations were chiefly the result of external circumstances, rather than of deliberate mass killing.[4] The Bataan Death March and other marches like it were not conducted in order to kill captives. Rather, the marches were badly managed attempts to move prisoners from one location to another. Furthermore, some

1. On the Nanjing Massacre, see Bob Tadashi Wakabayashi ed., *The Nanking Atrocity, 1937–38: Complicating the Picture* (Berghahn Books, 2nd ed., 2017).
2. Yuma Totani, *The Tokyo War Crimes Trial: The Pursuit of Justice in the Wake of World War II* (Cambridge University Press, 2015), 109, 158, 163–70.
3. Paul Ham, *Sandakan: The Untold Story of the Sandakan Death Marches* (Random House Australia, 2012), 347; Richard Braithwaite, *Fighting Monsters: An Intimate History of the Sandakan Tragedy* (Australian Scholarly Press, 2016), 357, 439, 464. National Archives of Australia (hereafter NAA), War Crimes Trial of Yamamoto Shoichi and Ten Others, Prosecutors Opening Address, 24.
4. Kevin C. Murphy, *Inside the Bataan Death March: Defeat, Travail and Memory* (McFarland and Company, 2014), 267–69.

death marches, including the Sandakan-Ranau Death Marches, took place when Japanese soldiers themselves were dying in large numbers from starvation, disease, and exhaustion.[5] As shown in this chapter, if Japanese military personnel wished to dispose of prisoners, they could do so in ways that posed less danger to Japanese troops than arduous marching.

For the purposes of this chapter, a massacre is defined as the deliberate killing of ten or more victims in one setting. I analyse the national tribunals' command responsibility prosecutions of junior and mid-level personnel for the crime of massacre, with a focus on four sets of trials, which are examined in chronological order: those for the killing of POWs at Ranau in North Borneo in 1945, the *sook ching* massacre of Chinese men in Singapore in early 1942, the killing of POWs at Palawan Island in the Philippines in 1944, and the massacre of civilians elsewhere in the Philippines in 1945.

Massacres were egregious offences, and the courts treated them as such, showing a determination to convict as many people as possible for their participation, regardless of the defendant's position in the chain of command. Massacres usually involved a fairly significant degree of planning and coordination amongst perpetrators, a targeted approach, and large numbers of victims. Thus, they were more likely to have occurred under the direct orders or direct supervision of officers.

As I demonstrate here, cases in which junior and mid-level officers were prosecuted for massacre as well as their co-accused senior officers were particularly complex. Typically, it could be shown that senior officers had issued orders for the crime, and that junior and mid-ranking officers, operating under the orders of those senior officers, had taken a direct part in organising or carrying out the massacre. Tribunals, nevertheless, did not focus on the direct contribution of the lower-ranking officers in assessing command responsibility. Despite the clear role of senior officers, when those in the middle of the hierarchy were in the dock, tribunals concentrated on the level of command they had held, and on what they ought to have done as responsible officers. Thus, junior and mid-level officers were rarely treated as the subordinates of their co-accused senior officers, but rather as part of a broader command structure that oversaw the carrying out of a massacre. Similarly, the enormity of the crime meant that courts were less willing to allow staff officers to escape prosecution because of their administrative function. Rather than accepting that they had been 'mere conduits' through whom orders had flowed, the courts treated staff officers as an integral part of the planning and carrying out of massacres. The inescapable conclusion is that the courts treated the crime of massacre as a joint offence of all or most of the

5. Ueno Itsuyoshi, *An End to a War: A Japanese Soldier's Experience of the 1945 Death Marches of North Borneo*, trans. Mika Reilly (Opus Publications, 2012).

Japanese military hierarchy. Trials for massacres, thus, came closer than other trials to prosecuting an entire chain of command.

This approach often meant holding multiple trials for the same crime with multiple defendants, with the result that responsibility was sometimes apportioned among those found guilty in contradictory ways. In some cases, junior officers in earlier trials were found to have exercised nearly complete command, only for later trials of their superiors to reassess where ultimate responsibility lay for the same offence. This reassessment of guilt meant that some massacre trials began to skirt around the edges of collective responsibility in a way that trials for other offences did not. Responsibility for massacres was considered to be almost absolute at each level of command; the failure of one officer to prevent, halt, or punish a massacre did not stop the tribunals from holding higher- or lower-ranking officers within the same chain of command responsible for the same failure.

Massacres in Context

Japanese servicemen massacred both civilians and military personnel, including guerrillas, army nurses, surrendering soldiers, and POWs. As on all sides of the war, POWs were particularly vulnerable to violence perpetrated by the enemy. Immediately after capture, frontline Japanese units would occasionally massacre POWs as revenge for unexpectedly stout resistance, or because the prisoners were inconvenient: many Japanese units, especially on small islands, did not have the resources or manpower to guard large numbers of captives.[6] Allied units behaved similarly with surrendering and captured Japanese soldiers.[7] In several battles, Allied soldiers were explicitly ordered to kill any Japanese soldier they encountered, even when the enemy was clearly defeated and attempting to surrender.[8] At the Battle of the Bismarck Sea, Allied aircraft and warships shot at Japanese troops stranded in the water after the sinking of several Imperial Japanese Navy transports and destroyers.[9] Both the Japanese and the Allies often

6. Joan Beaumont, *Gull Force: Survival and Leadership in Captivity 1941–1945* (Ure Smith, 1968), 54–56; Lynette Silver, *The Bridge at Parit Sulong: An Investigation of Mass Murder* (The Watermark Press, 2004); Bill Sloan, *Given up for Dead: America's Heroic Stand at Wake Island* (Bantam Books, 2004), xiv–xvi; Jayant Dasgupta, *Japanese in Andaman and Nicobar Islands: Red Sun Over Black Water* (Manas Publications, 2002), 88–91; Catherine Kenny, *Captives: Australian Army Nurses in Japanese Prison Camps* (University of Queensland Press, 1986), 30–35.
7. William Manchester, *Goodbye Darkness: A Memoir of the Pacific War* (Little, Brown and Company, 2008), 438–40.
8. Denis Warner and Peggy Warner, *The Sacred Warriors: Japan's Suicide Legions* (Avon, 1984), xi.
9. Douglas Gillison, *Royal Australian Air Force, 1939–1945* (Australian War Memorial, 1962), 694–95.

ignored international laws that protected personnel who were *hors de combat*, or incapable of carrying out military duties.[10]

Prisoners were also massacred towards the end of the war, usually on island garrisons, for example, at Palawan, Borneo, and Nauru. The exact motive can be difficult to determine, especially as few Japanese military personnel attempted to explain their actions at the post-war trials. Since Allied shipping had blockaded most Japanese-occupied islands at the end of the war, it is probable that some massacres were carried out to preserve the remaining food for Japanese soldiers. POWs might also have been perceived as a threat to their captors, as they seemed likely to rebel in the face of an Allied landing, which was constantly expected in the final stages of the conflict. In some POW camps, there may have been added incentive to kill prisoners before the end of hostilities to cover up years of ill-treatment.

Japanese forces also massacred large numbers of civilians on several occasions during the war. Chinese civilians living across the Asia-Pacific region were particularly vulnerable, as Japanese commanders viewed them with suspicion. Japan had been at war with China since 1937, so Japanese commanders assumed that Chinese civilians were deeply anti-Japanese and posed a threat to the stability and security of the Japanese occupation of conquered territories.[11] Doctors, nurses, and military patients at the Alexandra Barracks Hospital were also massacred during the fall of Singapore.[12] Japanese troops massacred Australian nurses on Bangka Island, off Singapore, on 16 February 1942.[13] Japanese forces killed US civilian workers who had been contracted for military projects on Wake Island in 1943, after US forces raided the island.[14] Other Japanese massacres of civilians occurred on Nauru, Ocean Island, and the Andaman Islands.[15]

---

10. John Dower, *War Without Mercy: Race and Power in the Pacific War* (W. W. Norton and Co., 1986), 74–76; Martin Caidin, *The Ragged, Rugged Warriors* (Bantam Books, 1985), 36–37.
11. Hayashi Hirofumi, 'The Battle of Singapore, the Massacre of Chinese and Understanding of the Issue in Post-War Japan', *The Asia-Pacific Journal: Japan Focus* 7 (2009): 1–3; S. C. Smith, 'Crimes and Punishment: Local Responses to the Trial of Japanese War Criminals in Malaya and Singapore, 1946–48', *South East Asia Research* 5 (1997): 46–48.
12. Sandra Wilson, Robert Cribb, Beatrice Trefalt, and Dean Aszkielowicz, *Japanese War Criminals: The Politics of Justice After the Second World War* (Columbia University Press, 2017), 14.
13. 'Majority Judgment', in *Documents on the Tokyo International Military Tribunal: Charter, Indictment and Judgments*, ed. Neil Boister and Robert Cryer (Oxford University Press, 2008), 545–50.
14. George J. W. Unwin, *Victory in Defeat: The Wake Island Defenders in Captivity* (Naval Institute Press, 2010), 312–13.
15. Yuki Tanaka, 'Japanese Atrocities on Nauru During the Pacific War: The Murder of Australians, the Massacre of Lepers and the Ethnocide of Nauruans', *The Asia-Pacific Journal: Japan Focus* 8 (2010): 7–14.

Japanese forces carried out massacres of local civilians as reprisals for guerrilla attacks.[16] In the Philippines, from October 1944 till the end of the war, the Japanese military committed large numbers of massacres while defending the archipelago, largely during anti-guerrilla operations, when civilians were caught up in the violence.[17] Some massacres were never prosecuted before the national tribunals. Often, it was simply because those who carried out the massacre did not live long enough to face prosecution. Some Japanese soldiers who perpetrated massacres killed themselves at the end of the war, likely aware that they would face prosecution. Others were killed in fighting or died from disease or starvation during the final months of the conflict.[18]

Range of Defendants

Massacre trials covered a broad range of defendants. They included enlisted soldiers and non-commissioned officers (NCOs), who were usually the ones who had carried out the killing, and other personnel all the way through the chain of command up to high-ranking officers from the general staff. If several trials were held for the same crime, those who had actively carried out the massacre would be tried alongside junior and mid-level officers who were held responsible on other grounds. Officers from the general staff, alongside their mid- and high-ranking staff officers, would then be tried separately.

There were probably several reasons for prosecuting high-ranking officers separately from their subordinates. Trying senior officers alongside a large number of lower-ranking personnel would necessarily lengthen a trial. Because tribunal judges were supposed to be of a rank equal to or higher than the accused, this would mean that senior Allied officers, who would have other duties to perform, would be forced to sit through the entirety of a long trial, considering evidence and defendants that they otherwise would not have needed to deal with.[19] In addition, trying senior officers was usually more complicated than

16. NAA, War Crimes Trial of Suzuki Naoomi and One Other, archived at [https://recordsearch.naa.gov.au/SearchNRetrieve/Interface/ViewImage.aspx?B=694873]; Jemima Garrett, *Island Exiles* (Sydney: ABC Books, 1996), 200.
17. James M. Scott, *Rampage: MacArthur, Yamashita, and the Battle of Manila* (W.W Norton and Co., 2018); Sharon Chamberlain, *A Reckoning: Philippine Trials of Japanese War Criminals* (The University of Wisconsin Press, 2018), 19–21, 28–35; Kelly Maddox, 'An Island of Killing and Slaughter: Anti-Guerrilla Warfare in Panay, 1943', *Journal of Contemporary History* 55, no. 3 (2020): 535–56.
18. Wilson, Cribb, Trefalt, and Aszkielowicz, *Japanese War Criminals: The Politics of Justice After the Second World War*, 51; Scott, *Rampage*, 412.
19. Philip R. Piccigallo, *The Japanese on Trial: Allied War Crimes Operations in the East, 1945–1951* (University of Texas Press, 1979), 36–37, 98, 125, 188.

trying lower-level personnel. It made sense to separate the more straightforward trials from the difficult ones.

Nonetheless, senior officers were sometimes tried alongside their lower-ranking subordinates, rather than separately, if they had directly ordered subordinates to carry out the massacre or had given subordinates discretion to do so. The US trial of Lieutenant-General Terada Seiichi and others has possibly the broadest array of accused of any of the post-war tribunals in the Asian theatre. The fifteen defendants ranged from Lieutenant-Generals to private soldiers. Many of them were junior and mid-level officers, ranging from lieutenants through to colonels.[20] In other trials, senior commanders from the Japanese general staff were prosecuted alongside junior officers. Although the focus of this book is on mid-level and junior officers, in massacre trials in which senior officers were tried alongside their subordinates, it is necessary to analyse how the senior officers were found guilty in order to understand the trial as a whole.

The Ranau Massacre Trials: Reassessing Guilt

On 29 May 1945, 536 Allied captives were marched approximately 260 kilometres from Sandakan POW Camp to Ranau, in the north of the island of Borneo.[21] During the march, which was carried out to escape from a looming Allied invasion, approximately 350 prisoners died because of inadequate provision of food and medicine, and poor health resulting from three years in captivity. After arriving at Ranau on 25 June, approximately 150 more prisoners died from starvation and exhaustion.[22] On 1 August 1945, Japanese army personnel massacred thirty-three surviving POWs at Ranau. The details of the massacre itself, and the events preceding it, were pieced together from the testimony of Japanese personnel and of six Australian POWs who had escaped during the march or just before the massacre. In 1946 the Australian military held several trials for the conditions on the march to Ranau, as well as the massacre itself.

Captain Takakuwa Takuo was the commanding officer during the march to Ranau and also during the massacre. On the march, Takakuwa had ordered that both Allied POWs and Japanese soldiers who could not keep up with the

20. National Archives and Records Administration, College Park MD (hereafter NARA), RG331, Supreme Commander of the Allied Powers, Legal Section, Prosecution Division, *USA versus Japanese War Criminals*, Case Files, 1945–48, Box 1638, *USA v Terada Seichi* [*sic*] *and Fourteen Others* (hereafter *USA v Terada*), Charge Sheet, 1–4.
21. This section draws on Paul Taucher, 'Command Responsibility at the Sandakan-Ranau War Crimes Trials' (Honours Thesis, Murdoch University, 2016), 19–32.
22. NAA, War Crimes Trial of Captain Takakuwa Takuo and Captain Watanabe Genzo (hereafter Takakuwa Trial, Charge Sheet, 3, archived at [https://recordsearch.naa.gov.au/SearchNRetrieve/Interface/ViewImage.aspx?B=693467].

group were to be killed.[23] No Japanese soldiers died on the march, though several other Japanese army units in the same area suffered high casualties during troop movements, due to starvation and disease.[24] On 1 August, after the group had arrived at Ranau, Takakuwa ordered several low-ranking enlisted soldiers to kill the surviving thirty-three prisoners, probably because of limited food supplies and the poor health of the captives. The captives were taken to several separate locations outside of Ranau, executed, and buried.[25]

From 3 to 5 January 1946, at Labuan, British Borneo, the Australian military tried Captain Takakuwa Takuo and one of his subordinates, Captain Watanabe Genzo, for the massacre of Australian POWs at Ranau, as well as for the ill-treatment of POWs on the march from Sandakan to Ranau.[26] The trial demonstrates two different understandings of command responsibility. The first way in which the doctrine was applied shows a commitment to the principle that a commander is responsible for the orders he issues: Takakuwa, as the formal commander of the march, had ordered that the massacre take place, and was held responsible as a direct participant because of his order. The second method focussed on where *de facto* command was located at the time of the actual massacre. Watanabe, rather than Takakuwa, was found to have been the *de facto* commander at the time and was held criminally responsible because of his position of command, rather than for any substantive crime. Takakuwa and Watanabe were both sentenced to death and executed. At Rabaul between 28 May and 2 June 1947, after the trial of Takakuwa and Watanabe had concluded, the Australian military also prosecuted Lieutenant-General Baba Masao, the overall Japanese commander on the island of Borneo when the massacre occurred.[27]

Taken together, the two trials show that in attempting to understand and define command, tribunals could be influenced by where in the chain of command the inquiry had begun. If the defendants in the first trial for a massacre were lower-ranking officers, the bench usually interpreted command in the field as a strict responsibility, as was the case with Takakuwa. When examining the same lower-ranking officers as part of trials of senior officers, however, the bench might deem junior officers not to have been fully in command or control, because of the action or inaction of the senior officers. In other words, command was analysed and prosecuted only with regard to those immediately on trial, and the level of command that an accused was determined to have had was rarely vitiated by the position of other officers in different positions within the same chain

23. Takakuwa Trial, Charge Sheet, 3.
24. Ueno, *An End to a War*, vii–viii.
25. Braithwaite, *Fighting Monsters*, 228.
26. Takakuwa Trial, Charge Sheet, 3.
27. NAA, War Crimes Trial of Baba Masao (hereafter Baba Trial), archived at [https://recordsearch.naa.gov.au/SearchNRetrieve/Interface/ViewImage.aspx?B=724239].

of command if they were not standing trial in the same proceedings. The result was that command responsibility was often applied opportunistically, with no regard for previous decisions about where responsibility lay for the same crime.

At his trial, Takakuwa argued that the massacre at Ranau had been an act of military necessity, as he had feared that the captives would escape and assist in combat against Japanese forces when the expected Allied landing took place.[28] Considering the extremely bad health of the prisoners, it is unlikely that Takakuwa was genuinely concerned about a prisoner uprising. The killing was more probably an attempt to cover up the poor treatment of the Allied captives: Sandakan POW Camp had one of the highest death rates of prisoners during the war in the Pacific and approximately 100 prisoners who could not keep pace on the march to Ranau had been shot or bayoneted. Furthermore, killing the remaining POWs was one of the few ways to maintain food for the Japanese soldiers at this late stage of the war. Allied militaries had effectively blockaded Borneo from late 1943 onwards, which meant that limited supplies were available to Japanese soldiers on the island.[29] On Borneo as in other places, more Japanese soldiers died from disease and starvation than from combat.[30]

The prosecution of Takakuwa for ordering the massacre was straightforward, as he had openly admitted to ordering the crime. Prosecuting the other officer, Captain Watanabe, required a more flexible understanding of how command, and thus command responsibility, operated. Watanabe was subordinate to Takakuwa. Although the two held the same rank, Watanabe's main role was as an adjutant, a type of staff officer; he did not have any formal command. He thus had had limited control over the march to Ranau and the subsequent massacre. The crux of the prosecution's argument appears to have been that as an officer within a relatively small unit, he had nevertheless exercised some degree of command, and that this degree of command was magnified by the fact that Takakuwa had been bedridden with illness at the time of the massacre. The court evidently agreed, as Watanabe was sentenced to death alongside Takakuwa.

Watanabe, like many of the Japanese defendants found guilty of war crimes, petitioned against the tribunal's findings, arguing that he had not been in command but had only served as Takakuwa's adjutant.[31] In other words, he claimed the defence of superior orders, which, as discussed in Chapter 1, could

28. Takakuwa Trial, Trial Transcript, 42.
29. Lizzie Collingham, *The Taste of War: World War II and the Battle for Food* (Penguin Press, 2012), 273–74.
30. Ooi Keat Gin, *The Japanese Occupation of Borneo, 1941–1945* (Routledge, 2011), 137.
31. Takakuwa Trial, Petition of the Accused, 9–10.

only act as a mitigating defence, rather than a total defence against a charge.[32] The Japanese Imperial Rescript to Soldiers and Sailors of 1882, however, which was still in force during the 1941–1945 war, explicitly stated that military personnel owed total obedience to their superiors. This instruction, together with the harsh discipline meted out in the Japanese army for disobedience, commonly featured in the defence used by accused war criminals, though Watanabe never explicitly relied on this defence during the trial or in his petition.[33]

The Judge Advocate General (JAG) did not consider Watanabe's petition to be convincing, stating that both the officers had exercised some degree of control and thus were jointly responsible for the massacre. He noted that Takakuwa had received no orders to carry out the killings. The JAG also made a definitive distinction between the officers' part in the massacre and that of the NCOs and enlisted soldiers who had actually shot the prisoners, stating that the lower ranks, who were not tried for the massacre, had a wholly different form of responsibility due to their obligation to obey Takakuwa.[34] The JAG, thus, recognised the force of superior orders, at least in relation to the enlisted men.

The JAG's assessment of responsibility and guilt shows the wide-ranging, yet at times contradictory, interpretations of the doctrines of command responsibility and superior orders. The soldiers and NCOs who had participated in the march and the massacre were declared not to have been fully responsible for what occurred, presumably because they did not have command or control over the situation. Yet Watanabe, who as a staff officer also had had only limited control over the events and had acted under the orders of a superior on that superior's admission, was found to be culpable for the prisoners' deaths, to the extent that he was executed. For the JAG, and presumably the trial bench, Watanabe's position as an officer attracted criminal liability, because of his duty to prevent war crimes, but how this duty interacted with his position as a subordinate staff officer was not explained in any of the trial material. As in so many other cases in which officers were put on trial, how exactly command created liability was never made clear, though the idea that command could attract some form of participatory or accessory liability, as seen in the previous chapter, was evidently attractive to Allied tribunals.

The argument that Takakuwa and Watanabe had both exercised discretion in their command was ignored at the later trial of Lieutenant-General Baba Masao. Baba was also tried for the deaths that had occurred during the march to

32. Bing Bing Jia, 'The Plea of Superior Orders in the Hong Kong Trials', in *Hong Kong's War Crimes Trials*, ed. Suzannah Linton (Oxford University Press, 2013), 169–75; Wilson, Cribb, Trefalt, and Aszkielowicz, *Japanese War Criminals*, 28–30.
33. Wilson, Cribb, Trefalt, and Aszkielowicz, 30; Takakuwa Trial, Petition of the Accused, 9–10.
34. Takakuwa Trial, JAG Report, 4.

Ranau, as well as on a separate 'death march' from Sandakan to Ranau in January 1945, and he was also prosecuted for the Ranau massacre.[35]

In Baba's trial, the prosecution argued that his negligent command had led to the massacre. According to the prosecution, because Baba had ordered the march, and the march itself was poorly planned, the massacre of the prisoners who had survived the march was essentially a natural consequence. That is, the prosecution maintained that Baba knew, or ought to have known, that there was inadequate food and medicine for the prisoners during the march and at Ranau, and that any prisoners who survived would be in such a poor state that killing them was likely. Prosecutors stated that in ordering that the march take place in such circumstances, Baba had put Takakuwa in a difficult situation, in which prisoners under his direct command would most likely die, in one way or another.[36] Surprisingly, the prosecution argued that Takakuwa's claim that he had acted out of military necessity in killing the prisoners who survived to reach Ranau had some degree of merit to it: food was limited, so killing the prisoners ensured that the remaining rations would last longer. This later acceptance of Takakuwa's defence was of no use to Takakuwa, who had been hanged the previous year, on 5 April 1946.[37]

The prosecution's successful argument makes it clear that neither the prosecution nor the tribunal at Baba's trial was interested in achieving consistency across the different proceedings. In arguing that Baba had placed Takakuwa in a difficult situation, and that Takakuwa's claims of military necessity had had some merit, the prosecution implicitly argued that Takakuwa had not been fully in command of what happened during the march and in the subsequent massacre. In other words, the killing of the prisoners happened at least partly because of circumstances outside of Takakuwa's control, and his decision to kill the prisoners was not wholly irresponsible. The prosecution did not need, however, to re-evaluate Takakuwa's responsibility to convict Baba: there was clear evidence that Baba had ordered the march and had known about the issues of supply and the difficult terrain. The prosecution's strategy was evidently to maximise the degree of responsibility that could be apportioned to Baba, just as the prosecution at the earlier trial had amplified the guilt of Takakuwa and Watanabe.

The Allied decision that the tribunals would not be strictly bound by precedent was intended to simplify court proceedings and to ensure that justice could be meted out quickly. There was thus no formal need for consistent application of the doctrine of command responsibility. In many cases, moreover, referring to previous decisions would have been no simple matter, even if benches had

35. Baba Trial, Charge Sheet, 1–4.
36. Baba Trial, Trial Transcript, 56–58.
37. Takakuwa Trial, Certificate of Promulgation, 1.

wanted to do so. The trials were held across a geographically vast region, often in areas with little supporting infrastructure. While the Australian trials held in Rabaul could easily have gained access to previous decisions made in the same location, accessing the outcomes of other Australian trials from Singapore, let alone US trials from Guam or Yokohama, or Philippine trials from Manila, would have been much more difficult. Even in major cities like Hong Kong, war crimes staff could not get copies of either the original Yamashita judgment, or the US Supreme Court appeal judgment.[38] Furthermore, taking into account the decisions of previous tribunals would have greatly lengthened each trial, as the defence, the prosecution, and the bench all would have had to wait on information about other proceedings that had dealt with similar issues, and then would have had to take time to analyse how legal concepts had been applied in earlier cases.

Command responsibility was an answer to the problem of how to hold individual officers liable for war crimes committed under their command. The focus on individual responsibility at the trials meant that the complexities of the military hierarchy were rarely considered in any detail. The cost of expediency was that any one trial focussed only on particular defendants who had occupied particular echelons of a command structure. Interpretations of command, and thus, of responsibility, were then restricted to those specific parameters. The interaction of decisions and actions taken by multiple officers across a chain of command was rarely analysed or was examined only in a limited way. As a result, liability for a single crime could be apportioned across several trials opportunistically, without reference to previous decisions on where command lay in respect of that crime.

The *Sook Ching* Massacre Trial in Singapore

In March 1947, a UK military court tried seven Japanese army officers for their role in the massacre of thousands of Chinese men in the weeks after the Japanese capture of Singapore on 15 February 1942.[39] The trial of the seven officers, all of whom had had some level of formal command during the massacre, demonstrates that tribunals relied on the doctrine of command responsibility to apportion responsibility and liability to officers even in cases in which the court accepted that they had acted under superior orders. In such proceedings, the officers' experience, rank, and level of control over the actions they had

38. NAA, War Crimes Trial of Tahara Susumu and Sixteen Others, vol. 3, archived at [https://recordsearch.naa.gov.au/SearchNRetrieve/Interface/ViewImage.aspx?B=4151688], Judge Advocate's Summation, 46.
39. The National Archives of the UK, Kew (TNA), WO 235/1004, *UK v Nishimura Takuma and Six Others.*

been ordered to carry out were key factors in determining responsibility, and thus guilt.

Some massacres perpetrated by Japanese military forces seem to have occurred with limited or no planning, and were isolated, local episodes. The *sook ching* massacre, by contrast, appears to have resulted from administrative orders, although it is unclear whether those orders actually called for suspects to be killed. General Yamashita Tomoyuki, commander of the Japanese army in Singapore, ordered that Chinese members of the military reserve Straits Settlement Volunteer Force, as well as government workers and members of organised crime groups, were to be rounded up and screened for anti-Japanese sentiment once Japanese forces had conquered the city. Some evidence suggests that it was one of Yamashita's staff officers, Colonel Tsuji Masanobu, who ordered that the civilians who had been rounded up and did not pass the screening were to be killed.[40] Tsuji managed to escape Allied forces after the war and was never tried for war crimes.

The massacre in Singapore was carried out over three weeks from 23 February 1942. The number of victims is unclear. British estimates after the war indicate that approximately 5,000 Chinese were executed. Upper estimates of deaths, according to the Singaporean Chinese community, suggested at the time that 30,000 were killed.[41] Those who carried out the executions were mostly members of the Kenpeitai, the Japanese military police. At the time of the massacre, the Kenpeitai formed the bulk of the Japanese military personnel in the city of Singapore: Japanese authorities had ordered other troops to stay out to lessen the chances of looting and other disorder. Some ordinary troops, however, supplemented Kenpeitai forces.[42]

The seven Japanese army officers tried by the UK military court for their role in the massacre were Lieutenant-General Nishimura Takuma, Lieutenant-General Kawamura Saburo, Lieutenant-Colonel Oishi Masayuki, Lieutenant-Colonel Yokota Yoshitaka, Major Jyo Tomotatsu, Major Onishi Satoru, and Captain Misamatsu Haruji.[43] Nishimura, who had commanded Japanese forces in the western half of the island of Singapore, was tried as an overall commander. So was Kawamura, who had been in command of the eastern half of Singapore. Oishi was Kawamura's immediate subordinate and was one of the planners of the

40. Cheah Boon Kheng, 'Japanese Army Policy Toward the Chinese and Malay-Chinese Relations in Wartime Malaya', in *Southeast Asian Minorities in the Wartime Japanese Empire*, ed. Paul Kratoska (Routledge-Curzon, 2002), 97.
41. Cheah Boon Kheng, *Red Star Over Malaya: Resistance and Social Conflict During and After the Japanese Occupation of Malaya, 1941–1946* (Singapore University Press, 1983), 20–24; E. F. L. Russell, *The Knights of Bushido: A Short History of Japanese War Crimes* (Cassell, 1958), 245–51.
42. Onishi Satoru, *Hiroku Shōnan kakyō shukusei kiken* (Tōkyō: Kongo shuppan, 1977), 63–67. (I thank Sandra Wilson for translating this source for me.)
43. WO 235/1004, JAG Review, 1.

massacre. The remainder of the accused had commanded units that had actually carried out the massacre and were themselves under the command of Oishi.

At the time of the massacre, international law did not give explicit guidance on how subversion, or potential subversion, should be treated in occupied territories. Considering that UK forces had surrendered Singapore, it is likely that under international law any agents of subversion would be considered as common criminals, rather than as recognised belligerents, and thus would be denied protection. Indeed, this seems to be the position that was accepted at the trial. In the JAG's review, one of the key issues was that the screening of potential anti-Japanese Singaporeans was 'so casual as to result in the killing of innocent persons'.[44] In the JAG's view, the screening of civilians was allowable, but for it to be legitimate, it needed to have been more systematic. It seems that the JAG acknowledged that some of those killed had been executed lawfully, though he acknowledged that many others had undoubtedly been civilians with no connection to subversive groups.

At the trial, the accused all relied on the same two grounds of defence. The first was that Yamashita's orders to screen civilians for subversive tendencies or activities had been lawful, as many of those who had been in the Straits Settlement Volunteer Force had either thrown away or hidden their uniforms, and thus were not identifiable as military personnel and had been entitled to no legal protection as POWs. Furthermore, it was reasonable to have assumed that former members of the Volunteer Force would have gone on to organise resistance to Japanese rule in Singapore. Carrying out the massacre was thus a legitimate military operational matter. The accused also claimed that Yamashita had ordered the massacre, though whether this was true is unclear.[45] There was an immediate benefit for the accused in claiming they had acted under superior orders, because it would lessen their culpability. In addition, Yamashita had already been executed, so could not refute the point. It is also possible that Tsuji ordered that the massacre take place but misled the accused into thinking that it was Yamashita's order.

Both the prosecution and the JAG sought to limit the extent to which superior orders might mitigate the defendants' responsibility for the massacre. They claimed that two factors meant that the defence of superior orders should either be ignored or have a limited application. First, the officers, except for Captain Misamatsu, were all experienced and relatively senior. For them, the defence of superior orders was less persuasive than it would have been for lower-ranking officers or enlisted soldiers. The implicit argument appears to be that since most of the accused were experienced, they ought to have been able to limit the

44. WO 235/1004, JAG Review, 21.
45. WO 235/1004, Trial Transcript, 137–38, 141–44, 152–58, 170–78, 198, 206, 208–10.

severity of the massacre, either by taking steps themselves to do so, or by discussing with their superiors whether the scope of the killings was necessary.[46] The second argument was that it should have been clear to the officers that the orders were not only illegal, but also excessively brutal.[47] Both arguments indicate a development in legal thinking that was central to the post-war trials: responsible command meant doing more than asking whether orders or actions technically were legal. It was also necessary to ask whether they ought to be legal.

Oishi and Kawamura were sentenced to be hanged, while the remainder of the defendants were sentenced to life imprisonment. The JAG's review makes clear the reason for the disparity. Kawamura not only passed on the order for the massacre to take place, but also allocated specific zones of Singapore in which specific commanders were to carry out the screening and killing. In doing so, he thus played a crucial role in organising the massacre. As for Oishi, it is unclear from the trial transcript whether he intended that so many civilians would be killed. The prosecution argued, however, that his planning of the operation was a large factor in explaining why so many died. Either Oishi intended the massacre to kill as many civilians as it did, or his lack of care in planning the operation created an opportunity for his subordinates to act excessively.[48] Thus, the prosecution adapted elements of command responsibility. In this instance, the crime was deemed to have occurred not because Oishi's subordinates were out of control: rather, the orders that Oishi gave were so vague as to allow the massacre to occur in the first place. In other words, the directions that Oishi gave were negligently or recklessly worded in a way that, as the JAG observed, allowed the killings to extend beyond legitimate operational matters, and into an illegal massacre.

It is surprising that five of the defendants were sentenced to life imprisonment – rather than receiving the death penalty – for the largest massacre perpetrated by Japanese forces outside of China. The JAG placed considerable emphasis on his finding that the massacre did have some, albeit limited, justification: the existence of Allied defenders remaining in the city was a legitimate threat to Japanese rule and security.[49] The fact that all the mid-level defendants had operated under superior orders, which survived in written form, was also a likely reason that so many were spared a death sentence. On the one hand, the command responsibility trials were designed to bring officers to account for the orders they had given, and for their failure to prevent war crimes. On the other hand, the trials often showed that what was legal and what was responsible

46. WO 235/1004, Trial Transcript, 712–16, 717–20, 202.
47. WO 235/1004, Trial Transcript., 704–10.
48. WO 235/1004, JAG Review, 1–4.
49. WO 235/1004, JAG Report, 3–4.

within a military could be complex matters that did not always fit neatly within a criminal trial.

For many civilians in Singapore, the sentences passed against the seven accused officers in the 1947 UK trial were inadequate. Several Chinese community groups, including the Chinese Chamber of Commerce, petitioned the British civilian and military authorities to modify the sentences of all seven accused to death sentences but were unsuccessful.[50] But not all public reaction called for harsher sentences. An editorial in the *Straits Times* noted that the defendants were not the actual perpetrators of the crimes, and for the most part had been in positions of command. The true cause of the massacre, for this editorial writer, was not the commanders but the 'Japanese military machine'.[51] The distinction between these commanders and the 'military machine' is at odds with the thinking behind the selection of defendants. Though the accused had certainly acted under superior orders, two of the officers had been on the general staff, and another four were experienced mid-level officers. Prosecuting officers such as those at the *sook ching* trial in fact represented the Allies' attempt to hold accountable the Japanese 'military machine' that had allowed such killings to take place. Just like the tribunal members, the editorial writer struggled to identify where responsibility for massacres lay, and what it meant to be in command during the commission of a war crime.

The *Straits Times* editorial also reflects the difficult balancing act that prosecutors had to perform. There were not enough resources to try every suspected war criminal, from direct perpetrators up to the general staff. For the Allies, prosecuting officers who had held command when crimes were committed was the most efficient way to reform Japanese society for the post-war era, and to demonstrate to their own soldiers and civilians that justice was being done. For the crime of massacre at least, the relatively low number of prosecutions of NCOs and enlisted soldiers was the price paid.

At his trial in Manila in late 1945, Lieutenant-General Yamashita Tomoyuki, commander of Japanese forces in Singapore, was not held accountable for the *sook ching* massacre, though he was convicted of responsibility for massacres perpetrated by his subordinates in the Philippines. The failure to prosecute Yamashita for the Singapore massacre illustrates the risks inherent in delegating international law to national jurisdictions. Jurisdictional boundaries worked against examining Yamashita's role in the Singapore killings: he was tried by the US, which had jurisdiction over crimes in the Philippines, while the British prosecuted Japanese personnel for crimes in Singapore. Convicted war criminals

50. Smith, 'Crimes and Punishment', 48–50.
51. 'The Massacre Trial', *The Straits Times*, 5 April 1947, https://eresources.nlb.gov.sg/newspapers/Digitised/Article/straitstimes1.

were sometimes handed over to other Allied authorities to be tried again for different crimes, but there was no opportunity to do this in Yamashita's case, as he was immediately executed. As a result, comprehensive justice for the Singapore massacre was never achieved, and the uncertainty over who had held ultimate responsibility for the order to kill so many civilians was never resolved.

Collective Responsibility: Trials for the Palawan Massacre

On 14–15 December 1944, the Japanese military massacred 139 American soldiers near Puerto Princesa, the largest city on Palawan Island, in the west of the Philippines. Liability for the massacre was pursued at three US military trials: two at Manila and one at Yokohama. The final trial for the Palawan massacre was held between 2 August and 8 November 1948 in Yokohama. Fifteen Japanese military personnel, of whom the highest-ranking was Lieutenant-General Terada Seiichi, were tried for the massacre. Along with Terada, Lieutenant-General Mikami Kizo, ten mid-ranking staff officers, one lieutenant, one NCO, and one enlisted soldier of the Japanese army were also charged with responsibility for the massacre. Subsidiary charges included forcing POWs to work on military projects, mistreating POWs, and covering up the massacre. Six of the accused were acquitted of all charges. The remaining nine were found guilty of multiple charges and received sentences ranging from two years' imprisonment to death.[52]

The last of the three trials for the Palawan massacre is the most important in demonstrating the malleability of command responsibility in court. Specifically, it shows that the application of the doctrine encouraged the courts to downplay procedural considerations in the interests of achieving convictions of commanders. That three separate trials were held, all of which saw senior officers face charges for the massacre, also demonstrates the Allies' level of determination in prosecuting massacres, and the difficulty in assessing where ultimate command, and thus responsibility, lay within a military hierarchy.

The victims had been on the island of Palawan since August 1942 when the Japanese military transported them there to build an airstrip and beach defences near Puerto Princesa. For most of the war, food rations for the prisoners on Palawan were steady. Medical supplies were in shorter supply on Palawan, and sick POWs were sent to Manila for treatment.[53] As the war progressed in favour of the Allies, it became clear to the Japanese military that the US would attack the Philippines, and Japanese military authorities wanted to move the POWs out of the way. On 22 September 1944, half of the prisoners on Palawan were

52. *USA v Terada*, Charge Sheets and JAG Report.
53. Bob Wilbanks, *Last Man Out: Glenn McDole, USMC, Survivor of the Palawan Massacre in WWII* (McFarland and Company, 2004), 45–56, 68–70.

transported to larger POW camps near Manila. The remaining 140 or so were expected to be shipped out soon after, but they never were.[54] The US military blockaded the island shortly after the first group was sent to Manila, and Japanese ships could no longer safely reach Palawan to pick up the prisoners.

In late November 1944, the Japanese garrison on Palawan sighted a US naval fleet, which Japanese forces suspected was part of a Palawan invasion force. The garrison unit planned to conduct long-term guerrilla fighting against invading US forces, rather than openly facing overwhelming enemy numbers and firepower.[55] In these circumstances, the presence of Allied POWs would be a serious hindrance. On 14 December 1944, the garrison, along with local Kenpeitai troops, sent the approximately 140 remaining US captives into underground air raid shelters, on the pretext that an attack was expected. Once the POWs were in the shelters, Japanese soldiers poured gasoline into the bunkers and threw in grenades. The prisoners who ran out of the shelters were shot at with rifles. Some prisoners managed to escape the initial killing.[56] Overnight and during the following day, Japanese forces searched the island for any survivors, finding several, but missing eleven. Philippine guerrillas rescued these eleven survivors and delivered them to the nearby US fleet.[57]

The Palawan massacre had already been raised in two previous trials. When Lieutenant-General Yamashita Tomoyuki was tried in December 1945, one of the charges was responsibility for the Palawan killings, of which he was found guilty.[58] The US military also used command responsibility to try Lieutenant-General Kou Shiyoku, the overall commander of POW and internment camps in the Philippines, for the massacre, in proceedings held at Manila in April 1946. Kou, the highest-ranking Korean in the Imperial Japanese Army, was convicted, and he was executed on 26 September 1946.[59]

The defence in the Terada proceedings placed great emphasis on the fact that both Yamashita and Kou had already been found guilty of command responsibility for the same massacre, but this argument ultimately failed to secure acquittals at the Terada trial. According to the defence, *res judicata*, a legal doctrine that means that once a court has reached a judgement on a matter, that same matter cannot be brought before another court, ought to have applied.[60] The defence argued that since two senior officers had previously been found guilty

54. Wilbanks, *Last Man Out*, 106–7.
55. *USA v Terada*, Trial Transcript, 850–55.
56. *USA v Terada*, Trial Transcript, 85, 88–95.
57. Wilbanks, *Last Man Out*, 134–38.
58. W. H. Parks, 'Command Responsibility for War Crimes', *Military Law Review* 62 (1973): 26.
59. Lydia N. Yu Jose, 'The Koreans in Second World War Philippines: Rumour and History', *Journal of Southeast Asian Studies* 43 (2012): 333–35; 'Japanese Sadists Pay the Penalty for Philippine Atrocities', *Cairns Post*, 25 September 1946, 4.
60. *USA v Terada*, Trial Transcript, 248.

under command responsibility for the crime, it was unacceptable for yet another command responsibility trial to be held for the same crime with new suspects. Command responsibility, in this view, had already been found to rest with Kou and Yamashita, and therefore could not be attributed to others. The law member, a member of the bench whose role was to rule on matters of law and procedure, held, however, that *res judicata* did not apply to the tribunal, so the prosecution of Terada and his co-accused could continue. His reasoning was based on broad principles. Rather than claiming that the facts of this trial meant that *res judicata* did not apply, the law member stated that the doctrine did not apply to war crimes tribunals in general.[61] So, much like the decision of Allied militaries to accept hearsay evidence at the tribunals, the Terada court rejected an aspect of domestic criminal law in Allied countries in the interest of establishing criminal liability for war crimes.

The law member's ruling implied that to achieve justice for war crimes, courts needed to move away from examining criminal acts strictly through the lens of individual responsibility and intent. Rather, they should consider collective or group responsibility. For prosecutors, investigators, and tribunals, massacres and other war crimes did not occur in a vacuum: aside from direct perpetrators, multiple members of the Japanese military had ordered, permitted, or ignored war crimes. Using command responsibility to prosecute the same crime at several different points in the command structure, after ultimate responsibility appeared already to have been adjudged, was a step towards holding the Japanese army collectively responsible for atrocities committed during the war. From this perspective, responsibility was not just attributable to the individuals most closely involved, whether they were direct perpetrators or commanders who had issued orders. Rather, responsibility was widely spread, and numerous individuals ought to be held accountable.

The rejection of *res judicata* appears to undermine the way command responsibility investigations and trials were intended, and indeed assumed, to progress. As discussed in Chapter 2, many investigators, prosecutors, and senior Allied authorities thought that command responsibility prosecutions began with those who had actually committed the crime before moving up through the ranks. The prosecution for the Palawan massacre, however, worked from the top down. The difference between theory and practice was likely due to practical concerns. On the one hand, the theory behind pursuing prosecutions from the bottom up through the chain of command probably represented an attempt to give structure and consistency to the overall trial process. At the same time, rigidly adhering to this policy would have undermined the original goal of the trials, which was to mete out 'stern justice' to the guilty: it would be wrong for a lower-ranking

61. *USA v Terada*, Trial Transcript, 252.

officer to escape prosecution simply because his superior had already been tried. Considering the readiness of Allied militaries to remove domestic procedural protections, like the rule against hearsay, ignoring the intended path of prosecutions would have been an easy step to take in the pursuit of responsibility for war crimes.

The defence in the Terada trial claimed that the proceedings were inherently unfair on the grounds that the fifteen defendants belonged to two different command structures and therefore should not appear in a joint trial. For the US military authorities, determining who was ultimately responsible for the Palawan massacre had presented serious difficulties. At the opening of proceedings in the Terada trial, the prosecution was still uncertain as to who had had formal jurisdiction over Palawan Island at the time of the massacre. In late November 1944, the Japanese army command structure in the Philippines had been reorganised. Due to sustained US aerial and naval bombardment, as well as personal conflict among Japanese commanders in the Philippines, the reorganisation was not efficiently carried out. Some commanders informally retained control of units that had officially been reallocated, and others never received formal orders transferring units to their command. Both in pre-trial interrogations and in the trial itself, Generals Terada and Mikami had each claimed that the other, along with his subordinate staff officers, had had command of Palawan at the relevant time, and was thus responsible for the massacre.[62] According to the defence, since both groups denied responsibility for and jurisdiction over Palawan when the massacre was carried out, there was an inherent conflict of defence, as each command group would attempt to prove that the other had been in command at the time the massacre occurred; the defence maintained that this circumstance made a joint trial procedurally unfair.[63]

In US, UK, and Australian domestic criminal trials, joint proceedings are held when the crime itself is the product of the common acts of the defendants. This was also the case in the majority of the war crimes prosecutions. At the Terada trial, however, the prosecution did not assert that the two commands had acted in common to carry out the massacre.[64] Instead, the prosecution's tactic was to charge both command units, probably in the hope that each group would be forced to defend itself by blaming the other. Though command responsibility was an excellent tool in linking the crimes of a subordinate to an officer, the doctrine relied on knowing who had exercised command. The prosecution in the Terada trial likely expected that the evidence raised by the two groups would allow the bench to understand which of the two command units had been in

62. *USA v Terada*, Trial Transcript, 17.
63. *USA v Terada*, Trial Transcript, 15–18.
64. *USA v Terada*, Trial Transcript, 20–22.

control of Palawan at the time of the massacre, and, thus, who was truly responsible. For the prosecution, charging both units when only one had had command at the relevant time, was a way of breaking open a deadlocked investigation.

The court refused the defence's request to try the two units in separate proceedings. The tribunal ruled that in practice, the two groups were being tried separately, and that the joint trial functioned merely to streamline the process. Trying the two groups together would mean that only one tribunal would be required, and that there would be no unnecessary repetition of evidence.[65] The tribunal members were probably also conscious that trying the two command units separately could result in two acquittals. If tried separately, each group would be more likely to convince a tribunal of its own innocence, as there would be less opportunity for the other unit to give an equivalent amount of counter-evidence that would disadvantage the first group.

The timing of the proceedings probably also affected the decision to run a joint trial. By 1947, the US military and government had begun to doubt whether continuing the prosecutions was in the best interests of the Allied governments. In the US especially, policy on Japan was shifting away from an emphasis on retribution and towards a desire to see the restoration of Japanese sovereignty. The trials were designed to show the Japanese public that what the Japanese military had done during the war was criminal. In March 1948, George F. Kennan, the director of the US State Department's Policy Planning staff, argued that the trials, including the Tokyo Trial, were taking too long. At this point, he believed the Japanese population sympathised with the defendants, at least at the national trials; those defendants were undergoing what Kennan described as 'endless and humiliating ordeals'.[66] Soon after, the US authorities began to wind down the American military tribunals. The IMTFE was ended in November 1948, despite the fact that additional proceedings before the international bench had originally been envisaged.[67]

By the time the Terada trial was held, also in November 1948, the Allied proceedings were well and truly winding down. Fewer trials were being held, and there were fewer staff to conduct them, as the Allied militaries demobilised and military funding fell. Jointly trying all the remaining suspects for the Palawan massacre was a pragmatic contribution towards ensuring that those still in Allied custody would be tried before the proceedings ended. In March 1949, the Far Eastern Commission, a body based in Washington D.C. that nominally oversaw

65. *USA v Terada*, Trial Transcript, 24.
66. George F. Kennan, 'Explanatory Notes, March 25, 1948', *Foreign Relations of the United States, 1948, Vol. 6, The Far East and Australasia*, United States Department of State (US Government Printing Office, 1948), 718–19; Wilson, Cribb, Trefalt, and Aszkielowicz, *Japanese War Criminals*, 20.
67. Wilson, Cribb, Trefalt, and Aszkielowicz, *Japanese War Criminals*, 117.

the Allied occupation of Japan, recommended that all Allied trials be ended by September 1949.[68]

In court, the prosecution succeeded in establishing that Terada had been in command at the time of the massacre. The evidence against Terada also served to substantiate findings of guilt against several of his staff officers. Evidence raised at the tribunal showed that Terada had ordered that the POWs on Palawan be 'disposed of' if they posed a threat to Japanese forces.[69] This order had itself been given to Terada by one of his superiors, General Tominaga Kyoji, though Tominaga was unavailable to present evidence at the trial, as he had been captured by Soviet forces at the end of the war and was still in Soviet captivity at the time of the trial.[70] Importantly for the prosecution's command responsibility argument, the order issued by Terada was not a direct instruction to kill the prisoners. Rather, Terada authorised the garrison commander on Palawan to use his discretion to decide whether the POWs were a threat to the Japanese soldiers and to kill the prisoners if he decided they were a threat.

The evidence that Terada had ordered the Palawan garrison to kill the prisoners if they posed a threat was the basis for the prosecution's command responsibility argument against both him and his subordinate staff officers. The prosecution argued that Terada and his staff officers were responsible for the massacre on two grounds. First, the order to kill the POWs was manifestly illegal, because there was no military benefit in killing them. Further, the order set the massacre in motion.[71] The prosecution thus acknowledged that Terada had not directly ordered the massacre on his own initiative but argued that he had nonetheless created circumstances in which a massacre was likely to occur. In relaying the order, the accused staff officers shared some responsibility for it. The second reason the accused were responsible was that all of the accused officers had failed to discharge their duty to protect the prisoners.[72] In making this argument, prosecutors asserted that staff officers have responsibilities similar to those of a commanding officer: the lead prosecutor maintained that while 'criminal responsibility rests initially and primarily with the commander', it was 'also shared by his staff officers and subordinate commanders'.[73] The effect of this assertion was to spread liability for the massacre across the command structure.

---

68. Wilson, Cribb, Trefalt, and Aszkielowicz, *Japanese War Criminals*, 115–20; Piccigallo, *The Japanese on Trial*, 46–47.
69. *USA v Terada*, JAG Report, 40; *USA v Terada*, Prosecution Exhibit 60, 22; *USA v Terada*, Prosecution Exhibit 62, 4.
70. *USA v Terada*, Trial Transcript, 914.
71. *USA v Terada*, Trial Transcript, 914–16.
72. *USA v Terada*, Trial Transcript, 918–26.
73. *USA v Terada*, Trial Transcript, 914.

Through this proposition, the prosecution argued for a form of collective responsibility for the massacre.

Rather than being held strictly liable for the massacre, three staff officers were essentially found guilty of committing a separate offence of the superior. The charges on which the three were found guilty focussed on the events leading up to the massacre and subsequent events, including failing to ensure that that the Palawan POW camp was placed under the command of a responsible officer, failing to ensure the murdered prisoners received a proper burial, and failing to inform the Japanese POW Information Bureau, the agency responsible for liaising with Allied governments about POWs, of the deaths.[74] Once again, holding the staff officers responsible under the separate offence interpretation of command responsibility allowed the tribunal to spread responsibility for the massacre across the chain of command to an extent that bordered on collective responsibility.

The post-trial review criticised the finding that Terada's staff officers were guilty of the ancillary charges under command responsibility.[75] The review lawyer argued that staff officers should not be held responsible for the decisions of their superiors, and that they did not have the effective authority to command. It appears that he intended to caution against the prosecution's attempt to extend command responsibility beyond individual liability and into collective responsibility for war crimes. Despite the review lawyer's concern, the staff officers' sentences, which ranged from four to twelve years' imprisonment, were confirmed.

The imposition of relatively light sentences on the staff officers was probably due to a combination of factors. Though the focus of the war crimes trials was on the end result rather than the procedure used to reach a verdict, the raising by the defence of *res judicata*, and the unfairness of trying the two command units together, likely contributed to the short prison terms. Nonetheless, the enormity of the crime of massacre led the tribunal as well as the confirming authority to accept that responsibility, and thus liability, for the offence was spread collectively amongst the Japanese leadership in the Philippines. In their view, some blame had to be placed at the feet of the staff officers as well as their superiors. Rather than being held collectively responsible for the substantive crime, the staff officers were held collectively responsible for the circumstances that allowed the crime to occur in the first place. In the end, the major concern of the Terada trial was to assign guilt to the command structure, and the method by which that goal was achieved was a secondary consideration, if a consideration at all.

The Terada trial shows that command responsibility was an effective prosecutorial tool in attributing guilt across the military hierarchy. The doctrine

74. *USA v Terada*, Trial Transcript, 848.
75. *USA v Terada*, JAG Report, 51–52.

enabled the prosecution to crack open a case with complex circumstances and assign guilt to officers who Allied legal personnel thought were truly responsible for the crime. At the same time, the trial shows that even relatively late in the trial program, tribunals struggled to articulate a clear understanding of what command was and who had wielded it. The defence's argument that the trial should be dismissed because ultimate responsibility for the massacre had already been apportioned to other officers could be seen as an attempt by defence lawyers to acquit their clients by any means necessary. The fact that the law member seriously considered this argument, however, and the rarity of similar arguments in other trials, indicates that defence lawyers had raised a genuine concern about the doctrine. The post-trial review that cautioned against using command responsibility against staff officers also demonstrates a legal expert's concern about the longer-term implications of the decision. The essential problem with the application of command responsibility in the Terada trial was the shift away from requiring a clear command relationship between those who had committed the substantive crime and those at more senior levels of the military hierarchy, in favour of a move towards a generalised, collective responsibility for the crime.

Massacre Trials Under the Philippines Government

Despite the large numbers of massacres reported to have been perpetrated by Japanese forces in the Philippines, these killings gave rise to comparatively few command responsibility trials, either under the Americans before 1947, or under the new Philippines government once it took over the trials.[76] The lack of US command responsibility trials in the Philippines is particularly striking in view of the relatively large number of command responsibility trials run by the US military for summary executions that had occurred during the liberation of the Philippines in 1945.[77]

There are two likely reasons for the limited number of command responsibility trials for massacres in the Philippines. First, many of the massacres appear to have occurred either immediately before or during vicious fighting between Japanese and Allied military forces. Thus, many mid- and junior-level officers who might have been tried under command responsibility would have died in the fighting. Second, the Philippine government, aware that trials were expensive and time consuming, may have been reluctant to repeat evidence and recall witnesses who had already had their day in court under the Americans in trials for a variety of offences. Many of the US command responsibility trials of

76. On war crimes in the Philippines, see Chamberlain, *A Reckoning*; Rafael Steinberg, *Return to the Philippines* (Time-Life Books, 1979), 140–45; Scott, *Rampage*.
77. Chamberlain, *A Reckoning*, 66.

senior officers had dealt with multiple crimes. In these senior officer trials, large numbers of witnesses had been produced to give evidence of the widespread commission of war crimes. At the Yamashita trial alone, nearly 200 prosecution witnesses, many of whom were Philippine civilians, appeared in court in person.[78] There was thus a reduced need for these same witnesses and victims to reappear and see that justice was being meted out.

In a March 1948 proceeding, Philippines authorities prosecuted one mid-ranking officer for two massacres using the doctrine of command responsibility. The trial shows that command responsibility, while a powerful prosecutorial tool, could still be limited by evidentiary and legal doubts and uncertainties. Lieutenant-Colonel Sato So was tried for the killing of sixteen civilians at Barrio Mission, in the province of Cagayan, on 30 June 1945, as well as the massacre of approximately 150 unnamed men, women, and children at Barrio Tapal, in the province of Bohol, on 1 July 1945. At the time of the massacres, Sato was a major; like many Japanese officers, he received a promotion in mid-1945, probably to replace superiors who had died. Sato, tried in Manila between 15 March and 6 May 1948, was found not guilty of the killings at Barrio Mission. Of the 150 dead at Barrio Tapal, he was found guilty of killing 30, some of whom were guerrillas.[79] The tribunal sentenced Sato to life imprisonment.[80]

The defence strategy for Sato was somewhat unusual for a trial that began at such a late stage of the Allied war crimes prosecutions. At this point, the conventions of war crimes trials, including differences from domestic criminal trials, were well established. The charges against the accused were not required to be specific. Indeed, prosecutors were even permitted to vary the charges midway through a trial to adapt to new evidence. Furthermore, the criteria for admissibility of evidence had been broadened, as shown in the large numbers of unsworn affidavits produced not only in the Sato trial, but in many other proceedings. Direct witness testimony could also be given under very relaxed conditions: tribunal benches accepted direct witness testimony that was patently hearsay evidence in nearly all cases in which it was available. Nonetheless, Sato's defence lawyers argued that the specificity of the charge and the quality and content of evidence were improper.[81]

The defence argument that the charge against Sato was invalid was based on the wording of the principal charge. In the post-war national trials, the main charge against an accused was almost invariably that he 'did violate the laws and

---

78. A. Frank Reel, *The Case of General Yamashita* (Octagon Books, 1971), 4.
79. NARA, RG331, Supreme Commander for the Allied Powers, Legal Section, Prosecution Division, *Philippines versus Various Japanese War Criminals*, Case File, 1947–1949, Box 1688, *Philippines v Sato So* (hereafter *Philippines v Sato So*), Charge Sheet.
80. Chamberlain, *A Reckoning*, 160.
81. *Philippines v Sato So*, Trial Transcript, 5–10.

customs of war'. Though the charge sheet would then lay out the specifics of the crimes, technically the accused was not on trial for those specific acts. Rather, he faced the broad charge of violating the laws and customs of war. The defence alleged that the charge against Sato was so broad that it contravened the explicit rights of the accused, which included the right to have 'a true copy of the charge and specifications clearly worded so to appraise the accused of each offense charged'. According to the defence, the charge, which did not cite any particular law or custom of war, was not legally specific enough to meet this criterion. The defence contended that the charge against the accused was the same as accusing a common domestic criminal of violating the Philippine Penal Code in its entirety, rather than any specific provision. The defence admitted that it was literally clear what Sato was accused of, but still maintained the charge was legally incoherent, and therefore the trial was invalid.[82]

Unsurprisingly, this argument failed. The Allied trials all relied on broad charges against the accused. Part of the rationale was that because the crimes had often taken place several years before they could be adequately investigated, let alone prosecuted, the exact nature of the crime was frequently vague or uncertain, though it was considered clear that some crime had been committed. The specific doctrine of command responsibility was also omitted both in the general charge and in the specifics, not only in Sato's trial, but indeed, in most command responsibility trials. The reason was that command responsibility is not a substantive crime, like murder or assault. Instead, it is a form of criminal responsibility: that is, it is a method of assigning guilt, rather than an actual criminal act.

Evidence connecting Sato to the first massacre of civilians, at Barrio Mission, was limited. The prosecution relied on the single affidavit of one Philippine civilian, who claimed that he had been interrogated by an officer named Captain Sato, and that during the interrogation, he saw Japanese soldiers kill several of the named victims. According to the witness, one of the identifying features of the Sato who interrogated him was that he wore glasses. At the trial, Sato stated that he did not ordinarily wear glasses, and a US military optometrist had examined him, and had found no defects in his vision.[83] It appears, however, that Sato had managed to outwit the prosecution, the bench and the optometrist: according to Sharon Chamberlain, Sato wore glasses in the mugshot taken before he was transferred from Japan to the Philippines for trial.[84] As well as the matter of the glasses, the defence also drew attention to the fact that Sato is a very common Japanese surname, claiming that forty soldiers called Sato were in Philippine custody, so it was more likely than not that there had been a mistake in this

82. *Philippines v Sato So*, Trial Transcript, 6–9.
83. *Philippines v Sato So*, Trial Transcript, 382–93.
84. Chamberlain, *A Reckoning*, 73.

case.[85] Attacking the credibility of the affidavit apparently worked, and Sato was found not guilty of the first massacre.

The circumstances in the larger massacre at Barrio Tapal show the difficulties that Japanese forces had confronted during the Battle of the Philippines in 1944–1945. Sato's unit had faced several small guerrilla attacks over two weeks. On 1 July 1945, a band of approximately forty guerrillas attempted to attack Sato's unit. However, the attacking force had limited small arms and was equipped mainly with machetes and bolo knives. After initiating the attack, the guerrillas quickly retreated from the better-equipped forces under Sato's overall command. Sato's troops pursued the retreating guerrillas and killed at least thirty of them. The exact circumstances in which the guerrillas were killed, however, was unclear. Some had certainly been killed in the retreat, while others appeared to have been rounded up and massacred. The prosecution insisted that the fact that approximately thirty of the guerrillas had died when they were no longer in combat constituted a violation of international criminal law. Sato and his defence lawyers maintained, on the other hand, that fighting during a war is not based on understandings of self-defence drawn from domestic law: in war, if there is an opportunity to kill retreating combatants, the opportunity should be seized.[86]

Unlike the UK and Australian tribunals, the Philippines tribunals occasionally gave reasons for their judgments. Though there was relatively little discussion of how specific laws had been applied, some courts attempted to rationalise both the finding of guilt and the sentence. In Sato's case, the tribunal held that the killing of approximately thirty guerrillas, who were poorly armed and retreating from superior forces, was an attack against personnel who were *hors de combat*.[87] Framers of international criminal law had made efforts to protect military personnel who were no longer an active threat to their opponents. Explicit protections were given to airmen who parachuted out of a damaged plane and sailors who had abandoned ship, even when such personnel were likely to return to combat.[88] Unarmed wounded soldiers were also included; retreating soldiers, however, were not explicitly protected.[89] Furthermore, all of these protections covered members of recognised militaries, not guerrillas.

The bench held that Sato's command responsibility for the massacre had arisen because he had not given strict limiting orders to his subordinates. The tribunal stated that he should have given a clear command to capture rather than kill guerrillas who had retreated or surrendered, and that he should have

85. *Philippines v Sato So*, Trial Transcript, 510.
86. *Philippines v Sato So*, Trial Transcript, 524–25, 538, 550.
87. *Philippines v Sato So*, Trial Transcript, 550–51.
88. Convention with Respect to the Laws and Customs of War on Land (Hague II), 29 July 1899, https://avalon.law.yale.edu/19th_century/hague02.asp.
89. A. P. V. Rogers, *Law on the Battlefield* (Manchester University Press, 1996), 7.

anticipated the need to do so, given the disparity in force between the guerrillas and the Japanese troops.[90] Such reasoning is legally unclear. All parties at the tribunal, including the bench, referred to the Philippine force as guerrillas, and guerrillas had limited protections under international criminal law. In wartime, guerrilla units can become a part of a recognised belligerent force, but otherwise, their right to military status and legal protection was not recognised.[91] At the time of the guerrilla attack against Sato's forces, there was no established liaison between the guerrillas and the US army or Philippine regular forces that operated alongside American troops. Sato's forces had killed the guerrillas immediately after an attack, when they were in possession of weapons; hence, the killing of the guerrillas was probably lawful.

The decision to hold Sato guilty because the orders that he gave his subordinates did not prevent war crimes is similar to the reasoning applied in the trial of Kawamura Saburo and his subordinates for the *sook ching* massacre. In both cases, the tribunal blended elements of command responsibility as applied in the Yamashita trial, where a commander is held liable for the crimes of his subordinate, with a more basic understanding of command responsibility, where an officer is held responsible for the orders that he gives. In both the Sato and Kawamura trials, the orders that were handed down were probably not *prima facie* illegal, but the accused officers failed to ensure that their orders were carried out lawfully. This theory of responsibility, however, was never clearly stated. Instead, the prosecution, and presumably the judges, entered the trials with a broad notion of what command meant or should mean, without raising in court any material that explicitly supported their position.

Sato's relatively light sentence demonstrates the important role of doubt and uncertainty in command responsibility trials. Given unreliable evidence connecting Sato to the first massacre, and the unclear legal status of the dead in the second massacre, the tribunal appears to have had difficulty in determining Sato's intent. In many of the command responsibility trials, particularly in cases of massacre and summary execution, the bench assumed a level of intent: that is, the tribunal held that the accused officer must have intended the crime to occur, even if there was little evidence in support of that conclusion. In Sato's case, however, there was not enough evidence for the tribunal to assume the same degree of intent as was assumed in other trials.

In another Philippines tribunal for command responsibility for massacre, held between 25 May and 12 September 1949, Lieutenant-Colonel Omura Yasuo

90. *Philippines v Sato So*, Trial Transcript, 551.

91. Lester Nurick and Roger W. Barrett, 'Legality of Guerrilla Forces Under the Laws of War', *The American Journal of International Law* 40 (1946): 563–69; Lassa Oppenheim, *International Law: A Treatise*, Vol. 2, *War and Neutrality* (Longmans, Green and Co., 2nd ed., 1912), 313–17.

and Captain Ono Masao were prosecuted in Manila for the massacre of civilians. The application of command responsibility against the superior officer, Omura, shows that in certain circumstances, the doctrine could operate in a straightforward manner, unencumbered by difficult questions of command, discretion, jurisdiction, and other legal matters. Such a smooth application of the doctrine, however, could only happen if the context of the crime were uncontested and the evidence clear.

Captain Ono, Omura's subordinate, faced charges relating to two massacres. The first, during which approximately one hundred civilians were killed, had been perpetrated in Barrio Fabrica, on the main island of Luzon, on 11 March 1945. As in other Philippine massacre trials, the number of victims was never conclusively proven, and the prosecution relied on estimates. The second massacre was committed on 7 April 1945 at Lafu Island, a small island in a river in Luzon. Approximately two hundred Philippine civilians were killed. Both massacres were carried out during punitive reprisals for guerrilla attacks against Japanese forces. Although Omura had been present at the same two massacres, he faced only one command responsibility charge, that of ordering or wilfully permitting the killings on Lafu Island.[92]

The prosecution's decision not to charge Omura with responsibility for the first massacre is surprising. As shown in the previous chapter, and established throughout this book, prosecutors regularly charged commanders with as many crimes as possible, presumably to increase the chances of conviction. Effectively, prosecutors threw as much as they could at the accused to see what would stick. In this case the prosecution established that Omura had been Ono's commander at the time of the first massacre and, furthermore, that he knew that the first massacre had occurred before the second was perpetrated.[93] The only plausible explanation for the prosecution's failure to charge Omura for the first massacre is that at the time that crime was committed, Omura had only just been given command, and so had not had the opportunity to prevent the crime from occurring. The prosecution presumably therefore considered him not to have had actual command, and thus, not to have had formal responsibility for the massacre. This explanation, however, is somewhat incomplete. Throughout the trials, many officers were tried for crimes that had occurred shortly after they had taken over a command structure, or in cases where they had not had the opportunity to prevent a crime from occurring.

92. NARA, RG331, Supreme Commander for the Allied Powers, Legal Section, Prosecution Division, *Philippines versus Various Japanese War Criminals*, Case File, 1947–1949, Box 1703, *Philippines v Omura Yasuo and One Other* (hereafter *Philippines v Omura*), Charge Sheet, 1–3.

93. *Philippines v Omura*, Trial Transcript, 426, 431–35.

Though Omura was not charged with responsibility for the first massacre, the prosecution did use this crime to seal his conviction for the second. The prosecution argued that since Omura knew that the first massacre had occurred, he had had a duty to ensure that his subordinates, in this case Ono, did not carry out further massacres, probably meaning that he should have both limited Ono's command and punished him for committing the first massacre.[94] According to the prosecution, the fact that the second massacre occurred, and that it was again carried out by Ono, was clear evidence that Omura had failed in his duty to prevent or halt the commission of a war crime.

In the Omura case, the prosecution applied a clear legal formula in relation to command responsibility, in a way that was relatively uncommon in the post-war trials. The prosecution first established that Omura's subordinate, Ono, had committed a massacre at Barrio Fabrica, and then established that Omura not only knew of this initial massacre but had taken no action to punish Ono. Thus, the prosecution showed two things: first, that Omura was on notice that war crimes were occurring within his command; and second, that his failure to punish the initial crime led to the second massacre occurring. That is, the prosecution interpreted command responsibility as a separate offence of the superior, where the action or inaction of the superior officer forms the criminal act. The tribunal agreed with the prosecution's argument, finding Omura not guilty of the original charge against him – ordering or wilfully permitting the first massacre to occur. Instead, when the bench announced its verdict, it amended the charge against Omura and found him guilty of failing to prevent the second massacre. Ono was sentenced to death by hanging, while Omura was sentenced to life imprisonment.[95]

The Omura trial is an important counterpoint to the majority of command responsibility trials. The prosecution could clearly establish Omura's command jurisdiction over the subordinates who had carried out the substantive crime. Omura was also proven to have had the requisite knowledge that members of his command were committing war crimes. Finally, although Omura had thus had an opportunity to exercise responsible command in preventing further crimes and punishing his subordinate, he did nothing to prevent the second massacre. He did not punish Ono for the first massacre, nor did he limit Ono's discretion in command. The application of command responsibility in this trial progressed in the manner that Allied trial personnel had expected or hoped for when the trials began. In reality, ideal circumstances rarely presented themselves to investigators and prosecutors, and instead, ideal circumstances were presupposed, and command responsibility was applied anyway.

94. *Philippines v Omura*, Trial Transcript, 539–41.
95. *Philippines v Omura*, Rationale, 4–5.

Conclusions

Command responsibility trials often turned out to be long-running, complicated affairs. They were almost guaranteed to be messy: prosecutors were using a doctrine that differed from domestic criminal law doctrines, in an unfamiliar legal system in which justice was measured by the sentence delivered, rather than by the correct application and interpretation of law, rules and processes. This was especially true in massacre trials because the crime often took place in, or close to, the heat and chaos of battle. It was difficult to establish who had had formal command, and when, as well as how many victims had died, and who they were.

Despite these difficulties, trials for massacres were more likely than trials for other offences to prosecute all available officers from the chain of command. Though many massacres appear to have gone untried, and many suspects escaped trial, when a massacre was brought to trial, large portions of the command structure were indicted and convicted. If a suspect in a massacre case were in Allied custody, there was a good chance he would be prosecuted. Prosecuting all suspects, however, came with its own problems, especially when command responsibility was involved.

The massacre proceedings show the difficulties that Allied tribunals faced in determining how to allocate responsibility at different levels of command. At the start of the trials, the idealised path of prosecutions – beginning with direct perpetrators and working up the chain of command – was meant to show that responsibility for crimes existed at multiple levels. Apportioning guilt across the hierarchy, however, turned out to be exceedingly complicated. Command was often split among multiple officers, with different ranks and different formal and informal positions, and thus, different degrees of control before, during, and after the crime. In these circumstances, it was hard to narrow down where exactly guilt lay, and how guilty each officer was. The trials often raised tough questions about the nature of command. How could tribunals apportion individual guilt across a chain of command, and was that desirable? How should partial responsibility be assessed when ultimate responsibility had already been apportioned? Did superior orders vitiate the command responsibility of lower-ranking officers?

The answers to these questions were different at each trial, because tribunals had varying understandings of what exactly the role of command was at each level; and there was no obligation, and little opportunity, to conform with precedent. The result was that guilt and liability were fluid, and tribunals may effectively have decided that ultimate, individual responsibility possibly did not exist: all officers, given that they were in command, could be held collectively responsible for a massacre. All officers, regardless of whether they had *de facto* or *de jure* command, or were staff officers exercising administrative discretion, were equally culpable, in this view. The consequence was that command was often considered, on the one hand, to be spread across multiple individuals within a unit, and on the other hand, to be almost absolutely wielded by individual officers.

5

Mistreatment of Prisoners

In late 1941 and early 1942, the Japanese military quickly captured large swathes of territory in the Asia-Pacific region. During their advance, Japanese forces took up to 350,000 Allied soldiers as prisoners of war (POWs). According to numbers from the prosecution case at the International Military Tribunal for the Far East (IMTFE), 132,134 white Allied POWs were held captive for the remainder of the war. Of the other soldiers taken prisoner, up to 220,000, were Asians – Indians, Filipinos, Indonesians, and others – fighting with or alongside Western troops. Approximately 173,000 Asian soldiers were set free relatively soon after capture.[1] Asian soldiers who remained captive were mostly British Indian soldiers and colonial soldiers from the Netherlands Indies.[2] For the rest of the war, Allied prisoners were either held in the countries in which they had been captured, or transported across the Japanese Empire, mostly to be used as a labour force.

POW camps were set up across the Empire, often within reach of factories, ports, mines, and construction sites. Prisoners were sometimes ill-treated when being moved to the camps in the first place. As we have seen, on the Bataan Death March, many prisoners died because of bad management of the operation by their captors, difficult weather, challenging geographical conditions, and the

1. International Military Tribunal for the Far East, Judgment, Chapter 8, 'Conventional War Crimes (Atrocities)', 1003, http://www.legal-tools.org/uploads/tx_ltpdb/JU01-07-1-01.pdf; Adachi Sumio, 'Kokusaijin dōhō saininshiki e no michi', *Hō to chitsujo* 74, no. 5 (Sept. 1983): 25, cited in Utsumi Aiko, 'Prisoners of War in the Pacific War: Japan's Policy', in *The Burma-Thailand Railway: Memory and History*, ed. Gavan McCormack and Hank Nelson (Allen & Unwin, 1993), 81n6; Iris Heidebrink, 'Prisoners of War (POWs)', in *The Encyclopedia of Indonesia in the Pacific War*, ed. Peter Post, William H. Frederick, Iris Heidebrink, and Shigeru Sato (Koninklijke Brill, 2010), 175–76.
2. G. J. Douds, 'Indian POWs in the Pacific, 1941–1945', in *Forgotten Captives in Japanese-Occupied Asia*, ed. Karl Hack and Kevin Blackburn (Abingdon, Oxon: Routledge, 2008), 74; Karl Hack and Kevin Blackburn, 'Japanese-Occupied Asia', in Hack and Blackburn, *Forgotten Captives*, 10.

poor health of the prisoners themselves.[3] Conditions at the camps were often very poor: terrain and climate could be inhospitable, food and medical supplies were unreliable, and work schedules were demanding. In addition, some prison staff meted out brutal treatment to prisoners. Death rates among prisoners in some areas were high. For Allied governments and militaries and the general public in Allied countries, prosecuting those who had mistreated POWs was a priority once the conflict ended.[4] The Potsdam Declaration of July 1945 had warned the Japanese government and military that 'stern justice shall be meted out to all war criminals, including those who have visited cruelties upon our prisoners'.[5] After surrender, Japanese camp guards, other staff, and commanders were automatically detained as war crimes suspects, as were personnel who had been involved in the transport of prisoners on ships.[6]

A great number of war crimes trials centred on the mistreatment of captured Allied soldiers, and command responsibility was frequently used as a prosecution tool. The strong determination to try Japanese personnel suspected of mistreating POWs, as well as time pressures, meant that some prosecutions were launched before a case had been properly prepared, and that prosecutors were more willing than they might otherwise have been to use evidence of dubious veracity. In such circumstances, command responsibility was particularly useful, because prosecutors did not need to have clear evidence that a commander had ordered a crime, or even knew about it: the mere fact that a crime had occurred was enough to convict an officer under the doctrine of command responsibility.

This chapter shows how command responsibility was used to prosecute crimes of mistreatment of POWs. Officers were regularly charged with responsibility for the physical beatings that subordinates had meted out to prisoners. In trials relating to labour camps, officers might also be held responsible for poor working conditions, including long hours; for forcing prisoners to do dangerous work; or for forcing sick prisoners to work. In nearly all trials for crimes committed in POW camps, commanding officers were prosecuted for providing inadequate food and medicine to the prisoners.

---

3. Kevin C. Murphy, *Inside the Bataan Death March: Defeat, Travail and Memory* (McFarland and Company, 2014), 267–69; National Archives of Australia (hereafter NAA), War Crimes Trial of Captain Yamamoto Shoichi and Ten Others, https://www.legal-tools.org/uploads/tx_ltpdb/ICWC1002ShoichiYamamotoetal01.pdfand.
4. Sandra Wilson, Robert Cribb, Beatrice Trefalt, and Dean Aszkielowicz, *Japanese War Criminals: The Politics of Justice After the Second World War* Columbia University Press, 2017), 42.
5. 'Proclamation by the Heads of Governments, United States, China and the United Kingdom', 26 July 1945, in *Foreign Relations of the United States: Diplomatic Papers: The Conference of Berlin (the Potsdam Conference), 1945* US Department of State (US Government Printing Office, 1945), 2:1476.
6. Wilson, Cribb, Trefalt, and Aszkielowicz, *Japanese War Criminals*, 48.

In addition to large numbers of POWs, the Japanese also interned approximately 130,000 Allied civilians, the great majority of whom had been captured in the Netherlands Indies and remained confined there.[7] Conditions in civilian camps could also be harsh, and civilian internees experienced many of the same hardships that POWs did. Among the US, UK, Philippine, and Australian trials, however, prosecutions for the mistreatment of captive civilians were much less common than those for captured Allied soldiers, and command responsibility rarely featured in such trials. Most trials for mistreatment of civilian internees were conducted by Netherland Indies authorities. Whereas Chapter 3 dealt with civilian victims of torture, this chapter, therefore, examines only cases involving POWs.

This chapter analyses trials held for camp conditions on Ambon Island in the Netherlands Indies, several camps along the Burma–Thailand Railway, one camp near Osaka in Japan, one camp in Manila, and one camp on Hainan Island. The cases examined provide an overview of conditions at different locations across the Japanese Empire during the war and are analysed in chronological order. I show that, with few exceptions, the post-war tribunals targeted camp commanders, who were usually junior and mid-level officers, for the poor conditions at POW camps, often interpreting the doctrine as a separate offence of the superior officer. Though this approach required a focus on what an accused officer had done or not done, it usually disregarded the circumstances in which decisions had been made. As a result, the tribunals did little to uncover the broader reasons for the terrible conditions that many POWs experienced, and individual officers were frequently held responsible for circumstances that had been beyond their control, especially the inadequate supply of food and medicine.

It is unlikely that the tribunals purposely ignored the wider circumstances that had contributed to the ill-treatment of captives. Rather, the expedited nature of the hearings, and the type of evidence that was available to both the defence and the prosecution, skewed the view of the camps that was presented in court. In consequence, the majority of the blame for the offences in question was attributed to individual camp commanders and other officers, rather than to the broader Japanese military and political system that was ultimately responsible for the conditions endured by POWs. As the trials analysed in this chapter demonstrate, moreover, the camp commanders who were held responsible for poor conditions among POWs had often had little authority, either formally within the command structure or informally amongst their subordinates.

7. Bernice Archer, *The Internment of Western Civilians Under the Japanese, 1941–1945: A Patchwork of Internment* (Routledge-Curzon, 2004); Christina Twomey, *Australia's Forgotten Prisoners: Civilians Interned by the Japanese in World War Two* (Cambridge University Press, 2007).

The trials selected here also show that Allied military authorities did recognise the difficulties Japanese officers had faced in supplying large numbers of prisoners, often in remote areas, and that their responses changed over time. For crimes committed in camps, tribunals appear to have handed down lighter sentences in cases that were scheduled later on in the trial program. While misgivings about the type of justice that was being meted out almost certainly played a part, the heavier sentences handed down at earlier trials also reflect the types of cases to which investigators and prosecutors had given priority. It seems that trials relating to camps in which large proportions of prisoners had died were held first, while trials for camps with fewer deaths were deferred to later stages of the prosecution program. This approach makes sense in view of the Allies' political goals. Part of the Allied intent in the trial process was to show to the Japanese public the extent and enormity of Japanese war crimes, and to demonstrate to Allied civilians that justice was being done.[8] Prosecuting cases based on egregious mistreatment of Allied POWs offered some of the clearest evidence to the Japanese public of the scope and severity of Japanese war crimes and also offered assurance to Allied civilians that the trials were being taken seriously.

As the trials continued into 1947 and 1948, it appears that tribunals, and more frequently, review lawyers, began to accept Japanese officers' claims that broader supply problems had been a significant reason for malnutrition and disease among captives. Such claims were made in nearly every trial for crimes committed at a POW camp, but were likely disregarded in the early trials as either desperate defences or as a refusal by the accused to acknowledge his criminality. As time went on, tribunals and review lawyers seem to have made greater allowance for the broader circumstances of the war when sentencing the accused. Other mitigating factors were also sometimes taken into account, including the commanding officer's competence and experience, and, in rarer cases, the condition of the prisoners before they had come under the accused's control. Overall, the camp trials offer the clearest evidence of an evolving definition of what command had meant during the war. The effect of these considerations on sentencing, however, was usually limited: officers were still held to very high standards of conduct.

The Doctrine of Command Responsibility and Ill-Treatment of Prisoners

Several factors separate the crimes that occurred in camps from summary executions, massacres, and torture. There were two key differences from summary execution and massacre. First, the intent of crimes against POWs was not to

8. Wilson, Cribb, Trefalt, and Aszkielowicz, *Japanese War Criminals*, 20–25.

kill them, even though many prisoners died as a result of the offences. Rather, the intent was usually to maintain discipline in the camps and to make prisoners work more productively, often in circumstances in which essential supplies were insufficient. A second point of contrast is that the crimes committed in camps had usually taken place over months or years, or at least were construed as ongoing crimes, whereas massacre and summary execution were discrete, specific events. The charge of inadequate provision of essential supplies normally referred to a prolonged period. Instances of physical mistreatment of captives, usually by beating them, could have been treated as discrete events but usually were not when officers were prosecuted. Instead, officers were tried for overseeing camps in which beatings were routine. With respect to torture, the key difference is that the mistreatment that POWs endured was incidental to their captivity, while victims of torture were captured for the explicit purpose of interrogation, if necessary, by force.

Because of these differences in the nature or perceived nature of the offences, prosecutors did not use the doctrine of command responsibility in the same manner as in trials for massacre, summary execution, or torture. Camp commanders were not always tried for the acts of their subordinates. Instead, they were held responsible for their own culpable negligence in the running of the camp, which meant that command responsibility in these trials was usually framed as a separate offence of the commanding officer. In charges for physical mistreatment of captives, the choice to try officers for overseeing camps where beatings were routine, or were presented as routine, probably reflects prosecutors' desire to frame the physical abuse as part of a long-term pattern that had been established under the officer's supervision, rather than as the acts of out-of-control subordinates.

For prosecutors in trials involving the mistreatment of POWs, command responsibility was indispensable in securing convictions. Some Japanese military personnel – usually non-commissioned officers and enlisted soldiers – did physically abuse prisoners. Most of the mistreatment of POWs, however, was the result of the general conditions of captivity and the severe requirements of work projects. Thus, in many cases, there was no clear direct perpetrator of a crime. Suspects were commonly tried for crimes of omission or negligence, rather than for substantive crimes that had involved direct action.

Command responsibility was also an exceptionally easy tool for prosecutors to use in cases based on crimes committed in camps, because, unlike in many of the trials for massacres and summary executions, and, to some extent, torture, prosecutors had access to abundant evidence. Allied prisoners of Japanese forces died in large numbers during the war, but approximately 70 per cent survived.[9]

9. International Military Tribunal for the Far East, Judgment, 1003.

Some survivors appeared personally in court to give evidence. Many were unavailable, as Allied militaries had prioritised sending prisoners home after the Japanese surrender, and those who had not yet been repatriated were usually recovering in hospital. Nevertheless, evidence was gathered from many former prisoners. British, Australian, and American war crimes investigators, in Japan and in the POWs' home countries, questioned almost every liberated prisoner on how they had been treated in the camps.[10] Furthermore, some captured officers, at great personal risk, had kept records on paper of ill-treatment and abuse. These notes and diaries were sometimes stashed in hiding places in camps, and occasionally in graves of deceased prisoners.[11] Thus, the prosecution in some trials had overwhelming evidence of the extent and nature of crimes that had been committed against POWs, even if not all the evidence was of the highest quality.

Prosecutors were easily able to demonstrate that there had been ongoing abuse of Allied personnel, whether in the form of physical beatings of individuals, collective punishment, a steady decrease in the quantity and quality of rations and medical supplies, or forcing sick prisoners to work. Once the evidence had been raised, the prosecutor only had to establish that the accused officer either knew, or ought to have known, that ill-treatment was occurring. Many specific charges accused officers of having had a direct policy to mistreat prisoners. In court, however, the prosecution was more likely to argue that the accused had had knowledge of ill-treatment, without asserting that there had been direct criminal intent. In such cases, the doctrine of command responsibility showed its worth to prosecutors: there was no need to prove criminal intent to prove criminal liability.

Modern international criminal law differentiates between crimes that occur through the actions of subordinates and those that occur because of general circumstances.[12] At the post-war national trials in the Pacific, however, this difference was rarely recognised. Allied tribunals took the view that Japanese officers could have kept prisoners supplied with food and medicine, even when the

10. Wilson, Cribb, Trefalt, and Aszkielowicz, *Japanese War Criminals*, 45.
11. Jack Holder Leemon, 'The Body Snatchers', unpublished manuscript, Australian War Memorial, MSS0811, 99.
12. Allison Marston Danner and Jenny S. Martinez, 'Guilty Associations: Joint Criminal Enterprise, Command Responsibility, and the Development of International Criminal Law', *California Law Review* 93 (2005): 166–69; Nina H. B. Jørgensen, 'On Being "Concerned" in a Crime: Embryonic Joint Criminal Enterprise?', in *Hong Kong's War Crimes Trials*, ed. Suzannah Linton (Oxford University Press, 2013), 139–61; Nina H. B. Jørgensen, 'Theories of Joint Criminal Responsibility at the Asian Tribunals', in *Trials for International Crimes in Asia*, ed. Kirsten Sellars (Cambridge University Press, 2015), 318–40; Cheah Wui-Ling, 'Post-World War II British "Hell-ship" Trials in Singapore: Omissions and the Attribution of Responsibility', *Journal of International Criminal Justice* 8, no. 4 (2010): 1035–42.

officers had had practically no control over the quantity and quality of supplies. The crimes committed in camps were interpreted as a failure of command, when, in many cases, the mistreatment of prisoners had occurred because of a much larger breakdown in supply. In trials for mistreatment of Allied captives, thus, the evidence overwhelmingly concerned the actions of individuals. As a result, junior and mid-level officers were held criminally responsible for wider systemic issues within the Japanese military, not just those over which they had had either official or actual control.

Conditions in the Camps: Dealing with External Factors

Central Japanese policies for dealing with prisoners were inadequate. At the outbreak of the war, neither the Japanese government nor the military had plans or policy in place to deal with captured Allied prisoners, in either the short or the long term.[13] Only in March 1942 did the Japanese military create the Prisoner of War Management Office (*Furyo kanribu*), as part of the Army Ministry, to handle all POW matters.[14] In April 1942 the Japanese Army decided that the prisoners would be used as a labour force. White prisoners had a further use: they would be paraded before local populations to demonstrate Japanese superiority over white soldiers and former colonisers. Even at this stage, however, limited directions were given on the actual treatment of POWs.[15] The failure of the Japanese government and military to adopt a clear policy on the treatment of captives, as well as the slow approach to implementing POW administration, no doubt contributed to the poor treatment of prisoners during the war.

The need to move prisoners around produced further hazards to the captives' welfare. Using Allied POWs as a labour force meant transporting them from the point of capture across the Japanese Empire, usually by ship. For many of the prisoners, the voyage was difficult. Crowded into transport ships on the way to wherever labour was needed, they faced squalid conditions and were often held below decks for the entirety of their journey. Cholera and dysentery were rife on some ships, and food and water were often inadequate. The vessels were not flagged as POW ships, and Allied air and naval forces sank a number of them, even when the Allied military was aware that POWs were likely to be

13. John Dower, *War Without Mercy: Race and Power in the Pacific War* (Pantheon, 1986), 65.
14. Utsumi Aiko, 'The Japanese Army and its Prisoners: Relevant Documents and Bureaucratic Institutions', Australia-Japan Research Project, Australian War Memorial, http://ajrp.awm.gov.au/ajrp/ajrp2.nsf/aa9b3f3247a3c8ae4a25676300078dee/d2e5732b8749d2e04a2567a8007b490c?OpenDocument.
15. Utsumi, 'Prisoners of War in the Pacific War', 69–73; Heidebrink, 'Prisoners of War', 174.

on board.[16] Over the course of the war, approximately 10,000 Allied prisoners of the Japanese died on transport ships or in the sea after shipwreck, in the latter case, mostly during Allied attacks. This death toll represents nearly one-third of all prisoner deaths in Japanese captivity.[17] Conditions on the ships became the subject of several US, UK, and Australian command responsibility trials.

The most significant factor affecting the welfare of POWs who were settled in camps was their location. Camps situated in remote places were often rudimentary, and there was no infrastructure for the long-term support of a large influx of prisoners. In many cases, this was because, although the region might have been strategically significant, the Allied colonial powers had done little during their earlier rule to build or improve roads, rail, and ports.[18] In other instances, Allied soldiers and local civilian administrators had destroyed existing infrastructure to deny it to the Japanese military.[19] During the construction of the Burma–Thailand Railway, as one notable instance, many prisoners were camped in remote jungle, with only the rail line that they were constructing to bring in supplies.

On the other hand, camps in Japan, Singapore, Hong Kong, Korea, and Taiwan were generally better than those on the fringes of the Empire, though food and medicine were sometimes scarce, and prisoners could be beaten.[20] These camps were situated in regions with established infrastructure and were further away from the fighting. Even along the Burma–Thailand Railway, camps close to towns and transport hubs had better conditions. Changi POW Camp in Singapore was considered by many POWs to be one of the best camps, due to limited oversight from Japanese guards; the fact that the camp occupied an

16. Lachlan Grant, 'Hellships, Prisoner Transport and Unrestricted Submarine Warfare in World War II', in *Beyond Surrender: Australian Prisoners of War in the Twentieth Century*, ed. Joan Beaumont, Lachlan Grant, and Aaron Pegram (Melbourne University Publishing, 2015), 207–12.
17. Gavan Daws, *Prisoners of the Japanese: POWs Of World War II in the Pacific* (William Morrow and Company, 1994), 297; Michael Sturma, 'Japanese Treatment of Allied Prisoners During the Second World War: Evaluating the Death Toll', *Journal of Contemporary History* 55 (2020): 517; Gregory Michno, *Death on the Hell-ships: Prisoners at Sea in the Pacific War* (Naval Institute Press, 2001), 87; Raymond Lamont-Brown, *Ships From Hell: Japanese War Crimes on the High Seas* (Sutton Publishing, 2002), 25–27.
18. I thank Professor Robert Cribb for this point.
19. Adrian Vickers, 'Dugas Jepengé/The Japanese Period: Bali Under the Japanese', in Post, Frederick, Heidebrink, and Sato, *The Encyclopedia of Indonesia in the Pacific War*, 87.
20. Sandra Wilson, 'Detention Camps in the Japanese Empire, 1941–1945', in *Detention Camps in Asia: The Conditions of Confinement in Modern Asian History*, ed. Robert Cribb, Christina Twomey, and Sandra Wilson (Brill, 2022), 209–12; Sarah Kovner, 'Allied POWs in Korea: Life and Death During the Pacific War', in *The Dismantling of Japan's Empire in East Asia: Deimperialization, Postwar Legitimation and Imperial Afterlife*, ed. Barak Kushner and Sherzod Muminov (Routledge, 2017), 107–12.

existing barracks, designed to hold large numbers of military personnel; and the presence of a hospital.[21]

Nearly all trials involving the mistreatment of prisoners included a charge of supplying inadequate food and medicine, and nearly all prosecutors treated the inadequate supply of food and medicine as the result of camp commanders' own orders or negligence. The fact that so many surviving prisoners from so many different camps reported shortages of food and medicine probably encouraged prosecutors to view this aspect of mistreatment as evidence of a broader pattern of criminality across the Japanese command: that is, they concluded that there had been a deliberate policy to mistreat captives.

Some camp commanders did deny food and medicine to prisoners with what appeared to be criminal intent. In the majority of cases, however, it is clear that inadequate supply was the result of a much bigger problem within the Japanese military. Over the course of the war the Japanese military's capacity to supply its own troops with enough food, medicine, and munitions practically collapsed. This failure was the direct result of unrestricted US naval warfare, which meant that any Japanese vessel, regardless of whether it was civilian or military, could and would be targeted. The consequences of unrestricted warfare were devastating: by the end of the war, over 75 per cent of Japanese shipping had been sunk, and most Japanese garrisons had been left with highly deficient long-term supplies of medicine and food.[22] The broader failure of supply and logistics affected POW camps, just as it did frontline Japanese units.

It is hardly surprising that the preponderance of evidence in camp trials dealt with individual actions, rather than broader circumstances that had contributed to mistreatment of prisoners. After all, the chief concern of the trials was to assign guilt to individuals: they were not inquiries into what had happened and how it had happened. In command responsibility cases, the prosecution almost invariably focused on what commanders had known about circumstances inside the camps they had controlled, and what they had done – or more frequently, had not done – to prevent, halt, or punish the mistreatment of prisoners, simply because that was the role of the prosecution. Information about the wider context of the war, and how external factors had affected the treatment of prisoners, in the broad sense, was not sought, and in any case would rarely have been available. Trials were often held relatively shortly after the war had ended. Defence lawyers did refer to the general situation of the war, but they did not have enough

21. R. P. W. Havers, *Reassessing the Japanese Prisoner of War Experience: The Changi POW Camp, Singapore, 1942–1945* (Routledge-Curzon, 2003), 166–70.
22. Joel Ira Holwitt, *'Execute Against Japan': The U.S. Decision to Conduct Unrestricted Submarine Warfare* (Texas A&M University Press, 2009), 164–66.

time or resources to collate information about the general circumstances that had led to mistreatment of POWs.

Tan Toey POW Camp Trial

The Australian trial for mistreatment of POWs at Tan Toey POW Camp on Ambon Island in the Netherlands Indies[23] is a good illustration of the Allied determination to prosecute those who had visited cruelties upon prisoners. It also illustrates of the trials' lack of capacity to account for factors outside of a commander's control. In terms of number of defendants, the Tan Toey trial was the largest conducted in the Asia-Pacific region after the Second World War.[24] A total of ninety-two defendants were indicted, ranging from the commander of the camp, Captain Shirozu Wadami, to low-ranking petty officers and a civilian interpreter, Ikeuchi Masakiyo.[25] All of the accused military servicemen were members of the Japanese navy. The trial was initially convened on Ambon Island, where the camp was located, between 2 January and 18 January 1946. It was then moved to Morotai Island, resuming on 25 January and closing on 15 February 1946, as the Dutch government had agreed to only four months of provisional control of the island by the Australian military.[26] Of the ninety-two defendants, fifty-five were acquitted, some midway through the trial, while the guilty received sentences ranging from death to one year of imprisonment. Shirozu, found guilty through command responsibility of both beating the captives and denying them adequate food and medicine, was sentenced to death by firing squad and was executed on 25 September 1947.[27]

The approximately 1,000 prisoners at Tan Toey were mostly a mix of Dutch and Australian soldiers, who had been captured after the Battle of Ambon (30 January–3 February 1942). Conditions at Tan Toey had initially been relatively good. The camp itself did not have a fenced perimeter, and prisoners could trade with local villagers for food and other items. There was comparatively little work to do. By late 1942, however, things had changed. In October, approximately 500 of the POWs, including the majority of officers, were sent to Hainan Island, off

23. Some material from this section has been published as Paul Taucher, 'Tan Toey Priisoner of War Camp: The Dilemmas of Command', in *Detention Camps in Asia: The Conditions of Confinement in Modern Asian History*, ed. Robert Cribb, Chritina Twomey, and Sanra Wilson (Brill-Nijhoff, 2022), 219–36.
24. Wilson, Cribb, Trefalt, and Aszkielowicz, *Japanese War Criminals*, 68.
25. National Archives of Australia (hereafter NAA), War Crimes Trial of Shirozu Wadami and Ninety-One Others, Part One (hereafter Shirozu Trial), Charge Sheet, 2–4, archived at [https://recordsearch.naa.gov.au/SearchNRetrieve/Interface/ViewImage.aspx?B=721016].
26. Georgina Fitzpatrick, 'The Trials on Morotai', in *Australia's War Crimes Trials 1945–1951*, ed. Georgina Fitzpatrick, Timothy McCormack, and Narrelle Morris (Brill-Nijhoff, 2016), 384–88.
27. Shirozu Trial, Appendix A: Accused Found Guilty Sentence and Date, 8.

the southeast coast of the Chinese mainland. For the Japanese military, it was common practice to remove officers from the relatively far-flung POW camps and send them closer to more secure Japanese territory: Allied officers were also removed from Sandakan POW Camp in North Borneo, and from various small camps in occupied Malaya and the Philippines.[28] When all ranks were in the same camp, officers provided some, albeit limited, protection from Japanese mistreatment, by organising and presenting complaints to their captors, as well as organising soldiers to support each other, so their removal almost certainly had a deleterious effect on the welfare of the remaining captives.

The adequacy of food, medicine, and clothing presented another set of issues. As the war progressed in favour of the Allies, provisions at Tan Toey steadily decreased, as fewer Japanese supply ships could safely reach Ambon. The trial, however, did not take this factor into account. Many prisoners on Ambon became sick with diseases such as dysentery and beriberi and contracted tropical ulcers. The official cause of death for the majority of POWs at Tan Toey was listed as beriberi, a disease resulting from poor nutrition. Two former prisoners, however, alleged that this cause of death was recorded at the insistence of Ikeuchi, a civilian interpreter, to cover up deaths from beatings and starvation, an allegation that Ikeuchi denied.[29] Immediately after the Japanese surrender in August 1945, according to evidence presented at the trial, the Japanese forces on Ambon inundated Tan Toey with food, medicine, and fresh clothes, thus proving, according to prosecutors, that supplies had been deliberately withheld during wartime.[30]

Deaths of prisoners also increased because of Allied bombing in the later stages of the war. International law required that POW camps be clearly marked as such,[31] but requests by Allied officers to have the Tan Toey camp marked were refused by their captors. In February 1943, approximately twenty POWs died when a munitions dump was blown up during an Allied air raid.[32]

Many prisoners died because of the nature of the work – and the amount of work – that they were forced to do. An additional factor was from being forced to work while sick. Several prisoners were killed when, despite their objections,

28. Paul Taucher, 'Command Responsibility at the Sandakan-Ranau War Crimes Trials' (Honours Dissertation, Murdoch University, 2016), 42; Heidebrink, 'Prisoners of War', 177; Daws, *Prisoners of the Japanese*, 105; Margaret Shennan, *Out in the Midday Sun: The British in Malaya 1880–1960* (John Murray, 2000), 275.
29. Shirozu Trial, Nominal Roll, 229–58; Shirozu Trial, Trial Transcript, 446.
30. Shirozu Trial, Charge Sheet, 2–4.
31. 'The Geneva Convention 1929', Article 12, http://avalon.law.yale.edu/20th_century/geneva02.asp#art12.
32. Joan Beaumont, *Gull Force: Survival and Leadership in Captivity 1941–1945* (Ure Smith, 1968), 103–5. The storage of munitions in a POW camp was also illegal under international law: see 'The Geneva Convention 1929', Article 9.

they were forced to defuse unexploded ordnance with metal hammers instead of wooden or rubber hammers. Prisoners worked on constructing barracks and other buildings, which involved carrying construction material over eight miles of rough terrain: the heavy manual labour, combined with a poor diet, would have rapidly weakened the prisoners. Sick POWs, suffering from a range of tropical diseases, vitamin deficiencies and injuries, were forced out of a makeshift hospital to work. Of the approximately 540 Australian and Dutch prisoners held on Ambon for the duration of the war, approximately 130 survived.[33] The death rate at Ambon was thus one of the highest of the war in the Pacific.

At the Tan Toey war crimes trial, all ninety-two of the defendants were charged with ill-treating Australian and Dutch POWs by physically beating and torturing them, compelling sick and infirm POWs to work, failing to ensure the proper provision of food supplies, and failing to ensure the proper provision of medical supplies and medical care.[34] Captain Shirozu Wadami, the overall commander of Tan Toey Camp from December 1943 until the end of the war, was the most senior of the accused. As a naval captain, it was somewhat unusual for Shirozu to have been responsible only for a single POW camp: colonels, the equivalent army rank, were often in charge of multiple camps.[35] The Imperial Japanese Navy lacked a dedicated system for dealing with POWs, and Shirozu had probably ended up with responsibility for the prisoners simply because he was already in command of the Ambon garrison.[36] Shirozu was charged with beating POWs and failing to provide adequate food. No evidence was raised, however, to suggest that he had personally hit any prisoner during his command. Instead, the prosecution presented evidence to show that he either knew, or ought to have known, that his subordinates were beating prisoners. Shirozu was thus tried for command responsibility.

Physical punishment of captives was not unusual at Japanese-run POW camps. In some camps, beatings could be brutal, resulting in severe injuries, including broken bones, and sometimes death.[37] In other camps, it appears that prisoners were slapped across the face, or received a single punch or kick.[38] Both

---

33. Shirozu Trial, Charge Sheet, 2–4.
34. Shirozu Trial, Charge Sheet, 2–4.
35. Felicia Yap, 'Prisoner of War and Civilian Internees of the Japanese in British Asia: The Similarities and Contrasts of Experience', *Journal of Contemporary History* 47 no. 2 (2012): 336; Robin Rowland, 'Command Ability and Command Responsibility: Lt Col. Hirateru Banno and the "F Force" Trials' (Master's thesis, York University, 2003), 2–5.
36. Ooi Keat Gin, 'Of Permanent Possession: Territories Under the Imperial Japanese Navy', in Post, Frederick, Heidebrink, and Sato, *The Encyclopedia of Indonesia in the Pacific War*, 71, 85.
37. Alan B. Lyon, *Japanese War Crimes: The Trial of the Naoetsu Camp Guards* (Australian Military History Publications, 2000), 19–23; Richard Reid, *Laden, Fevered, Starved: The POWs of Sandakan, North Borneo* (Commonwealth Department of Veteran Affairs, 1999), 22–23.
38. Sarah Kovner, *Prisoners of the Empire: Inside Japanese POW Camps* (Harvard University Press, 2020), 83–84.

the navy and the army used summary beating by non-commissioned and commissioned officers as an immediate response to real or perceived indiscipline among prisoners, as opposed to relying on a formal written warning or imposition of menial labour or imprisonment – forms of punishment to which Allied soldiers would have been accustomed.[39]

Physical punishment was also common within the Japanese military. In nearly every trial in which charges of beating prisoners were laid, the defence maintained that such treatment was a standard punishment across the Japanese military. Shirozu made the same claim, downplaying his responsibility for the beatings by arguing that because physical punishment was a core part of the Japanese military's system of discipline, it was normal rather than exceptional.[40]

Shirozu took the argument one step further, however, asserting that he did not have legal responsibility for the beatings in any case. His reasoning was that his duty to halt, prevent, or punish crimes committed by his subordinates would only have been triggered if there had been evidence of regular, ongoing abuse. At Tan Toey, the worst beatings had occurred under a previous commander, referred to in the trial only as Captain Ando, who allegedly was responsible as commander for the beating of thirty-three prisoners, of whom three died, in July 1942. Under Shirozu's command, beatings appear to have been limited to less severe incidents, though wooden staffs and axe handles were occasionally used to hit prisoners, and prisoners were commonly slapped.[41] According to Shirozu, one hundred beatings over three years ought to have been viewed as one hundred single instances, rather than as a pattern of behaviour. Through this argument, Shirozu probably sought to appeal to a statement made at the Yamashita Tomoyuki tribunal in Manila in December 1945. Upon finding Yamashita guilty of war crimes, the American tribunal held that when crimes committed by a commander's subordinates had been particularly widespread, or not sporadic in nature, then a commander could be held liable for these crimes.[42]

Shirozu was also charged with failing to provide adequate food for the prisoners. Though food supply had initially been good, the situation had changed in mid-1943. Supply ships arrived less frequently at Ambon, so the prisoners were ordered to farm their own crops – mostly sweet potato and tapioca – a practice

39. Gavan McCormack, 'Apportioning the Blame: Australian Trials for Railway Crimes', in McCormack and Nelson, *The Burma-Thailand Railway*, 87; Colin Sleeman, ed., *Trial of Gozawa Sadaichi and Nine Others* (William Hodge and Company, 1948), xxiv–xxvi; Wilson, Cribb, Trefalt, and Aszkielowicz, *Japanese War Criminals*, 75.
40. Shirozu Trial, Trial Transcript, 451–53.
41. Shirozu Trial, Trial Transcript, 5–6.
42. Richard L. Lael, *The Yamashita Precedent: War Crimes and Command Responsibility* (Scholarly Resources, 1982), 96.

that was widespread amongst island garrisons across the Japanese Empire.[43] With limited farming tools, however, and a labour shortage caused by the fact that the prisoners were already working elsewhere on the island in building defences and an airstrip, the farm alone could not sustain the captives.

By late 1944, the prisoners' rations were substantially less than those of their Japanese guards. This situation was a direct breach of the 1929 Geneva Convention, which stipulated that captives were to be given food equivalent in quantity and quality to that of their guards.[44] In August 1944, Shirozu had ordered that the POWs' rations be cut, following the destruction of food stores during an Allied bombing raid. In court, Shirozu argued that restocking of food supplies had been impossible due to an Allied blockade of the island, which meant that food for both POWs and Japanese soldiers needed to be reduced.[45] Shirozu had been placed in a difficult position: there was not enough food to keep his own soldiers in fighting condition and to give adequate sustenance to the captives as well. He chose to maintain the condition of his own soldiers at the expense of the Allied prisoners.

Shirozu's implicit argument was that the decision to cut the prisoners' food fell under the defence of military necessity. Prior to the Second World War, the doctrine of military necessity was commonly held to allow both enlisted soldiers and officers a carte blanche for military acts considered to be essential to victory,[46] though the defence of military necessity would later be rejected at the Tokyo Trial in relation to mistreatment of POWs.[47] The timing of Shirozu's trial, which concluded over two years before the IMTFE ended, meant that there was no clear consensus amongst the lawyers on the validity of the doctrine of military necessity, nor on how it should interact with command responsibility charges. Neither Shirozu nor his defence lawyer explicitly articulated to the tribunal the idea that food rations had been cut to maintain the fighting capabilities of Japanese soldiers. It is unclear why Shirozu's argument was incomplete, but the fact that there were ninety-two defendants at the trial meant that the defence counsel was overworked to a point where even key issues may have been neglected.

The prosecution of Shirozu for providing inadequate food and medical supplies was based on two understandings of command responsibility. On the one hand, the charge based on Shirozu's direct decision to limit the food supplies for

---

43. Aaron William Moore, 'An Insatiable Parasite: Eating and Drinking in WWII Armies of the Asia-Pacific Theatre (1937–1945)', in *Food and War in Mid-Twentieth Century Asia*, ed. Katarzyna J. Cwiertka (Ashgate, 2013), 124–25.
44. 'The Geneva Convention, 27 July 1929', Article 11.
45. Shirozu Trial, Petition of Captain Shirozu Wadami, 24.
46. Hilaire McCoubrey, *International Humanitarian Law: The Regulation of Armed Conflicts* (Dartmouth Publishing Company, 1990), 198–203.
47. Neil Boister and Robert Cryer, *The Tokyo International Military Tribunal: A Reappraisal* (Oxford University Press, 2008), 243.

prisoners was a standard application of command responsibility, where officers are held criminally responsible for the commands that they issue. On the other hand, the prosecution's concern with the deteriorating supplies throughout 1944, before Shirozu had directly ordered the lowering of the prisoners' rations, and with his failure to take steps to alleviate the situation, shows that the prosecution was also pursuing him for a crime of omission.

The fact that Shirozu was found guilty on both charges shows the value of command responsibility to Allied tribunals pursuing justice for what had happened to POWs during the war. For the prosecutor and the judges, the purpose of the trial was to identify and punish members of the Japanese military who had committed crimes against prisoners. Shirozu had held some form of command of a camp that had one of the highest death rates during the war in Asia. The fact that shortages of food and medicine occurred not because of the acts of members of Shirozu's command, but because of wider problems within the Japanese military, was not relevant for the tribunal, especially as this was an early trial, held at the beginning of 1946. So soon after the end of the war, the Australian judges and prosecutors would have been particularly outraged at the treatment of Allied prisoners: Australian newspaper reports throughout 1945 had been dominated by reporting on Japanese atrocities.[48] In this environment, greater attention was inevitably paid to the crimes of mistreatment, rather than the circumstances in which they had occurred. Furthermore, in the legal system that the Allied governments had set up for the post-war trials, guilt was assigned to individuals, rather than entire organisations.[49] Within this framework, command could not be separated from the circumstances in which it had operated.

The Burma–Thailand Railway Trial of Banno Hirateru

The UK trial of Lieutenant-Colonel Banno Hirateru shows that tribunals in command responsibility proceedings could, in fact, take account of contextual issues that had contributed to the mistreatment of prisoners. In this case, the tribunal recognised problems with supply and, in addition, the unusual factor of an accused officer's personal incompetence when commanding his subordinates. The Banno trial was an outlier in the application of command responsibility, at least in the early stages of the trial program: when assessing liability, at this stage tribunals rarely gave much weight to supply problems and an officer's capacity to command.

48. Dean Aszkielowicz, *The Australian Pursuit of Japanese War Criminals, 1943–1957: From Foe to Friend* (Hong Kong University Press, 2017), 25–26.
49. Wilson, Cribb, Trefalt, and Aszkielowicz, *Japanese War Criminals*, 1, 18–19, 27.

Between 25 September and 23 October 1946, a UK military tribunal tried Banno and six others for crimes committed against Australian and British prisoners, members of a formation known as F Force, while they were building the Burma–Thailand Railway. It was not the first time Banno had been tried. A Dutch tribunal had previously found him guilty of crimes against POWs in Sumatra and had sentenced him to two years' imprisonment.[50] In the UK trial, Banno, the overall commander of the camps at which F Force had been stationed, was charged with 'the inhumane treatment of POWs, resulting in the death and suffering of many', and with responsibility for the unhygienic conditions at several work camps along the railway.[51] The charge of inhumane treatment of POWs covered the lack of supplies at the camps, as well as the physical beating of prisoners and of sending sick prisoners to work, all of which occurred under the command of Banno's subordinates. Tried under the doctrine of command responsibility, Banno was found guilty of both charges and sentenced to three years' imprisonment.[52] Considering that Banno was essentially held responsible for the deaths of over 3,000 POWs, he received an extremely light sentence.

The Japanese military constructed the Burma–Thailand Railway between June 1942 and October 1943 to support the Japanese invasion of Burma. The railway, which linked the rail hubs of Ban Pong in Thailand and Thanbyuzayat in Burma, was over 400 kilometres long, crossing remote jungle and mountain passes. Labour was provided by approximately 270,000 Asian civilian labourers, known as *romusha*, as well as some 60,000 Allied prisoners of war.[53] Japanese operations in Burma were hampered throughout the war by poor supply lines and limited infrastructure, and the same problems created supply issues for the railway. During its construction, approximately 11,000 POWs and over 73,000 romusha died from a combination of starvation, disease, ill-treatment, and overwork. An unknown number of civilians and POWs also died from Allied 'friendly fire', either during transportation to the railway in ships and trains, or during Allied air attacks on the railway itself.[54] Following the Japanese surrender, the Australian, UK, and Dutch militaries held fifty-five trials for crimes committed

50. National Archives of Japan, 'Oranda sensō saiban gaikenhyō', Hōmu-Heei-11-4A-21-7130, 37, cited in Yuma Totani, *Justice in Asia and the Pacific Region, 1945–1952: Allied War Crimes Prosecutions* (Cambridge University Press, 2015), 224, n. 65.

51. The National Archives of the UK, Kew (hereafter TNA), WO 235/1034, *UK v Banno Hirateru and Six Others*, Charge Sheet, 3.

52. WO 235/1034, Trial Transcript, 751–57.

53. Paul H. Kratoska, 'General Introduction', in *The Thailand-Burma Railway, 1942–1946: Documents and Selected Writings, Vol. 1*, ed. Paul H. Kratoska (Routledge, 2006), 1–3. See also Nakahara Michiko, 'Malayan Labour on the Thailand Burma Railway', in *Asian Labour in the Wartime Japanese Empire: Unknown Histories*, ed. Paul H. Kratoska (M.E. Sharpe, 2005), 249–66.

54. Kratoska, 'General Introduction', 11–14, 39.

during the construction of the railway.[55] Command responsibility was used in these trials to indict not only commissioned officers throughout the chain of command, but also non-commissioned officers.[56] The doctrine was mostly used to prosecute officers for poor working conditions and inadequate supply of food and medicine, and for the physical beatings of prisoners by subordinate soldiers.

In April 1943 approximately 6,000 UK and Australian prisoners, captured when Japanese forces conquered Singapore in February 1942, were transported to the Thailand-Burma border to work as F Force to construct the railway. The prisoners worked on a particularly challenging section of the railway in a mountain range. At the time of their arrival at the worksite, they were approximately 300 km from the nearest functioning rail line. During the long march from the existing line to the worksite, there were outbreaks of cholera and dysentery, diseases that would plague the captives throughout their work on the line, as well as malaria and beriberi.[57] The prisoners were distributed across five camp sites, which had limited drainage, no sanitation facilities, and only basic bamboo huts.[58]

The captives were immediately put to work, building bridges and cutting passes through the mountains. The heavy labour was made even more difficult by insufficient rations: the further away a camp was from either the Burmese or the Thai rail hub, the smaller and poorer the rations were. In May 1943, Japanese command brought forward the deadline for the project's completion, which meant that the prisoners worked longer hours. Japanese guards and engineers beat prisoners for not working hard enough, or when it was suspected that they were feigning illness to avoid work. During this period, sick prisoners were forced out of the rudimentary hospitals to work.[59] By the time F Force returned to Changi in December 1943, 3,096 of the original 7,062 captives, or 44 per cent, had died.[60]

Tried jointly with Banno were subordinates under his command, including direct commanders of individual camps, guards, and a medical officer. Captain Fukuda Tsuneo, one of Banno's subordinates, had commanded two F Force

55. Georgina Fitzpatrick, 'The Trials in Singapore', 585; Sybilla Jane Flower, 'Captors and Captives on the Burma-Thailand Railway', in *Prisoners of War and their Captors in World War II*, ed. Bob Moore and Kent Fedorowich (Berg, 1996), 233; Rowland, 'Command Ability and Command Responsibility', 2; Yasuko Kobayashi, 'Japanese Documents Concerning the War Crimes Trials (esp. General Ishida and Others) Relating to the Burma-Siam Railway', in *The Thailand-Burma Railway, 1942–1946: Documents and Selected Writings Vol. 6*, ed. Paul H. Kratoska (Routledge, 2006), 19–26.
56. TNA, WO 235/817, *UK v Aoki Toshio*.
57. T. Wilson and J. A. Reid, 'Malaria Amongst Prisoners of War in Siam ("F" Force)', *Transactions of the Royal Society of Tropical Medicine and Hygiene* 43 no. 3 (1949): 258–61.
58. Rowland, 'Command Ability', 125–29.
59. Don Wall, *Singapore and Beyond* (2/20 Battalion Association, 1985), 188.
60. TNA, WO 235/1034, Reports on Activities of AIF 'F' Force, 1070–71.

camps, first at Upper Sonkrai and later at Lower Sonkrai. He was tried under the doctrine of command responsibility for the conditions at the two camps, and for the conduct of his subordinate guards.[61] Fukuda's prosecution relied on similar arguments to those raised in the proceedings against Captain Shirozu Wadami in the Tan Toey trial: both were held responsible for the acts of their subordinates, as well as for the overall supply situation. As he was an immediate subordinate of Banno, the charges against Fukuda formed the foundation of the charge against Banno. Captain Tanio Susumu, the medical officer, was tried for the inadequate supply of medicine, while the remaining accused were tried for the harsh working conditions on the railway and the direct physical ill-treatment of prisoners, and for directly forcing sick captives to work.

The decision to try both Banno and his subordinate Fukuda under command responsibility at the same trial was probably the best outcome for the two officers. In other cases where multiple command responsibility trials were held for the same crime, prosecutors were inconsistent, and indeed, opportunistic, in their arguments about how guilt ought to be applied: a prime example was at the two trials for the Ranau massacre, discussed in Chapter 3. Trying the two officers at the same time meant that the tribunal would have been presented with all the relevant evidence against both accused, which, in turn, would have given the tribunal the most accurate view of what had happened, and who was responsible. It probably also would have reduced the opportunity to blame both defendants for the same crimes.

In addition to Banno's subordinates, Lieutenant Abe Hiroshi, a railway engineer, was also accused at this tribunal of crimes committed against prisoners of F Force. Abe was not under Banno's command and was not involved in running or overseeing the POW camps. As an engineer, he was responsible for directing work on the railway, which meant determining the kind of work that the prisoners did and establishing how many prisoners were required to work on each section of the line.[62] The prosecution argued that Abe had directly ordered sick prisoners to work and had personally beaten them.[63]

The prosecution's case against Banno was based on his failure to prevent, halt, or punish war crimes across seven camps for which he had been responsible.[64] The prosecution raised evidence to show that his subordinates had been negligent or actively criminal. Fukuda was said to have taken little or no action to

61. WO 235/1034, Charge Sheet, 3–4.
62. WO 235/1034, Trial Transcript, 641–43.
63. For retrospective comments by Abe on his work on the railway, his trial and his sentence, see Abe Hiroshi, 'Building the Burma-Siam Railroad', in *Japan at War: An Oral History*, ed. Haruko Taya Cook and Theodore F. Cook (New York Press), 99–105; Abe Hiroshi, 'Death Row at Changi Prison', in Cook and Cook, *Japan at War*, 420–27.
64. WO 235/1034, JAG Review, 3.

improve the hygiene and sanitation at the campsites he commanded, and to have made no efforts to stop guards from beating prisoners, including those who were sick.[65] A great deal of evidence was brought before the court to show that one of the accused civilians, Toyoyama Kisei, a Korean guard, had been especially violent, and that the prisoners had made numerous formal complaints about Toyoyama not only to Captain Fukuda, but also to Banno himself.[66] On multiple occasions, POWs had also reported to Banno about the harsh treatment and overworking of prisoners under Lieutenant Abe's supervision and command.[67] The prosecution argued that although Abe was not Banno's formal subordinate, Banno still ought to have taken steps to prevent his abuse of prisoners.[68]

The prosecution's argument against Banno was essentially that he had been aware that his subordinates were directly committing war crimes, and he was also aware that Fukuda, his co-accused, was neglecting his duty to prevent, halt, or punish the commission of war crimes.[69] Such an argument demonstrates the potential reach of command responsibility up the chain of command, even within a single trial. In this view, Fukuda had failed in his duty as a commander; the fact that Banno had not corrected or punished his subordinate's failures of command then formed the basis of the charge against Banno himself.

The prosecution's claim that Banno should be held liable for Abe's crimes was based on two factors. The first was that Banno was a colonel, a relatively senior officer, while Abe was only a lieutenant, the lowest-ranking commissioned officer in the army. Regardless of whether Abe had been under his formal command or not, Banno should have been able to exert some degree of control over Abe, in this view. The other factor was that Banno had had command of the prisoners.[70] Thus, Banno had had a responsibility to ensure that the captives were not mistreated, regardless of whether it was by one of his subordinates or not. The prosecution thus drew an implicit parallel between the responsibility that an officer owes to his own soldiers, and the responsibility that a camp officer has to his prisoners.

According to Banno and his lawyer, there were at least two reasons that Banno had been unable to adequately carry out his duties as the commander of the POWs. First, while Banno had had command of the POWs while they were in the camp, the prisoners, while working, were essentially 'on loan' from the camp to the military engineers who supervised the building of the railway.

65. WO 235/1034, Affidavit of Captain Ronald Harry Mastin, 1–2; WO 234/1034, Affidavit of William Bruce Bowring.
66. WO 235/1034, Affidavit of Noel McGuffie Johnston, 1–3; Affidavit of Captain R. W. Pearce, 1.
67. WO 235/1034, Mastin Affidavit, 3–5.
68. WO 235/1034, Trial Transcript, 725–27.
69. WO 235/1034, Trial Transcript, 723–25.
70. WO 235/1034, Trial Transcript, 386–87.

The majority of the beatings took place while prisoners were working on the line. Banno was thus unable to prevent the beatings, or to ameliorate the harsh working conditions, as he was not responsible for the prisoners when they were outside the camp. Second, F Force was stationed at the end of a long and difficult supply line, and it was likely that other units stole rations along the way that had been allocated to Banno's prisoners. This situation was beyond his control.[71]

Banno's defence also relied on another point, which was perhaps one of the more sophisticated, if unusual, arguments raised at a command responsibility case in the national tribunals. Though many officers argued that they had not truly been in command or had had limited scope to make effective changes to conditions, Banno's defence went one step further. His lawyer argued that the crimes occurred not because Banno had been wilfully negligent, but rather because he had not had the personal qualities necessary to stop the crimes. In other words, Banno's defence relied on assertion of his incompetence as a commander. Banno's lawyer, who wrote Banno's petition, claimed that lack of ability is not a crime, and that there is 'no law that punishes a man who failed to save a drowning person because he was not a good swimmer'.[72]

Some evidence suggests that Banno was indeed not up to the job. He appears to be an example of what Utsumi Aiko has identified as a 'permanent colonel': that is, an officer who had been passed over for promotion to higher ranks and pushed into what army authorities considered to be an insignificant role commanding POW camps.[73] It was not unusual for the Japanese army to utilise poor quality or inexperienced staff in POW camps. From a purely military point of view, it did not make sense to allocate capable and efficient officers to guard prisoners; it was important that the best quality staff directly assisted fighting operations. As a result, officers like Banno who were relatively senior, yet apparently incapable, were given the job of commanding prison camps, a duty that was considered comparatively unimportant.[74] Similarly, very junior officers could be given command of large numbers of prisoners and guards, perhaps in their first experience of command. In addition to encountering difficulties in supervising so many prisoners and guards, inexperienced junior officers also had to deal with a hierarchy of command within the army as a whole, in which their junior rank even further reduced their already-limited capacity to improve the situation of prisoners.

Banno's sentence for command responsibility was certainly more lenient than was typical for defendants facing similar charges in other POW trials.

71. WO 235/1034, Trial Transcript, 722–25.
72. WO 235/1034, Petition of Accused Banno Hirateru, 4.
73. Utsumi Aiko, 'Japan's World War II POW Policy: Indifference and Irresponsibility', *The Asia-Pacific Journal: Japan Focus* 3, no. 5 (2005): 1–2.
74. Aiko, 'Japan's World War II POW Policy', 2; Kovner, *Prisoners of the Empire*, 61, 105.

Commanders of other camps, where the death rate of prisoners had been substantially lower, were sentenced to death, or received lengthy prison terms, despite having dealt with problems similar to those Banno had faced, with less drastic outcomes.[75] The tribunal in this case clearly took account of Banno's apparently limited capacity as a commander, after both a former Australian captive, Lieutenant-Colonel Charles Kappe and the prosecutor, Captain Oliver Dixon, described Banno as an 'incompetent, fatuous old man'.[76] Moreover, the tribunal appears to have understood that genuine supply difficulties had beset the camps that Banno had commanded. The problem was that this stance had not been consistent across the national war crimes tribunals as a whole, or even across the batch of trials conducted by any particular military jurisdiction.

More surprisingly, Banno's sentence of three years' imprisonment was also considerably more lenient than the sentences handed down to his subordinates. The tribunal sentenced Abe, Fukuda, Toyoyama, and one other accused to death for their role in the mistreatment of POWs. In his review, the Judge Advocate General (JAG) gave his view that Banno's sentence was appropriate, but he also acknowledged that 'the case of Banno has rendered more difficult a proper assessment of punishment in the case of his subordinates'. In other words, the JAG struggled to reconcile the low level of criminal responsibility assigned to Banno with the higher levels attributed to his subordinates. Based on this consideration, he recommended that the findings and sentences be confirmed, but that the death sentences be commuted to terms of imprisonment ranging from fifteen years to life, recommendations which the confirming officer ultimately accepted.[77]

Banno's sentence is relatively easy to understand when considered in isolation. He was simply not an effective commander, and, furthermore, external factors could not have been fixed. The fact the JAG considered Banno's sentence to be appropriate, and the confirming authority did nothing to increase the sentence, indicates some level of acceptance of these points across the board. In Banno's case, the judges and the legal reviewers were more interested in his individual capacity to command than in any more general assessment of what a colonel should have and could have done. Banno's sentence, however, becomes much more difficult to understand when compared with those handed down in other trials. As seen in the trial of naval Captain Shirozu Wadami, who held the equivalent rank and was executed, tribunals did not always accept that command could be vitiated by personal or external circumstances.

---

75. See, for example, TNA, WO 235/952, *UK v Hachisuka Kunifusa and Twenty-Three Others*; TNA, WO 235/886, *UK v Anami Sanso and Thirteen Others*.
76. WO 235/1034, Trial Transcript, 359, 578.
77. WO 235/1034, JAG Review, 6.

The leniency granted to Banno was a potential risk to the perceived legitimacy of earlier war crimes trials. UK, US, and Australian tribunals had already passed the death sentence on camp officers who had been tried under command responsibility for the mistreatment of POWs, in cases in which similar defence arguments about supply issues and ability to command had been made, even if, in other trials, the defence had not asserted that the commander had been incompetent. If the leniency that Banno received became standardised, it would essentially constitute an Allied admission that the war crimes trials had changed to a new standard in measuring and applying guilt and responsibility. If it did not become standardised, it would be a glaring example of inconsistency in sentencing.

Banno's sentence, surprisingly, received little coverage in the press. Several Australian reports on the trial mentioned that Banno had been sentenced to prison, but none of them gave the length of the prison term. Banno's case appears to have gone unreported in UK papers.[78] It is likely that the limited reporting of the trial was due to some level of censorship, either by the press itself, or by Allied authorities, in an attempt to avoid public backlash at lenient sentences for Japanese war criminals. In Australia, supposedly light sentencing at several trials held in Darwin in March 1946 had resulted in a storm of criticism in newspapers across the nation.[79] From late 1946 onwards, the press in Australia, Singapore, the UK, and elsewhere criticised cases in which sentences were relatively harsh but fell short of the death penalty. As seen in the previous chapter, criticism of the allegedly lenient sentencing at the *sook ching* trial of Lieutenant-General Nishimura Takuma and others, for example, was relatively well-covered in the Singapore press.[80] In the case of the Banno trial, the Allied authorities, or the press, or both, may have wished to avoid any similar backlash, and may therefore have restricted reporting on the trial or at least on its outcomes.

The Trials of Nogi Naraji and Nakanishi Yoshio

The Banno trial was unusual; in their judgements, war crimes tribunals normally did not separate criminal responsibility from an accused's personal capacity to command. Two US trials at Yokohama of relatively junior officers, both of whom had had limited experience of operating in military chains of command,

78. 'Four Japs to Die', *Singleton Argus*, 11 November 1946, 1; 'Four Japs to Die for Brutalities on Burma Railway', *The Canberra Times*, 9 November 1946, 1; 'Four Japs to Die; Three Gaoled', *Newcastle Morning Herald and Miners' Advocate*, 9 November 1946, 3. A search in the Times Index revealed no articles relating to Banno's trial.
79. Aszkielowicz, *The Australian Pursuit of Japanese War Criminals*, 60–61.
80. 'The Massacre Trial', *The Straits Times*, 5 April 1947, 7, archived at https://eresources.nlb.gov.sg/newspapers/Digitised/Article/straitstimes1.

illustrate this point. Captain Nogi Naraji and Second-Lieutenant Nakanishi Yoshio had both been given command during the war of a situation they could not change, at a time when war crimes were committed. Both were given lengthy prison sentences for their command responsibility for war crimes. Cases like those of Nogi and Nakanishi demonstrate the approach that tribunals normally took in command responsibility trials for the mistreatment of POWs. The accused were assessed on what they had or had not done to prevent war crimes, according to an inflexible standard under which commanders were assumed to have had complete control over both their subordinates and the broader external circumstances.

At Yokohama between 16 and 24 January 1947, the US military tried Captain Nogi Naraji of the Imperial Japanese Army for failing to provide adequate food and medical care to Allied POWs at Bilibid Prison Hospital in Manila and for personally beating sick prisoners. Nogi was also charged with refusing to make use of the Bilibid Hospital facilities to help sick and injured POWs.[81] Nogi had been the commandant of Bilibid Prison Hospital. The hospital was part of the Bilibid Prison Complex, which also housed a Japanese military police interrogation centre and a separate POW camp. Though Nogi had certainly been in command of the hospital, he was primarily a doctor rather than a military officer. Nogi was found not guilty of refusing to make use of the medical facilities, but guilty of neglecting to provide adequate food and medicine and of beating prisoners and was sentenced to twenty-five years' imprisonment.[82] Evidence at the trial indicated that Nogi had acted as a hospital administrator rather than a commanding officer. Nonetheless, military command responsibility was used to convict him. His case thus demonstrates that command responsibility could be extended to quasi-military positions. The case also suggests that former prisoners sometimes exaggerated evidence against an officer, likely because of long-standing resentment of their captivity.

Though many camp commanders were tried for the inadequate supply of medicine, far fewer were held to account more broadly for the quality of medical care that prisoners received. In most camps, medical staff among the Allied prisoners voluntarily treated and cared for their own sick and injured. The principal reason seems to be that Japanese medical staff were considered to have less medical training, many did not speak English, and POWs did not trust Japanese staff to treat Allied personnel properly, even if they were capable of doing so. In a few areas, Japanese authorities provided POWs with a dedicated hospital – at

81. National Archives and Records Administration, College Park MD (hereafter NARA), RG331, Supreme Commander of the Allied Powers, Legal Section, Prosecution Division, *USA versus Japanese War Criminals*, Case Files, 1945–48, Box 1576, *USA v Nogi Naraji*, Charge Sheet, 1–2.
82. *USA v Nogi Naraji*, Trial Transcript, 285–86.

Changi, for instance, and at Batavia in the Netherlands Indies.[83] These hospitals were staffed by a combination of Japanese and Allied medical personnel.[84] Though the welfare and treatment of prisoners at the hospitals was often far better than elsewhere, Allied military tribunals nonetheless pursued Japanese military medical personnel for abuses at these hospitals too.[85]

Four former American prisoners testified in court as prosecution witnesses against Nogi, all of whom had been patients at Bilibid from early June 1942 until February 1945, when US forces liberated the prison.[86] Two were enlisted soldiers, one was a lieutenant-colonel, and one was a civilian. The remainder of the prosecution case relied mostly on unsworn affidavits from other former prisoners, as well as records that Allied medical staff had kept and hidden during their captivity. A significant part of the prosecution relied on evidence from the diary of Dr Thomas Hayes, a US POW who was interned in the camp from 1942 until liberation.[87] Unlike the testimony of the four witnesses, Hayes's diary was relatively sympathetic to Nogi. Indeed, Hayes considered the behaviour of some Allied prisoners at the hospital to have had a more detrimental effect on the POWs than Nogi's command had had. Many prisoners did not share extra food that they had smuggled into the hospital, while others stole from hospital supplies.[88]

According to the prosecution witnesses, the level of rations at the hospital was designed to starve the patients, albeit slowly, and at no time was the food adequate to sustain life.[89] This claim was made even though all of the prosecution witnesses had survived in Bilibid Hospital from June 1942 until liberation. According to the enlisted men, the rice ration was of inferior quality, and at times was as low as six grams per person, per day.[90] Lieutenant-Colonel W. H. Waterous, however, stated that the daily rice ration, initially 400 grams, had fallen to 50 grams by February 1945.[91] The rice ration had been supplemented with corn and soybeans. Though these and other vegetables were always available, they were often of poor quality. There was little meat or fish, and when it was available, prisoners described it as mostly inedible dried fish.[92] The apparent difference in rice rations between the enlisted soldiers and the more senior

83. Rosalind Hearder, 'More Complex than a Stereotype: Australian POW Doctors and the Japanese in Captivity, 1942–45', *Health and History* 6, no. 2 (2004): 78–80.
84. Havers, *Reassessing the Japanese Prisoner of War Experience*, 31.
85. See, for example, WO 235/1039, *UK v Ori Masami and Three Others*.
86. Richard Connaughton, John Pimlott, and Duncan Anderson, *The Battle for Manila: The Most Devastating Untold Story of World War II* (Bloomsbury, 1995), 96–100.
87. The diary was later published: see A. B. Feuer (ed.), *Bilibid Diary: The Secret Notebooks of Commander Thomas Hayes, POW, the Philippines, 1942–1945* (Archon Books, 1987).
88. Feuer, *Bilibid Diary*, 13, 92, 122, 126–27, 169, 177.
89. *USA v Nogi Naraji*, Trial Transcript, 23–27.
90. *USA v Nogi Naraji*, Trial Transcript, 26.
91. *USA v Nogi Naraji*, Trial Transcript, 88.
92. *USA v Nogi Naraji*, Trial Transcript, 66.

officer can be explained by either or both of two possibilities. On the one hand, either Waterous, or, more likely, the enlisted soldiers, were lying: the ordinary soldiers may have received more food than they claimed. On the other hand, as an officer, Waterous may have received more food than the lower-ranking prisoners, a relatively common occurrence in captivity.[93]

From the prosecution witnesses' testimony and other evidence, it does not appear that Japanese camp staff implemented a policy of deliberate starvation. Rather, the prisoners were supplied with food relatively similar in quantity and quality to what Philippine civilians were used to: that is, the food that was locally available. Many of the patients, unaccustomed to the food, initially refused to eat at all, or only ate what was palatable to them; and it was likely that many prisoners considered that being supplied with food that was unpalatable was the same as being supplied with no food[94] – hence the claims about deliberate starvation. No doubt, the refusal to eat much of the food when it was available meant that disease and illnesses caused by malnutrition occurred earlier than would otherwise have been the case.

The prosecution witnesses stated that Nogi had been the overall commander of the hospital, even though none of them had had any direct contact with him. Nor were they entirely sure of what his position actually was, apart from the fact that he was the head Japanese doctor.[95] All the prosecution witnesses held him responsible for the inadequate food supply, as well as for the overall conditions in the hospital and the conduct of the guards, who beat patients for minor infractions of rules. The prosecution even attempted to hold Nogi responsible for beatings that had occurred outside of the hospital. Allied prisoners from other camps in the Manila area who had received life-threatening beatings were sent to the hospital to recover. The witness Waterous attributed many of the deaths at the hospital to Nogi, on the grounds that the patients had failed to survive beatings received outside of the camp because of the care given to patients at Bilibid, and because Nogi had not admitted injured or sick POWs earlier. In the defence's cross-examination of Waterous, he admitted that he did not know whether Nogi had had any actual authority to admit patients – the trial record indicates that it was up to other POW camp commanders – and further admitted that he had no idea to what extent Nogi had been constrained by regulations and higher orders.[96]

The prosecution's accusation that Nogi was responsible for deaths of patients who did not recover from injuries sustained elsewhere was an attempt to hold

93. Hank Nelson, 'Measuring the Railway: From Individual Lives to National History', in McCormack and Nelson, *The Burma-Thailand Railway*, 17–18; McCormack, 'Apportioning the Blame', 110.
94. Moore, 'An Insatiable Parasite', 120–23.
95. *USA v Nogi Naraji*, Trial Transcript, 28–32, 55–57, 98.
96. *USA v Nogi Naraji*, Trial Transcript, 95–99.

him strictly liable for all deaths that had occurred under his command. Such a strategy rested on a far-reaching interpretation of command responsibility: the life-threatening beatings had not been carried out by Nogi's subordinates, nor was any substantial evidence offered in the trial to suggest that Nogi had had any real control over who was admitted to the hospital. According to Waterous, upon whom the prosecution principally relied to push this argument, the practical limitations of a military position ought to have no impact on 'questions of judicial actions in humanitarian affairs'.[97] In other words, the fact that Nogi had had no control over Japanese personnel outside the hospital was irrelevant; the deaths occurred in Nogi's hospital, so he was responsible.

Waterous's scathing testimony about Nogi is at odds with the evidence in Lieutenant-Commander Hayes's diary. While Hayes did criticise the treatment of the sick and injured, he considered that Nogi had done the best he could in his position and that he had made constant attempts to procure additional medical and food supplies. In fact, Hayes was more critical of Waterous than of Nogi. Waterous had had access to additional food because of personal wealth and outside contacts; Hayes was livid that Waterous, and other senior Allied officers in a similar position, had made only token efforts to share their personal supplies with the entire hospital. It is likely that Waterous's aggressive testimony was an attempt to cover up some of his own behaviour during captivity. Waterous later faced recriminations from former Bilibid prisoners for his testimony against Nogi, and was encouraged to recant it, which he never did. Evidently, many former prisoners considered Nogi to have done his best in a difficult situation.[98]

Nogi's defence was well prepared. Evidence was raised that prisoners had stolen additional rations for themselves, especially canned goods, from the hospital stockpile. Defence lawyers further claimed that the decrease in food and medicine from mid-1943 onwards, as well as increasingly harsh punishments, were attributable to the intensification of US military operations in and near the Philippines: less food reached the hospital, and the guards were more and more concerned with maintaining discipline among the prisoners in the face of the growing number of Allied attacks. The defence also highlighted the fact that the Bilibid complex had served as a way station for prisoners waiting to be shipped to other locations in the Japanese Empire. Sudden influxes of transient prisoners naturally depleted food stores that had been intended for the patients.[99] Significant numbers of Allied prisoners were indeed shipped from the Philippines to other locations from 1944, and many of them would have gone

97. *USA v Nogi Naraji*, Trial Transcript, 97.
98. John A. Glusman, *Conduct Under Fire: Four American Doctors and their Fight for Life as Prisoners of the Japanese, 1941–1945* (Penguin, 2006), 481.
99. *USA v Nogi Naraji*, Trial Transcript, 97–98, 101–3.

through Bilibid, at the same time as Bilibid Hospital rations began to fall.[100] Finally, the defence argued that despite his military rank, Nogi had been nothing more than a hospital administrator, claiming that he had had no genuine scope of command over the day-to-day lives of the prisoners and was incapable of navigating military bureaucracy.[101] Nogi's defence, like Banno's, was that he was incompetent. Despite these arguments, the tribunal handed down the sentence of twenty-five years.

Between 12 and 16 May 1947, a US military court at Yokohama tried Nakanishi Yoshio, a fifty-year-old Second-Lieutenant, for the ill-treatment of Allied POWs between October 1944 and August 1945 at three camps he had commanded near Osaka, on the Japanese island of Honshu.[102] In relation to Notogawa POW Camp, Nakanishi was charged with failing to provide adequate food and medicine, failing to provide adequate accommodation, and failing to discharge his duty as commanding officer to restrain his subordinates from physically abusing POWs. In relation to the camps at Yodogawa and Sakurajima, he was charged with failing in his duty as a commanding officer by permitting POWs under his command to do work directly related to the Japanese operation of the war: under the 1929 Geneva Convention, POWs could not be required to do war-related labour.[103] The prisoners had worked alongside Japanese civilians at a steel mill, making oil drums for the Japanese military. Nakanishi was found guilty of failing to supply adequate food and suitable accommodation, and of failing to restrain members of his command from beating POWs, all at Notogawa POW Camp, and was sentenced to fifteen years' imprisonment. He was acquitted of both charges relating to Yodogawa and Sakurajima camps, because, although the oil drums were used by the Japanese military, they were deemed to be not directly related to Japan's war effort.[104]

The prosecution's case against Nakanishi was based entirely on affidavits from former prisoners at the camps, a situation that was not unusual at the post-war trials. All the affidavits supported the general charge that the food at Notogawa had been of poor quality, that there was limited medicine available, and that the accommodation had been mostly inadequate.[105] In some descriptions, the latrines at Notogawa were in the main sleeping quarters, and consisted of a basic hole in the floor, with no partition from the floor mats on which captives

100. Kovner, *Prisoners of the Empire*, 89–92.
101. *USA v Nogi Naraji*, Trial Transcript, 207–10, 227.
102. NARA, RG153, Records of the Office of the Judge Advocate General (Army), War Crimes Branch, Case Files, 1944–1949, Box 815, *USA v Nakanishi Yoshio*.
103. *USA v Nakanishi Yoshio*, Trial Transcript, 71; 'The Geneva Convention, 27 July 1929', https://avalon.law.yale.edu/20th_century/geneva02.asp.
104. *USA v Nakanishi Yoshio*, Trial Transcript, 86–90, 28–33.
105. *USA v Nakanishi Yoshio*, Affidavit of John Appenzeller, 12 February 1946, 2–3; *USA v Nakanishi Yoshio*, Affidavit of Donald McRae, 14 August 1946, 1.

slept. In other descriptions, the latrines were partitioned, or were outside the main buildings.[106] Affidavit evidence on Nakanishi himself was also inconsistent, and at times appears to have been fabricated. Some prisoners said that Nakanishi had visibly enjoyed watching prisoners being beaten.[107] Others stated that beatings only seemed to occur when Nakanishi was not present, though he had been aware that beatings had been administered.[108]

There are several reasons why the evidence was inconsistent at Nakanishi's trial. Indeed, inconsistency in evidence from POWs at camp trials was not unusual.[109] After release, many captives probably placed the majority of blame for any mistreatment they had experienced on the camp commander, and some may have distorted evidence to ensure a successful prosecution.[110] Prisoners in Japan, as elsewhere in the Empire, rarely spent the entirety of their captivity at one camp, so prosecutors would receive evidence that was specific to a particular span of dates: the latrines may have been inside at one point, but outside at another. Furthermore, prisoners had varying experiences and different expectations of captivity. Some prisoners were aware that conditions in the Japanese military, and indeed, in the countries in which they were imprisoned, were worse than the conditions they were used to, and that high standards could not be expected in the camps. Other prisoners were clearly resentful that a seemingly inferior military and inferior race of people held them captive.[111] Moreover, many prisoners, especially enlisted soldiers, would have had little appreciation of the difficulties faced by camp commanders, or of what kinds of things were outside of an officer's control.

Evidence that the POWs had less food than their guards was almost certainly true. It is unlikely, however, that the difference in rations was intentional. The rations the POWs received were not markedly different from those of most civilians in wartime Japan. Japanese civilians had undergone rationing since early 1941, and further cuts to food occurred throughout the war: by the end, the average daily intake of calories was 17 per cent less than at the start of the war in

106. *USA v Nakanishi Yoshio*, Affidavit of Eric Mitchell, 14 October 1946, 1; *USA v Nakanishi Yoshio*, Appenzeller Affidavit, 2–3; *USA v Nakanishi Yoshio*, Affidavit of Hugh Murdock, 20 August 1946, 1.
107. *USA v Nakanishi Yoshio*, Mitchell Affidavit, 3.
108. *USA v Nakanishi Yoshio*, Affidavit of John Eric Olsen, 28 September 1945, 4.
109. Sarah Kovner, 'Captivity on the Home Front: Allied Prisoners of War in Fukuoka During the Second World War', in *Detention Camps in Asia: The Conditions of Confinement in Modern Asian History*, ed. Robert Cribb, Christina Twomey, and Sandra Wilson (Brill-Nijhoff, 2022), 237–38.
110. Lynette Silver, *Sandakan: A Conspiracy of Silence* (Sally Milner Publishing, 1998), 275; Wilson, Cribb, Trefalt, and Aszkielowicz, *Japanese War Criminals*, 82–85.
111. Wilson, Cribb, Trefalt, and Aszkielowicz, *Japanese War Criminals*, 10; Kovner, 'Captivity on the Home Front', 238–39; Wilson, 'Detention Camps in the Japanese Empire', 204.

the Pacific.[112] In the final months of the war, fresh vegetables had become increasingly difficult to source, and rice, the staple food, had usually been replaced by barley or wheat. Eventually, some people ate wild grasses instead of rice.[113] Thus, the situation that most prisoners faced was relatively similar to, if not slightly better than, that faced by the Japanese civilian population.

Nakanishi was tried for and found guilty of the mistreatment of POWs that occurred in camps he commanded from October 1944 through to the end of the war. By this stage, the Japanese home islands had been effectively cut off from overseas supply, which meant that food and medicine were inadequate practically everywhere. From January 1945 onwards, the US air force had intensified its firebombing of Japanese cities, killing thousands of civilians, further destroying Japanese road and rail networks, and making millions of Japanese homeless.[114] Notogawa camp was on the outskirts of Osaka, a city that the US military bombed heavily throughout the final months of the war.[115] Faced with such circumstances, it is difficult to understand what Nakanishi could have done to improve the conditions of the prisoners' captivity. The situation he had to deal with went beyond poor logistics and poor planning: he operated as a commander at a point where the Japanese military, economy, and society were on the verge of collapse.

Nakanishi was also found guilty of failing to restrain his subordinates from beating the prisoners. Some evidence suggested not only that he had known the beatings were occurring, but also that he had allowed them to happen when he was in the camp and enjoyed seeing prisoners getting hit. Other evidence implied that Nakanishi did prevent his soldiers from beating POWs when he could: the beatings were said to have occurred only when he was away from camp, implying that his subordinates were aware that Nakanishi did not want the prisoners to be hit. Furthermore, Nakanishi claimed that he had instructed his subordinates to treat the prisoners kindly and not to hit them. On balance, it seems probable that the evidence purporting to show that Nakanishi encouraged or allowed beatings was fabricated, and that in fact, beatings only took place when he was away. Former prisoners would likely have exaggerated an accused commander's degree of knowledge and participation in any beatings, as a form of revenge for their captivity; by contrast, there seems to be limited motivation for former prisoners to downplay a commander's role in the harsh treatment they

112. Thomas R. H. Havens, *Valley of Darkness: The Japanese People and World War Two* (University Press of America, 1986), 115, 118, 132.
113. Havens, *Valley of Darkness*, 127–32; Moore, 'An Insatiable Parasite', 125; Lizzie Collingham, *The Taste of War: World War II and the Battle for Food* (Penguin Press, 2012), 303–8.
114. Sandra Wilson, Michael Sturma, Arjun Subrahmanyan, Dean Aszkielowicz, and J. Charles Schencking, *The U.S. and the War in the Pacific, 1941–45* (Routledge, 2022), 68–75.
115. Havens, *Valley of Darkness*, 177, 182–86.

received, and thus, the evidence claiming that Nakanishi discouraged violence is more convincing.

As an inexperienced officer, with little command authority owing to his junior rank, it is hardly surprising that Nakanishi was unable to prevent his subordinates from beating prisoners. Nonetheless, his inability to prevent the beatings would likely have been irrelevant to the tribunal. It was clear that prisoners had been hit and that Nakanishi knew about it. For the tribunal, a commander's role was to prevent war crimes from occurring, and Nakanishi had failed to do so.

Both the Nogi and the Nakanishi trials demonstrate the difficult position in which many Japanese officers found themselves during the war and in its immediate aftermath. Both were junior officers, with limited experience of military command. This circumstance reduced their capacity to make any meaningful change to the POW camp system, either in the way that prisoners were treated by guards, or in the extraction of supplies from other units. Nonetheless, they had both been in formal positions from which they ought theoretically to have been able to improve the quality of treatment of the prisoners. In many of the Allied tribunals, including these two, the practical ineffectiveness of such officers was treated as an individual criminal failure of their command. Though the punishment could be harsh, as seen in Nakanishi's and Nogi's lengthy terms of imprisonment, death sentences were rarely handed down for offences committed in camps where there had been relatively few or no deaths. In camps where prisoners had died in larger numbers, however, death sentences were more likely, regardless of the fact that the overall circumstances of the camp, which might have suffered from long-term supply problems, poorly trained staff, and poor discipline amongst prisoners, had been either broadly similar or worse.

The differences in sentencing between Nogi and Nakanishi on the one hand, and Banno on the other hand, are difficult to reconcile. The evidence presented at the Nogi and Nakanishi trials shows not only that both defendants were junior officers given command outside of their capacity, but also that they were held responsible for a wide range of factors that had been beyond their control, and that officers of their rank would have been unable to change. Banno, by contrast, was an officer of long experience, and his senior rank suggested that he should have been able to effect changes. The difference appears to lie in the tribunals' assessment of how responsibility arose. Many tribunals, like those in the Nogi and Nakanishi trials, appear to have prosecuted according to the official position of the accused – that is, the tribunals held the military office itself accountable. In the case of Banno, however, it appears that the tribunal separated the formal rank that Banno had held from the 'fatuous old man' who appeared in court.

Holding an officer responsible because of the position that he had held could be justified on the basis of the longer-term purpose of the trials. They were intended to create a broad precedent, so that future militaries would be held responsible for the crimes that they perpetrated. Ultimately, this meant holding commanders responsible. The trials were also designed to act as a deterrent: an inflexible approach that single-mindedly held commanders responsible for abuses that occurred under their control would ideally ensure that officers across the chain of command would take steps to prevent war crimes in the future. This approach to command responsibility conflicted with traditional understandings of criminal guilt, in which individuals are held responsible for what they had control over, and what they deliberately did.

The Hainan POW Camp Trial

Some of the longer-running command responsibility trials for mid-level officers took place in 1948, after the initial rush of trials had begun to lessen. Command responsibility trials held in 1948 became increasingly complicated, as the defence produced large quantities of evidence to support its arguments. It is unclear whether such an approach was a genuine attempt to exonerate the accused, by providing as much evidence as possible to counteract the charges, or whether it was merely a delaying tactic. Some defence lawyers would have been aware that the trials were beginning to wind down, and that the harshness of sentences might decrease as the trials became more distant from the time at which the crime had been perpetrated. Perhaps defence lawyers were hopeful that, if trials dragged on, tribunals would be more inclined to leniency than to 'stern justice'.

Between 5 January and 22 June 1948, the Australian military tried seventeen members of the Imperial Japanese Navy in Hong Kong for the ill-treatment of 263 Australian and Dutch POWs on Hainan Island, in the South China Sea, some of whom had been removed from Tan Toey POW Camp on Ambon in October 1942.[116] Seventy-two Australians died, but it is unclear how many, if any, Dutch prisoners died. It was the longest running of the Australian trials, creating over 2,600 pages of transcript and documentary evidence. As was common at POW camp trials, the accused had held a range of positions across the chain of command, from junior enlisted soldiers through to camp commanders. The accused were charged with failing to supply adequate food and medicine, physically beating the prisoners, forcing the prisoners to carry out work directly related to the war, and, unusually for an Australian tribunal, causing mental harm to the prisoners.[117] What exactly 'causing mental harm' meant was not elaborated on in

116. NAA, War Crimes Trial of Tahara Susumu and Sixteen Others (hereafter Trial of Tahara), Volume 1, Charge Sheet, 1–3, archived at https://recordsearch.naa.gov.au/SearchNRetrieve/Interface/ViewImage.aspx?B=739675.

117. Tahara Trial, Volume 1, Charge Sheet, 1–3.

the trial. The three most senior officers amongst the accused, the naval captains Tahara Susumu, Kawamura Shinichi, and Aoyama Shigeo, had all commanded the Hainan camp at different times during the war and now faced command responsibility charges for the ill-treatment of the prisoners.[118] Kawamura and Tahara were also tried for the use of prisoner labour on military projects. Though the tribunal handed down severe sentences to the accused officers, post-trial review lawyers recommended that the sentences be reduced, likely because they had a more nuanced understanding than did the bench of the problems that Japanese commanders had faced during the war.

The defence lawyers at the Hainan trial were more prepared than other Japanese lawyers to argue on technical procedural points. They probably raised such arguments to drag out the trial, since they must have been well aware that some of their objections would be flatly rejected. The first three days of the proceedings consisted solely of the defence lawyer objecting to prosecution evidence.[119] The defence objected to the use of what it considered to be hearsay evidence. Unsurprisingly, as the tribunals had been explicitly designed to allow hearsay evidence, these objections were unsuccessful.[120] The defence further objected to the inclusion in written evidence of material not germane to the trial.[121] Many documents offered in war crimes proceedings contained such material, because a single statement might represent an investigator's attempt to gather evidence for possible use in a range of trials, in which case it would contain material about different incidents, conditions, or camps. In this case the defence was successful in having selected evidence removed from the proceedings. The fact that the defence was so assiduous in objecting to evidence in this trial perhaps reflects not only a desire to prolong the trial, but also a growing confidence among Japanese defence lawyers in their handling of command responsibility cases under an unfamiliar system.

As in most of the camp trials, the prosecution's primary focus was on the inadequate supply of food and medicine. According to affidavits and witnesses, the prisoners had complained about the state of supplies to all three accused captains throughout their captivity. Though there was initially a relatively large farm outside the camp boundary, from 1944 onwards it was replaced as a means of augmenting food supplies by a smaller farm inside the camp perimeter. Survivors blamed a Japanese non-commissioned officer for this change to a less productive farm. Captain Tahara argued that the change had been necessary to protect the captives, as local Chinese guerrillas had increased their

118. Tahara Trial, Precis of Evidence, 2–5.
119. Tahara Trial, Vol. 1, Trial Transcript, 1–37.
120. Tahara Trial, Vol. 1, Trial Transcript, 23–26.
121. Tahara Trial, Vol. 1, Trial Transcript, 67.

activity in the area.[122] As for medical conditions, most of the prisoners suffered from beriberi, because of a lack of vitamin B in their diet and the prisoners had been forced to rely on the limited care that could be provided within the camp. Although there was a Japanese military hospital on Hainan, captives were rarely sent there.[123]

The circumstances that had led to limited supply of food and medicine at the Hainan camp were remarkably similar to those experienced at other island POW camps. As elsewhere, supplies had initially been good, and the prisoners were allowed to supplement their standard rations from the farm and through purchases from a canteen. As the war progressed, however, the quantity and quality of supplies decreased, contributing to the deaths of many prisoners. As in other camps, immediately after the Japanese surrender, the prisoners received large supplies of food, as well as an increase in the quantity and quality of medicine. At the trial, the prosecution argued that the dwindling of the rations, followed by an immediate increase, were proof of the accused officers' intent to kill the prisoners during the war. The accused officers maintained, that in fact, the decrease in supplies had been caused by the circumstances of the war: few supply ships could get to Hainan, and the garrison had been forced to subsist on what had already been stored and the limited produce grown in the camp. With the war over, there was no need to stockpile resources for a protracted future battle, and the commander's priority shifted from maintaining the health of Japanese soldiers so that they could fight to ensuring the survival of the remaining POWs.[124]

In addition to failing to provide adequate supplies of essential goods, the three captains, together with a lieutenant, were also charged with responsibility for beatings that had been inflicted on the prisoners. Though the guards did beat the prisoners, there was relatively limited evidence of substantial beatings in the camp. The prosecution focused mainly on beatings that had been inflicted while the prisoners were working on outside projects, under the supervision of units that were not part of the camp's own chain of command. In this case, the central legal issue was that the prisoners had not been beaten by the accused commanders' subordinates. The prosecution contended that the accused knew that the beatings were happening, but either did nothing, or did not do enough, to prevent or halt the abuse. This was a mixed argument. On the one hand, it was clear that the commanders were legally responsible for beatings carried out by their subordinates. On the other hand, the prosecution also contended that the accused had had a duty to ensure that prisoners under their command were

---

122. Tahara Trial, Vol. 1, Trial Transcript, 452.

123. NAA, War Crimes Trial of Tahara Susumu and Sixteen Others, Volume 2, Trial Transcript, 1094, https://recordsearch.naa.gov.au/SearchNRetrieve/Interface/ViewImage.aspx?B=4151688.

124. NAA, War Crimes Trial of Tahara Susumu and Sixteen Others, Volume 3, Defence's Closing Address, 8, https://recordsearch.naa.gov.au/SearchNRetrieve/Interface/ViewImage.aspx?B=4151689.

not mistreated by others. In the prosecution's view, their failure to prevent soldiers from outside of their command from mistreating prisoners was a failure of this duty.

Tahara and Kawamura, one of the other two commanders of the Hainan camp, faced charges of using prisoner labour on prohibited projects – that is, projects that had contributed to Japan's war effort. During their captivity, the prisoners constructed bunkers on potential landing sites, from which Allied attacks could be countered, as well as anti-aircraft emplacements.[125] International law allowed POWs to be used as labour, provided that the work was not directly related to the war effort. Though the line could be blurred, because a state of total war made it necessary for nearly everything produced by a nation to be directed to the war effort, there was no ambiguity at the Hainan trial. Building military fortifications was a direct use of prisoner labour for military gain. The question at the trial was to what extent the accused commanders had been responsible for the prisoners' work on these projects.

There was no conclusive evidence to show that either Kawamura or Tahara had ordered that the prisoners should work on military projects. From the trial transcript, it appears that the POWs were treated as a convenient source of labour for multiple purposes on the island and were utilised by a number of separate units to build roads and unload ships, and in general construction.[126] Both Kawamura and Tahara had been responsible for a wide range of administrative and command duties, and they appear to have paid little attention to the nature of the work that prisoners did.[127] This lack of attention, however, goes to the heart of command responsibility charges. By not knowing, or not taking steps to know, the accused had failed in their role as commanders, albeit at an earlier stage than other officers accused of command responsibility. While other commanders had known that a crime was occurring, and had done nothing, or did not do enough to rectify the situation, Kawamura and Tahara did not even discharge their initial duty to be aware of what the prisoners were doing. They were found guilty on this charge. With no written judgment, and with inconclusive evidence, however, it is difficult to determine whether the court found them guilty by reason of strict command responsibility, or because the judges believed they had specifically ordered that the prisoners work on military projects.

The chief issue at the trial was the high number of Australian prisoners who had died. For the tribunal, the key point in determining culpability was when, and in what circumstances, they had died. Tahara had been in command from December 1943 until November 1944, and was immediately succeeded

125. Tahara Trial, Volume 1, Trial Transcript, 382–83.
126. Tahara Trial, Vol. 1, Trial Transcript, 414–18; Tahara Trial, Vol. 2, Trial Transcript, 828.
127. Tahara Trial, Vol. 1, Trial Review, 31–38.

by Kawamura, who had command of the camp until March 1945. Following Kawamura's departure, Aoyama was in command until the end of the war. During Aoyama's command sixty-seven Australian prisoners had died from disease and starvation, out of a total of seventy-two Australian deaths.[128] Exactly when the other five prisoners died is unclear from the trial record.

The Judge Advocate at the trial, whose role was to assist the bench on points of law, took a more prominent role than many other Judge Advocates. Lieutenant-Colonel John Truman Brock was evidently a well-respected Australian legal officer: he had previously sat as Judge Advocate at the so-called senior officer trials held in Rabaul in 1947, including the trial of Lieutenant-General Baba Masao, discussed in Chapter 3.[129] At the end of the trial, Brock gave the court his 169-page summation of both the facts of the case, and what he considered to be the relevant and applicable law, including comments on how he thought command responsibility operated. According to Brock,

> Responsibility is not absolute. It does not attach to a commander merely by virtue of his appointment, for not only must he command, but he must also have the means in his power to exercise that command and carry out his duties and responsibilities . . . The law does not demand the impossible.[130]

For Brock, the evidence of the accused commanders that they had faced serious and ongoing supply issues was critical in determining whether they were responsible for mistreating prisoners, and if they were, to what extent.

Brock argued that command could be limited by the circumstances of the war, as well as the failure of superior officers to give the accused the necessary means to carry out their duties. Brock cautiously agreed with the defence's submission that the ultimate cause of the POWs' suffering was that Hainan had been cut off from supply, and that the POW camp was situated in an inhospitable part of the island. He also, however, stated that the tribunal was free to decide that the accused could still be held responsible if they could have done more to alleviate the conditions in the camp with the resources available to them.[131] The overall tenor of Brock's summation was that while the accused commanders could be held responsible, the level of command that they exercised had been limited, and, thus, their liability ought to be mitigated. It was not the Judge Advocate's role, however, to make specific recommendations on sentencing.

The tribunal sentenced Tahara to twelve years' imprisonment, while Kawamura received a sentence of just six months. The disparity in sentencing

---

128. Tahara Trial, Vol. 1, Trial Review, 1–5.
129. Caroline Pappas, 'Law and Politics: Australia's War Crimes Trials in the Pacific, 1943–1961' (PhD thesis, University of New South Wales, 1998), 240.
130. Tahara Trial, Vol. 3, Trial Review, 41.
131. Tahara Trial, Vol. 3, Trial Review, 39, 45–52, 166–69.

between Tahara and Kawamura is probably because Kawamura had a much shorter command of the camp – just four months or so. Furthermore, Kawamura was bedridden for three months, during which period he was not replaced, meaning the camp had to run itself. Aoyama was sentenced to death by hanging. Considering that Aoyama was only in command for five months, this is a significant increase in the severity of punishment compared with Tahara's and Kawamura's. The likely reason for such a harsh sentence is that Aoyama was in command during the final months of the war, when the death rate was highest. The judges evidently found that he was ultimately responsible for these deaths.

The judges' decision to sentence Aoyama to death contradicts Brock's summation. Brock expressed the view that much of the POWs' mistreatment was caused by the conditions of captivity, rather than any particular action or inaction of the accused commanders. The gap between Brock's argument and the judges' sentence shows a fundamentally different understanding of how command responsibility operated, and of what a commander could be held liable for. For the bench, an officer was totally liable for the actions that occurred during his command, regardless of external factors.

The post-trial review was favourable to both Aoyama and Kawamura. According to the review, which was compiled by a legal officer from the Judge Advocate General's staff, the tribunal's decision that Aoyama should be executed ignored the long-term circumstances of the prisoners' captivity. The reviewer conceded that the prisoners had not had enough food and medicine during Aoyama's command. He argued, however, that ample evidence showed that this had also been the case during Kawamura's and Tahara's periods of tenure. Thus, the deaths could not be attributed solely to Aoyama; they were the result of prolonged ill-treatment under multiple commanders. The reviewer recommended that Aoyama's sentence be reduced to twelve years' imprisonment, the same as Tahara's. He also recommended that Kawamura's sentence be remitted, due to time already served: the length of the trial was over six months, and all the accused had been in custody during this period. The confirming authority accepted both recommendations.[132]

The difference between the sentence that the tribunal handed down to Aoyama and both Brock's summation and the sentence as adjusted on the legal reviewer's recommendation raises serious questions about the capacity of military tribunals not only to pass appropriate sentences, but also to deal more broadly with the effect of external factors on the doctrine of command responsibility. Such a significant difference in sentence recommendations implies that the judges made serious errors in their attribution of responsibility. To both the legal officer and the confirming authority, it was clear that the tribunal had interpreted

132. Tahara Trial, Vol. 1, Trial Review, 5–6.

command responsibility as a strict liability. That is, since the deaths occurred under Aoyama's command, he had been held to be necessarily responsible for them. By now, such an interpretation of command responsibility was considered too simple to address a complicated chain of events that had extended over a considerable period of time.

It appears that legally trained personnel who regularly encountered the tangle of legal, moral, and philosophical issues that command responsibility raised had gradually developed a more refined understanding of the doctrine. By this stage, they would most likely have analysed multiple command responsibility trials, and, over time, would have identified similar circumstances affecting a range of POW camps. Nearly every officer accused of supplying inadequate food and medicine to prisoners claimed that there had simply not been enough supplies to go around. While such claims may have seemed like desperate defence ploys to tribunal members, who did not always sit through multiple trials, they would probably have become more and more convincing to review lawyers. Furthermore, review lawyers would likely have become aware that camp conditions were not the same everywhere: some camps had better food supplies than others, which meant that in cases where food supply was poor, the mistreatment that prisoners faced could be understood as the result of external circumstances, rather than of intentional starvation.

Conclusions

The command responsibility trials for the mistreatment of POWs raised complicated considerations with which the trial system, for the most part, was unable to deal adequately. On the one hand, large numbers of Allied captives had died, often in horrific conditions. Many of those who returned were emaciated and suffered from serious diseases. Others had endured beatings or other forms of physical mistreatment. To the Allied authorities, it was clear that there was something fundamentally wrong with how the Japanese military had treated prisoners, and that pursuing officers was one of the most effective ways of achieving justice. The early trials were certainly coloured by moral outrage and the desire for severe retribution. On the other hand, as the trials progressed, and claims of inadequate supply lines and assertions that staff had been incapable or out of their depth became increasingly familiar, it grew clearer that what was fundamentally wrong with the Japanese military went deeper than action – or inaction – by individuals. Command responsibility focused criminal liability on to individuals, many of whom were important parts of the Japanese military at an institutional level, but at the same time, ignored the widespread failures at an institutional level that had given rise to the crimes in the first place.

As time went on, tribunals, and, more commonly, review lawyers, began to accept that important elements of the circumstances that had led to the ill-treatment of POWs had been outside of a commander's control, and that what an officer could legitimately be held accountable for was limited. Because there was no fixed understanding of what command meant, and what a commander could be expected to do, camp commanders received wildly different punishments for similar crimes that had been perpetrated under similar circumstances across the Japanese Empire. In the post-war trials for war crimes, precedent was not strictly followed, and written judgments were only occasionally published. As a result, tribunals were free to hand down harsh punishment even in trials of commanders who had been in exceptionally difficult situations, but, equally, they could change their assessments. The stern justice initially handed down at the command responsibility trials for mistreatment of prisoners did not last long. In normal circumstances, changes to the interpretation and application of law, and, thus, changes in sentencing outcomes, take a relatively long time. The limited oversight of the war crimes trials, however, meant that the tribunals could quickly adjust to changing understandings of law and justice.

Though POW camp commanders received lighter sentences as the trials continued into 1947 and 1948, the extent of this shift was likely limited by the harsher sentencing of earlier trials. While the tribunals were under no obligation to conform with the sentencing decisions of previous courts, a sudden shift from harsh to light sentencing for what were essentially the same crimes would have raised difficult questions for Allied authorities to answer, both from their own civilian and military populations, and from Japanese civilians and convicted war criminals. On the one hand, for those Allied personnel still motivated by vengeance, a last-minute revision of how guilt was attributed to commanders, with the effect of reducing sentences, would have been unacceptable. On the other hand, for Japanese personnel whose family members had already been executed, or for those convicted and sentenced to lengthy terms of imprisonment, it would have seemed manifestly unjust and unfair if war criminals convicted in later trials received lighter punishment on the grounds that tribunals and review lawyers had developed a more sympathetic understanding of the influence of external factors on the effectiveness of command. For these reasons, a change in sentencing that reflected the changes in understanding of how command responsibility operated would have undermined the legitimacy of the Allied trial project.

The command responsibility trials for camp conditions are the clearest example of Allied legal authorities' growing discomfort with the doctrine of command responsibility. Trials for other crimes would have seemed different to both tribunal judges and legal reviewers. In cases of massacre, summary execution, and torture, direct perpetrators had all displayed clear intent to commit the crimes. Tribunals could then feasibly apportion some degree of intent to an accused officer through command responsibility, perhaps based on an underlying suspicion that the accused commander had ordered the crime to occur. But Allied authorities eventually recognised that many of the conditions in camps had resulted from factors outside of a commander's control. Holding commanders criminally responsible to an extent that warranted death sentences or lengthy terms of imprisonment became increasingly difficult to justify as the trials continued.

Conclusion

On 16 November 1998, the International Criminal Tribunal for the former Yugoslavia (ICTY) handed down a judgment against four Bosnian military personnel.[1] The four defendants had been charged with the murder, torture, and cruel treatment of Serbian prisoners at the Čelibići prison camp in Bosnia between April and December 1992. Two of the accused were charged under the doctrine of command responsibility for crimes committed in the camp, while the other two were tried for directly committing the crimes. The Čelibići proceedings were the first international proceedings to use command responsibility since the trials held from crimes committed in the Second World War.

The crimes that had been perpetrated at Čelibići prison camp would have been familiar to Allied personnel who had worked on the post-war trials of suspected Japanese war criminals. The captives in Bosnia had been given inadequate food and were kept in cramped and unsanitary accommodation. They had been harshly beaten, and tortured with electric shocks and cigarette burns. Several prisoners had been shot or bayoneted. Female captives had been raped. Though the nature of the crimes committed had not changed, however, the public record of the Čelibići trial was far removed from what the Allies had produced at the command responsibility trials of Japanese junior and mid-level officers after the Second World War.

The trial judgment at Čelibići ran to over four hundred pages. It provided a systematic analysis of what command meant, who was considered to have wielded it in the Bosnian prison camp, and what commanders could and should do in the face of atrocities committed by their own side. The Čelibići judgment provided a clear explanation of how the doctrine of command responsibility

1. International Tribunal for the Prosecution of Persons Responsible for Serious Violations of International Humanitarian Law Committed in the Territory of the Former Yugoslavia since 1991 (hereafter ICTY), *Prosecutor v. Zejnil Delalić and Three Others* (hereafter *Prosecutor v Delalić*), archived at [http://www.legal-tools.org/doc/6b4a33/].

operated. There was little mystery about whether the trial had been fair, what the commanders had done to deserve conviction, and what exactly they had been convicted of. Other command responsibility trials have followed in the wake of the Čelibići decision. They have applied the same interpretation and reasoning as in Čelibići, and have reached comparable outcomes.[2] The Čelibići tribunal relied on the Yamashita trial, the Hostages Trial, the High Command Trial, and the Toyoda Trial, which are discussed in the Introduction to this book, as evidence that command responsibility was a 'well-established norm of customary and conventional international law'.[3] The fact that the doctrine had lain dormant for some fifty years was neither questioned, nor considered relevant to the case at hand.

Between the Allied post-war trials and the ICTY, legal scholars had sporadically considered whether the doctrine of command responsibility might be redeployed. One of the more notable instances was a suggestion by Telford Taylor, who had been the US prosecutor at the Subsequent Nuremberg Trials, that is, the twelve US trials of Nazi suspects held between 1946 and 1949, after the closure of the International Military Tribunal at Nuremburg. Taylor argued in 1970 that several US officers, and potentially even the US president, could be held responsible under the doctrine for the 1968 Mỹ Lai massacre in Vietnam,[4] in which US forces killed 350–500 Vietnamese civilians.[5] Nothing came of this argument, however, and no superior officer faced command responsibility charges for the massacre. Nor were any other officers held responsible for the crimes of their subordinates in other conflicts, until the ICTY opened.

In the post-war trials of Japanese war criminals, the Allies had gone to enormous lengths to prosecute commanders, both for their own direct crimes, and for the crimes of their subordinates through command responsibility. Hundreds of officers were investigated, indicted, tried, and convicted in an ambitious and wide-ranging trial program that was both financially expensive and time-consuming. The costs of the trials initially appeared worth it. The doctrine of command responsibility had proved to be a malleable prosecutorial tool that enabled the Allies to secure convictions across the entirety of the military chain of command, for a wide range of crimes, that had been perpetrated in a variety circumstances. In the immediate aftermath of the trials, it seemed clear that the command responsibility proceedings had created a straightforward, legally

2. See for example ICTY, *Prosecutor v Tihomir Blaškić*, archived at [http://www.legal-tools.org/doc/e1ae55/]; ICTY, *Prosecutor v Dario Kordić and One Other*, archived at [https://www.legal-tools.org/doc/738211/].
3. *Prosecutor v Delalić*, 122.
4. Telford Taylor, *Nuremberg and Vietnam: An American Tragedy* (Quadrangle Books, 1970).
5. Howard Jones, *My Lai: Vietnam, 1968, and the Descent into Darkness* (Oxford University Press, 2017), 1.

enforceable duty of commanding officers to halt, prevent, or punish the commission of war crimes.

The frequent use of the doctrine, beyond just senior officers like Yamashita Tomoyuki, was in part a response to the apparently widespread commission of war crimes by the Japanese military. Reports from escaped prisoners and liberated civilians, together with the investigations of Allied war crimes staff during the conflict, pointed towards something fundamentally wrong with how the Japanese military had conducted the war. Such widespread crimes, authorities believed, could not have been solely the result of out-of-control enlisted soldiers, but rather, they reflected a broader failure of the military chain of command to prevent war crimes from occurring, or perhaps even indicated that Japanese officers had acquiesced or participated in the crimes in some way. Prosecuting such officers was thus seen as necessary if true justice for the crimes were to be achieved. In other words, reckoning with Japanese war crimes meant reckoning with the complex question of how to attribute blame across the military hierarchy.

Despite the clear intention of the Allies to use the doctrine of command responsibility widely, relatively little had been done to prepare for this work. Though international laws and customs were amended, and the type of permissible evidence was expanded, Allied legal authorities made few attempts to clarify what command responsibility actually meant. Legal planners most likely thought that the doctrine was straightforward in both its interpretation and its application. Immediately, however, its complexity became apparent: no one was quite sure whether Yamashita was held responsible simply because he was the superior officer, or because he knew, or ought to have known, that crimes were occurring under his command, and he did nothing about it. From the very outset, consistency was missing from the trial program.

Command responsibility then proved difficult to apply consistently in court. The work of investigators, prosecutors, and judges was impeded by the overwhelming scope of the trials, complex legal questions about the doctrine itself, and a strong desire to convict officer-defendants. Essentially, the complexities underlying attempts to bring officers to justice for crimes they had not personally committed were never resolved. As the trials proceeded, command responsibility quickly transformed from a basic principle into a tangled legal web of uncertainties about defendants' intent, level of control of their subordinates and of the broader circumstances in which the crimes had been committed, and the extent of their participation in offences. All these considerations then had to be related to and judged against a complex military hierarchy. One consequence was that, taken as a whole, the legal proceedings did not impose clear limits on when accountability for a crime had finally been reached, so that, in effect, any and all relevant commanders could be held fully accountable for the same crime.

Moreover, because the Allies had entered the trials with no consensus on what command meant, interpretation of the doctrine had been left to the preconceptions, whims, and imperfect efforts of individual prosecutors, judges, and legal review staff.

Some Allied lawyers did attempt to clarify command responsibility, either in court or at the review stage. But there was no consensus on how the doctrine should function on a legal level. It was unclear whether command responsibility operated as a strict liability, or, alternatively, officers were held responsible for a separate offence based on what they had or had not done. Moreover, difficult questions arose across the trials about whether the doctrine also imparted some form of participatory liability under either interpretation.

Strict liability was attractive to tribunals because it was easy to apply. When using this interpretation, the trial process rarely differentiated between liability and guilt. That is, the commander was considered just as guilty as if he had personally carried out the direct crime, even though the liability for that crime arose solely from his formal position in the military hierarchy. Strict liability was also potentially useful because it created a strong deterrent: under strict liability, an officer would be convicted simply for being in command of subordinates who committed war crimes. Thus, it was expected that future commanders would go to immense efforts to ensure that their subordinates did not contravene the laws and customs of war.

Strict liability, moreover, suited Allied personnel who assumed, whether consciously or not, that the entire Japanese military was responsible for war crimes. It was also useful in cases where there was simply not enough evidence to convict an officer of directly perpetrating a crime, even if prosecutors believed that he had done so. The idea that officers were ultimately responsible for the crimes committed during the war evolved, perhaps naturally, into a suspicion amongst some Allied personnel that many Japanese officers had, in fact, directly ordered their subordinates to commit war crimes. The possibility that enlisted soldiers had executed captives, tortured civilians, and beaten prisoners without orders, yet in a modern military had faced no punishment or reprimand from their own superiors, would have seemed unfathomable to most prosecutors and judges. It was often impossible, however, to establish whether an order to carry out a crime had ever been issued. Allied personnel, faced with the possibility that those whom they genuinely believed had committed the crime might escape punishment, turned to command responsibility as a strict liability in order to secure convictions.

When the doctrine was understood as a separate liability, guilt was correlated with what tribunals considered an officer should have done to prevent war crimes. In making this evaluation, however, tribunals were often either unable, or unwilling, to take account of factors that may have mitigated a commander's guilt: problems of securing an adequate supply of essential goods for prisoners, poor communication, poor training, and other circumstances of command during the war all appear to have been ignored or downplayed in the great majority of cases. In other words, the questions of what a commander could have done in the subjective circumstances within which he had operated was disregarded, and instead he was judged on what he should have done according to undefined objective standards.

Reconciling varying or competing understandings of command responsibility was made even harder by the scope of the trial program. Thousands of officers were tried in hundreds of trials across the Asia-Pacific region. Individual Allied legal personnel were left with little direction on how to conduct trials and which interpretation of command responsibility to use. Keeping track of who had been found responsible for what, and how, was an almost impossible task, made even more difficult by the lack of formal written judgments, itself a necessary practical requirement considering that most judges had no legal training. Over time, the changing political environment in Japan, principally the 'Reverse Course', would also have had an impact; though Allied policymakers never directly interfered in individual trials, for many military lawyers and judges, it would appear clear which way the political winds were blowing.

Attempts to determine where responsibility and guilt rested in proceedings instituted on such a massive scale, with such a loose framework and external pressures, were almost guaranteed to produce inconsistent results. The desire to secure convictions, moreover, played another part: many legal reviewers would have been relatively unconcerned with exactly how an officer was found guilty at trial, because of an underlying assumption that such officers were guilty of something.

Beyond all these practical and legal considerations sat a much more difficult problem to tackle, one that went to the heart of command responsibility. What exactly command was, and what it had meant or should have meant during the war, were never made certain. Command was assumed by Allied legal planners to be a straightforward concept, where the power to order came with the power to oversee. But the Allies appeared unprepared to face the reality that many Japanese officers had faced during the war. Military hierarchies were complex systems, with the power to order and to oversee split and shared across many individuals with varying levels of competence and experience. These qualities of command were themselves difficult to measure, and the Allies had no established system of doing so. Some Japanese officers had been required to oversee relatively simple operations. Others were given almost unmanageable commands: they were required to control their own troops plus large numbers of enemy prisoners, possibly including civilians, often in remote locations with little or no external support.

What command meant to the individuals running the trials, whether they were defence lawyers, prosecutors, judges, or legal reviewers, played a greater role in determining how tribunals assessed responsibility and guilt than did the desire to convict, the legal complexity of the doctrine, or the scope of the trials. At a basic level, all prosecutors and judges believed that command came with a heavy responsibility to prevent, halt, or punish war crimes. But under what circumstances these duties arose was a matter subject to various understandings. Some legal personnel felt that the duty was held by individual officers and entire command structures at the same time. Others considered that command could be situational, and that, at the end of the day, Japanese officers were people who had been thrust into difficult, if not impossible, situations; and that these situations were themselves the product of a broader context, over which the Japanese officers had exercised limited control. These individual interpretations of what command meant informed the way in which tribunals reached their decisions. Some tribunals struggled to separate the objective role of an ideal officer from the individual before the court, while others displayed a surprising degree of leniency towards relatively junior officers who had been given what appeared to be an overwhelming task.

Assessing whether the command responsibility trials were fair is a vexed undertaking. For the Allied personnel taking part, the trials certainly seemed fair – Japanese forces had committed widespread atrocities during the war, and there was a clear need for a reckoning with those who had had some level of power to prevent those atrocities but had failed to do so. Many Japanese officers who were tried under the doctrine had effectively done nothing to control the worst urges of their subordinates, or had come so close to taking a part in the crime as to be almost accessories, if not participants. There was a clear need, and indeed, an existing mandate, to punish the Japanese military, and criminal trials were the prime mechanism. At the same time, the Pacific War had been fought on the Japanese side predominantly by men forced into military service, who had been given inadequate training, unruly subordinates or impossible tasks, and limited support. The overwhelming firepower and industrial might that the Allies brought to bear upon Japan, moreover, destroyed both the Japanese military's chain of command and its support system while the conflict still raged.

The twenty trials closely analysed here show that in later proceedings Allied legal personnel exhibited a degree of trepidation about command responsibility, especially in trials for mistreatment of prisoners. The punishment that went along with conviction under command responsibility began to be tempered by legal reviewers. It seems that, upon assessing the scope of the trials and the large number of officers convicted under the doctrine, Allied legal officers became wary of what the trials had created. The duty of command as understood in the post-war proceedings was too broad and too easily triggered. The relative comprehensiveness of the command responsibility trials, in terms both of the crimes committed and of the number of accused commanders, was staggering. It left some legal experts wondering where the future of the doctrine lay. Did the entire chain of command face retribution for the acts of rogue soldiers? The same factors that made command responsibility so successful in prosecuting command were also potentially the doctrine's undoing.

On the one hand, considering all the time, willpower, and resources put into establishing command responsibility in the trials of Japanese war crimes suspects, as well as their counterparts in Europe, it is surprising that the doctrine was so quickly discarded after the post-war trials. On the other hand, the state of the doctrine at the end of the trials, and the process of getting to that point, gave the Allies every reason to walk away from command responsibility. The doctrine had been applied inconsistently, with no clear limits on accountability for a crime. In many cases, it appeared to have been used as a convenient way of securing convictions, rather than as a dispassionate legal tool. Moreover, the tangle of legal, moral, and philosophical problems that arose when the doctrine was applied was left essentially unresolved at the end: there was still no clear consensus on what it meant to be in command or on what could and should be expected of officers.

The ICTY's decision to apply command responsibility was perhaps unsurprising, despite the numerous difficulties that the Allies had experienced in using the doctrine after the Second World War – and the fact that they had chosen to walk away from the standard they had set. The Allies' creation and application of the doctrine at the post-war trials was a legal solution to the intractable problem of assigning responsibility to complex military hierarchies. Notwithstanding the array of practical, moral, and philosophical problems that arose in the interpretation and application of command responsibility, the doctrine proved to be an effective tool in assigning guilt beyond direct participants in situations in which it was clear that something fundamentally wrong had occurred in the chain of command.

Appendix A

TABLE OF RANKS

	Imperial Japanese Army	*Imperial Japanese Navy*
Enlisted Soldiers	Private	Seaman
	Corporal	Leading Seaman
Non-Commissioned Officers	Sergeant	Petty-Officer
	Warrant-Officer	Chief Petty-Officer
Junior (Company) Officers	Lieutenant	Sub-Lieutenant
	Captain	Lieutenant
Mid-level (Field) Officers	Major	Lieutenant-Commander
	Lieutenant-Colonel	Commander
	Colonel	Captain
General Staff	Major-General	Rear-Admiral
	Lieutenant-General	Vice-Admiral
	General	Admiral
	Field Marshal	Grand-Admiral

Bibliography

Archives

Australia

Australian War Memorial, Canberra (AWM)

Leemon, Jack Holder, 'The Body Snatchers', Unpublished Manuscript, Australian War Memorial, MSS0811.

National Archives of Australia, Canberra and Melbourne (NAA)

Series: A471 – Courts-Martial files [including war crimes trials]
80734. War Crimes Trial of Shinohara Eitaro and Two Others, Rabaul, 30 March–1 April 1946.
80756. War Crimes Trial of Odamura Toshitake, Morotai, 14–15 January 1946.
80771. War Crimes Trial of Takakuwa Takuo and One Other, Labuan, 3–5 January 1946.
80777. War Crimes Trial of Hoshijima Susumu, and Sixteen Others, Labuan 8–20 June 1946.
80796. War Crimes Trial of Suzuki Naoomi and One Other, Rabaul, 15–16 April 1946.
81029. War Crimes Trial of Yamamoto Shoichi and Ten Others, Labuan, 23–28 January 1946.
81207. War Crimes Trial of Kawasaki Matsuhei, Rabaul, 17–18 June 1947.
81209. War Crimes Trial of Okada Tametsugu, Rabaul, 23–24 June 1947.
81245. War Crimes Trial of Obana Yoshimasa and Seven Others, Singapore, 2–11 September 1946.
81630. War Crimes Trial of Yutani Yujiro and Two Others, Darwin, 19 March–10 April 1946.
81631. War Crimes Trial of Baba Masao, Ranau, 28 May–2 June 1947.
81644. War Crimes Trial of Ichise Shinichi and Five Others, Morotai, 16–20 February 1946.
81709. War Crimes Trial of Shirozu Wadami and 92 Others, Ambon 2–18 January 1946 and Morotai, 25 January–15 February 1946.

81950 PART 1. War Crimes Trial of Tahara Susumu and Sixteen Others, Vol. 1, Hong Kong, 5 January–22 June 1948.
81950 PART 2. War Crimes Trial of Tahara Susumu and Sixteen Others, Vol. 2, Hong Kong, 5 January–22 June 1948.
81950 PART 3. War Crimes Trial of Tahara Susumu and Sixteen Others, Vol. 3, Hong Kong, 5 January–22 June 1948.
80977. War Crimes Trial of Endo Shinichi, Morotai, 23–31 January 1946.

National Library of Australia, Canberra (NLA)

Papers of D. C. S. Sissons, (1950–2006), MS3092.

United Kingdom

The National Archives, Kew (TNA)

WO 203/5620, Treatment of Prisoners of War by Japanese, General Information POWS.
WO 235/862, *UK v Takasaki Shinji and One Other*, Singapore, 2–6 May 1946.
WO 235/872, *UK v Toyoda Akiichi*, Singapore, 3–9 July 1946.
WO 235/883, *UK v Abe Keiichi and Three Others*, Labuan, 29 April–4 May 1946.
WO 235/886, *UK v Anami Sanso and Thirteen Others*, Singapore, 3–26 July 1946.
WO 235/890, *UK v Murakami Seisaku and Three Others*, Singapore, 14–17 August 1946,
WO 235/931, *UK v Higashigawa Yoshinobu and Thirty-Four Others*, Penang, 30 August–28 September 1946.
WO 235/952, *UK v Hachisuka Kunifusu and Twenty-Three Others*, Singapore, 24 July–6 September 1946.
WO 235/953, *UK v Ogata Tsuyoshi*, Kota Bahru, 21–24 October 1946.
WO 235/993, *UK v Kishi Yasuo and Fourteen Others*, 28 March–25 April 1946.
WO 235/1004, *UK v Nishimura Takuma and Six Others*, Singapore, 10 March–2 April 1947.
WO 235/1007, *UK v Shibata Shigeo and One Other*, Hong Kong, 10 February 1947.
WO 235/1034, *UK v Banno Hirateru and Six Others*, Singapore, 25 September–23 October 1946.
WO 235/1039, *UK v Ori Masami and Three Others*, Kuala Lumpur, 24 July–25 August 1947.
WO 235/1041, *UK v Ushiyama Yukio and Three Others*, Hong Kong, 7 July–12 August 1947.
WO 235/1102, *UK v Fukudome Shigeru and Five Others*, Singapore, 9–27 February 1946.

United States

National Archives and Records Administration, College Park MD (NARA)

RG125, Records of the Judge Advocate General (Navy)

Box 3, Records Re Interrogations of Japanese Witnesses and Defendants in War Crimes Cases, 1945–1949, Folder Kobayashi Masashi.

Box 8, War Crimes Branch, Case Files of the Pacific Area War Crimes Trial 1944–49, Case of Captain Tanaka Masaharu and Two Others, Guam, 5 November 1946.

RG153, Records of the Office of the Judge Advocate General (Army)

Box 815, War Crimes Branch, Case Files, 1944–1949, *USA v Nakanishi Yoshio*, Yokohama, 12–16 May 1947.

Box 881, War Crimes Branch, Case Files 1944–49, *USA v Ichinoe Kimiya and Six Others*, Yokohama, 22 December 1947–16 January 1948.

Box 1385, Office of the Judge Advocate General, Case Files, 1944–1949, *USA v Toyama Minoru and Two Others*, Manila, 17–28 January 1947.

RG331, Records of Allied Operational and Occupation Headquarters, World War II

Box 2 SCAP Legal Section, International Prosecution Section, International Military Tribunal for the Far East, Judgment.

Box 1350, SCAP, Legal Section, Administrative Division, War Crimes Files, 1945–49, Publications, Richard Rudisill 'History of the Investigation Division'.

Box 1576, SCAP, Legal Section, Prosecution Division, *USA Verses* [*sic*] *Japanese War Criminals*, Case Files, 1945–49, *USA v Nogi Naraji*, Yokohama, 16–24 January 1947.

Box 1579, SCAP, Legal Section, Prosecution Division, USA Verses Japanese War Criminals, Case File, 1945–49, *United States of America vs Akira Nagahama*, Manila, 25 January–11 March 1946.

Box 1638, Supreme Commander of the Allied Power, Legal Section, Prosecution Division, *USA versus Japanese War Criminals, USA v Terada Seichi and Fourteen Others*, Yokohama, 2 August–8 November 1948.

Box 1688, SCAP Legal Section, Prosecution Division, *Philippines versus Various Japanese War Criminals*, 1947–1949, *Philippines v Sato So*, Manila, 15 March–6 May 1948.

Box 1690, SCAP Legal Section, Prosecution Division, *Philippines versus Various Japanese War Criminals*, Case File, 1947–1949, *Philippines v Nakamura Hideichi and Twelve Others*, 24 October 1947–27 May 1948.

Box 1694, Supreme Command for the Allied Powers, Legal Section, Prosecution Division, *Philippines versus Various Japanese War Criminals*, Case File, 1947–1949, *Philippines v Shimamura Katsuji and One Other*, Manila, 23 August–9 October 1948.

Box 1703, Supreme Command for the Allied Powers, Legal Section, Prosecution Division, *Philippines versus Various Japanese War Criminals*, Case File, 1947–1949, *Philippines v Omura Yasuo and One Other*, Manila 25 May 1949–12 September 1949.

Box 1728, SCAP Legal Section, Prosecution Division, *Philippines versus Various Japanese War Criminals*, 1947–1949, *Philippines v Fujita Takefumi*, Manila, 5 September–10 November 1947.

Box 1728, SCAP Legal Section, Prosecution Division, *Philippines versus Various Japanese War Criminals*, 1947–1949, *Philippines v Fujisaki Saburo*, Manila, 14 November 1947–23 December 1947.

Box 1857, SCAP Legal Section, Prosecution Division, *USA versus Japanese War Criminals, USA vs Tomoyuki Yamashita*, Vol. I.

Box 1859, SCAP Legal Section, Prosecution Division, *USA versus Japanese War Criminals, USA vs Tomoyuki Yamashita*, Vol. XXXIV.

Online Legal Archives

International Tribunal for the Prosecution of Persons Responsible for Serious Violations of International Humanitarian Law Committed in the Territory of the Former Yugoslavia since 1991, *Prosecutor v. Zejnil Delalić and Three Others*, archived at [http://www.legal-tools.org/doc/6b4a33/].

International Tribunal for the Prosecution of Persons Responsible for Serious Violations of International Humanitarian Law Committed in the Territory of the Former Yugoslavia since 1991, *Prosecutor v Dario Kordić and One Other*, archived at [https://www.legal-tools.org/doc/738211/].

International Tribunal for the Prosecution of Persons Responsible for Serious Violations of International Humanitarian Law Committed in the Territory of the Former Yugoslavia since 1991, *Prosecutor v Tihomir Blaškić*, archived at [http://www.legal-tools.org/doc/e1ae55/].

'The Geneva Convention 1929', [http://avalon.law.yale.edu/20th_century/geneva02.asp#art12].

'Convention with Respect to the Laws and Customs of War on Land (Hague II) 1899', [https://avalon.law.yale.edu/19th_century/hague02.asp].

Newspapers

'Four Japs to Die for Brutalities on Burma Railway', *The Canberra Times*, 9 November 1946, 1.

'Four Japs to Die', *Singleton [NSW] Argus*, 11 November 1946, 1.

'Four Japs to Die; Three Gaoled', *Newcastle [NSW] Morning Herald and Miners' Advocate*, 9 November 1946, 3.

'Jap Conqueror of Philippines Indicted', *The Tweed [NSW] Daily*, 10 December 1945, 3.

'Japanese Barbarism at Hong Kong', *The Tweed [NSW] Daily*, 12 March 1942, 4.

'Japanese Sadists Pay the Penalty for Philippine Atrocities', *Cairns Post*, 25 September 1946, 4.

'The Massacre Trial', *The Straits Times*, 5 April 1947, 5.

'VC Award Would be a Mockery, Historian Warns Tribunal', *The Sydney Morning Herald*, 13 March 2012, 1.

Legislation and Proclamations

'Proclamation by the Heads of Governments, United States, China, and the United Kingdom' 26 July 1945, archived at [http://www1.edu/History-old/figal/hist371/assets/pdf/Potsdam.pdf].

Royal Warrant 0160/2498, 18 June 1945 (UK), archived at [https://ihl-databases.icrc.org/applic/ihl/ihl-nat.nsf/xsp/.ibmmodres/domino/OpenAttachment/applic/ihl/ihl-nat.nsf/8CB72E81A52C0130C1256B350031779F/TEXT/Regulations%20for%20the%20Trial%20of%20War%20Criminals%201945.pdf].

War Crimes Act 1945 (Australia), archived at [https://www.legislation.gov.au/Details/C1945A00048].

Books, Articles, Chapters, and Theses

Abe, Hiroshi. 'Building the Burma-Siam Railroad'. In *Japan at War: An Oral History*, edited by Haruko Taya Cook and Theodore F. Cook. New York Press, 1992.

Abe, Hiroshi. 'Death Row at Changi Prison'. In *Japan at War: An Oral History*, edited by Haruko Taya Cook and Theodore F. Cook. New York Press, 1992.

Akashi, Yoji. 'Japanese Policy Towards the Malayan Chinese 1941–1945'. *Journal of Southeast Asian Studies* 1 no. 2 (1970): 61–89.

Ara, Satoshi. 'Food Supply Problem in Leyte, Philippines, During the Japanese Occupation (1942–44)'. *Journal of Southeast Asian Studies* 39 (2008): 59–82.

Archer, Bernice. *The Internment of Western Civilians Under the Japanese, 1941–1945: A Patchwork of Internment*. Routledge-Curzon, 2004.

Aszkielowicz, Dean. *The Australian Pursuit of Japanese War Criminals 1943–1957: From Foe to Friend*. Hong Kong University Press, 2017.

Baxter, R. 'So Called "Unprivileged Belligerents": Spies, Guerrillas, and Saboteurs'. *British Yearbook of International Law* 28 (1951): 323–45.

Beaumont, Joan. *Gull Force: Survival and Leadership in Captivity 1941–1945*. Allen and Unwin, 1988.

Beevor, Antony. *The Second World War*. Little, Brown and Company, 2012.

Boas, Gideon, and Lisa Lee. 'Command Responsibility and Other Grounds of Criminal Responsibility'. In *Australia's War Crimes Trials 1945–51*, edited by Georgina Fitzpatrick, Timothy McCormack, and Narrelle Morris. Brill-Nijhoff, 2016.

Boister, Neil, and Robert Cryer. *Documents on the Tokyo International Military Tribunal: Charter, Indictment and Judgments*. Oxford University Press, 2008.

Boister, Neil, and Robert Cryer, eds. *The Tokyo International Military Tribunal: A Reappraisal*. Oxford University Press, 2008.

Borch, Fred, L. *Military Trials of War Criminals in the Netherlands East Indies, 1946–1949*. Oxford University Press, 2017.

Caiden, Martin. *The Ragged, Rugged Warriors*. Bantam Books, 1985.

Carrell, Michael. 'Australia's Prosecution of Japanese War Criminals: Stimuli and Constraints'. Unpublished PhD thesis, University of Melbourne, 2005.

Chamberlain, Sharon. 'Justice and Reconciliation: Postwar Philippine Trials of Japanese War Criminals in History and Memory'. PhD thesis. George Washington University, 2010.

Chamberlain, Sharon. *A Reckoning: Philippine Trials of Japanese War Criminals*. University of Wisconsin Press, 2019.

Cheah, Kheng Boon. 'Japanese Army Policy Toward Chinese and Malay-Chinese Relations in Wartime Malaya'. In Paul H. Kratoska, *Southeast Asian Minorities in the Wartime Japanese Empire*. Routledge-Curzon, 2002.

Cheah, Kheng Boon. *Red Star Over Malaya: Resistance and Social Conflict During and After the Japanese Occupation of Malaya, 1941–1946*. Singapore University Press, 1983.

Cheah, Wui-Ling. 'Post-World War II British "Hell-ship" Trials in Singapore: Omissions and the Attribution of Responsibility'. *Journal of International Criminal Justice* 8, no. 4 (2010): 1035–58.

Clague, Peter. *Bridge House: The True, Chilling Story of a Shanghai Chamber of Horrors*. South China Morning Post, 1983.

Clapson, Mark. *The Blitz Companion: Aerial Warfare, Civilians and the City Since 1911*. University of Westminster Press, 2019.

Cohen, David. 'The Singapore War Crimes Trials and their Relevance Today'. *Singapore Law Review* 31 (2013): 3–38.

Collingham, Lizzie. *The Taste of War: World War II and the Battle for Food*. Penguin Press, 2012.

Connaughton, Richard, John Pimlott, and Duncan Anderson. *The Battle for Manila: The Most Devastating Untold Story of World War II*. Bloomsbury, 1995.

Cormier, Monique, and Sarah Finnin. 'Obedience to Superior Orders and Related Defences'. In *Australia's War Crimes Trials 1945–51*, edited by Georgina Fitzpatrick, Timothy McCormack, and Narrelle Morris. Brill-Nijhoff, 2016.

Cribb, Robert. '"Conventional War Crimes": The International Military Tribunal for the Far East and the Ill-Treatment of Prisoners of War and Civilian Internees'. In *The Tokyo Tribunal: Perspectives on Law, History, and Memory*, edited by Viviane E. Dittrich, Kerstin von Lingen, Philipp Osten, and Jolana Makraiová. Torkal Opsahl Academic EPublisher, 2020.

Daniels, Gordon. 'The Great Tokyo Air Raid, 9–10 March 1945'. In *Modern Japan: Aspects of History, Literature and Society*, edited by W. G. Beasley. Charles E. Tuttle Company, 1976.

Danner, Allison Marston, and Jenny S. Martinez. 'Guilty Associations: Joint Criminal Enterprise, Command Responsibility, and the Development of International Criminal Law'. *California Law Review* 93 (2005): 75–169.

Dasgupta, Jayant. *Japanese in Andaman and Nicobar Islands: Red Sun Over Black Water*. Manas Publications, 2002.

Daws, Gavan. *Prisoners of the Japanese: POWs of World War II in the Pacific*. William Morrow & Company, 1994.

Dorr, Robert F. *Mission to Tokyo: The American Airmen Who Took the War to Japan*. Voyageur Press, 2012.

Douds, G. J. 'Indian POWs in the Pacific, 1941–1945'. In *Forgotten Captives in Japanese-Occupied Asia*, edited by Karl Hack and Kevin Blackburn. Routledge, 2008.

Dower, John. *War Without Mercy: Race and Power in the Pacific War*. Pantheon, 1986.

Drea, Edward J. *Japan's Imperial Army: Its Rise and Fall, 1853–1945*. University Press of Kansas, 2009.

Drea, Edward J., and Hans van de Ven. 'An Overview of Major Military Campaigns During the Sino-Japanese War, 1937–1945'. In *The Battle for China: Essays on the Military History of the Sino-Japanese War of 1937–1945*, edited by Edward J. Drea and Hans van de Ven. Stanford University Press, 2012.

Durham, Helen, and Narrelle Morris. 'Women's Bodies and International Criminal Law: From Tokyo to Rabaul'. In *Beyond Victor's Justice? The Tokyo War Crimes Trial Revisited*, edited by Yuki Tanaka Tim McCormack and Gerry Simpson. Martinus Nijhoff Publishes, 2010.

Earl Mountbatten of Burma. 'Foreword'. In *Trial of Gozawa Sadaichi and Nine Others*, edited by Colin Sleeman. William Hodge and Company, 1948.

Evatt, Herbert Vere. *The Royal Prerogative*. The Law Book Company, 1987.

Fellows, Jamie. 'Law at a Critical Juncture: Retribution and Criminal Responsibility at the US Army War Crimes Trials in the Philippines, 1945–1947'. PhD thesis. James Cook University, 2020.

Feuer, A. B., ed. *Bilibid Diary: The Secret Notebooks of Commander Thomas Hayes, POW, the Philippines, 1942–1945*. Archon Books, 1987.

Fitzpatrick, Georgina. 'The Trials in Singapore'. In *Australia's War Crimes Trials 1945–51*, edited by Georgina Fitzpatrick, Timothy McCormack, and Narrelle Morris. Brill-Nijhoff, 2016.

Fitzpatrick, Georgina. 'The Trials on Morotai'. In *Australia's War Crimes Trials 1945–51*, edited by Georgina Fitzpatrick, Timothy McCormack, and Narrelle Morris. Brill-Nijhoff, 2016.

Fitzpatrick, Georgina, Tim McCormack, and Narrelle Morris, eds. *Australia's War Crimes Trials 1945–51*. Brill-Nijhoff, 2016.

Flower, Sybilla Jane. 'Captors and Captives on the Burma-Thailand Railway'. In *Prisoners of War and Their Captors in World War II*, edited by Bob Moore and Kent Fedorowich. Berg, 1996.

Francis, Timothy Lang. 'To Dispose of the Prisoners: The Japanese Execution of American Aircrew at Fukuoka, Japan, During 1945'. *Pacific Historical Review* 66 (1997): 469–501.

Garrett, Jemima. *Island Exiles*. ABC Books, 1996.

Gillison, Douglas. *Royal Australian Air Force, 1939–1945*. Australian War Memorial, 1962.

Gin, Ooi Keat. 'Of Permanent Possession: Territories Under the Imperial Japanese Navy'. In *The Encyclopedia of Indonesia in the Pacific War*, edited by Peter Post, William H. Frederick, Iris Heidebrink, and Shigeru Sato. Koninklijke Brill, 2010.

Gin, Ooi Keat. *The Japanese Occupation of Borneo, 1941–1945*. Routledge, 2011.

Glusman, John A. *Conduct Under Fire: Four American Doctors and Their Fight for Life as Prisoners of the Japanese, 1941–1945*. Penguin, 2006.

Grant, Lachlan. 'Hellships, Prisoner Transport and Unrestricted Submarine Warfare in World War II'. In *Beyond Surrender: Australian Prisoners of War in the Twentieth Century*, edited by in Joan Beaumont, Lachlan Grant, and Aaron Pegram. Melbourne University Publishing, 2015.

Green, L. C. 'Command Responsibility in International Humanitarian Law'. *Transnational Law and Contemporary Problems* 5 (1995): 319–41.

Guy, George F. 'The Defense of Yamashita'. *United States Air Force Academy Journal of Legal Studies*, 6 (1950): 215–36.

Hack, Karl, and Kevin Blackburn. 'Japanese Occupied Asia from 1941 to 1945: One Occupier, Many Captives and Memories'. In *Forgotten Captives in Japanese-Occupied Asia*, edited by Karl Hack and Kevin Blackburn. Routledge, 2008.

Ham, Paul. *Sandakan: The Untold Story of the Sandakan Death Marches*. Random House Australia, 2012.

Hamai, Kazufumi, and Peter Mauch. 'The Wartime Destruction of the Japanese Diplomatic Record in Historical Perspective'. In *Defamiliarizing Japan's Asia-Pacific War*, edited by W. Puck Brecher and Michael W. Myers. University of Hawaii Press, 2019.

Hartendorp, A. V. H. *The Japanese Occupation of the Philippines, Vol. 1*. Bookmark, 1967.

Havens, Thomas R. H. *Valley of Darkness: The Japanese People and World War Two*. University Press of America, 1986.

Havers, R. P. W. *Reassessing the Japanese Prisoner of War Experience: the Changi POW Camp, Singapore, 1942–1945*. Routledge-Curzon, 2003.

Hearder, Rosalind. 'More Complex than a Stereotype: Australian POW Doctors and the Japanese in Captivity, 1942–45'. *Health and History* 6, no. 2 (2004): 75–91.

Heidebrink, Iris. 'Prisoners of War (POWS)'. In *The Encyclopedia of Indonesia in the Pacific War*, edited by Peter Post, William H. Frederick, Iris Heidebrink, and Shigeru Sato. Koninklijke Brill, 2010.

Heller, Kevin Jon. *The Nuremberg Trials and the Origins of International Criminal Law*. Oxford University Press, 2011.

Hogan, David W. *U.S. Army Special Operations in World War II*. Centre of Military History, Department of the Army, 1992.

Holwitt, Joel Ira. *'Execute Against Japan': The U.S. Decision to Conduct Unrestricted Submarine Warfare*. Texas A&M University Press, 2009.

Hirofumi, Hayashi. 'The Battle of Singapore, the Massacre of Chinese and Understanding of the Issue in Post-War Japan'. *The Asia-Pacific Journal: Japan Focus* 7 (2009): 1–20.

Itsoyoshi, Ueno. *An End to a War: A Japanese Soldier's Experience of the 1945 Death Marches*. Translated by Mika Reilly. Opus Publications, 2012.

James, David H. *The Rise and Fall of the Japanese Empire*. Routledge, 1951.

Jia, Bing Bing. 'The Plea of Superior Orders in the Hong Kong Trials'. In *Hong Kong's War Crimes Trials*, edited by Suzannah Linton. Oxford University Press, 2013.

Johnston, B. F. *Japanese Food Management in World War II*. Stanford University Press, 1953.

Jones, Howard. *My Lai: Vietnam, 1968, and the Descent into Darkness*. Oxford University Press, 2017.

Jørgensen, Nina H. B. 'On Being "Concerned" in a Crime: Embryonic Joint Criminal Enterprise?' In *Hong Kong's War Crimes Trials*, edited by Suzannah Linton. Oxford University Press, 2013.

Jørgensen, Nina H. B. 'Theories of Joint Criminal Responsibility at the Asian Tribunals'. In *Trials for International Crimes in Asia*, edited by Kirsten Sellars. Cambridge University Press, 2015.

Jose, Lydia N. Yu. 'The Koreans in Second World War Philippines: Rumour and History'. *Journal of Southeast Asian Studies* 43 (2012): 324–39.

Kennan, George F. 'Explanatory Notes, March 25, 1948'. In *Foreign Relations of the United States, 1948, Vol. 6, The Far East and Australia*. United States Department of State. US Government Printing Office, 1948.

Kennedy, Joseph. *British Civilians and the Japanese war in Malaya and Singapore, 1941–45*. W. Hodge, 1951.

Kenny, Catherine. *Captives: Australian Army Nurses in Japanese Prison Camps*. University of Queensland Press, 1986.

Kerr, E. Bartlett. *Flames Over Tokyo: The U.S. Army Air Force's Incendiary Campaign Against Japan, 1944–1945*. D. I. Fine, 1991.

Kerr, E. Bartlett. *Surrender and Survival: The Experience of American POWs in the Pacific, 1941–1945*. William Morrow and Company, 1985.

Kobayashi, Yasuko. 'Japanese Documents Concerning the War Crimes Trials (esp. General Ishida and Others) Relating to the Burma-Siam Railway'. In *The Thailand-Burma Railway, 1942–1946: Documents and Selected Writings Volume 5*, edited by Paul H. Kratoska. Routledge, 2006.

Kramer, Alan. 'The First Wave of International War Crimes Trials: Istanbul and Leipzig'. *European Law Review* 14 (2006): 441–55.

Kratoska, Paul H. 'General Introduction'. In *The Thailand-Burma Railway, 1942–1946: Documents and Selected Writings Volume 5*, edited by Paul. H. Kratoska. Routledge, 2006.

Kovner, Sarah. 'Allied POWs in Korea: Life and Death During the Pacific War'. In *The Dismantling of Japan's Empire in East Asia: Deimperialization, Postwar Legitimation and Imperial Afterlife*, edited by Barak Kushner and Sherzod Muminov. Routledge, 2017.

Kovner, Sarah. *Prisoners of the Empire: Inside Japanese POW Camps*. Cambridge University Press, 2020.

Kovner, Sarah. 'Captivity on the Home Front: Allied Prisoners of War in Fukuoka During the Second World War'. In *Detention Camps in Asia*, edited by Robert Cribb, Christina Twomey, and Sandra Wilson. Brill-Nijhoff, 2022.

Kushner, Barak. 'Chinese War Crimes in Trials of Japanese, 1945–1956: A Historical Summary'. In *The Historical Origins of International Criminal Law: Volume I*, edited by Morten Bergsmo, Cheah Wui-Ling, and Yi Ping. Torkel Opsahl Academic Publisher, 2014.

Kushner, Barak. *Men to Devils, Devils to Men: Japanese War Crimes and Chinese Justice*. Harvard University Press, 2015.

Lael, Richard L. *The Yamashita Precedent: War Crimes and Command Responsibility*. Scholarly Resources, 1982.

Lamont-Brown, Raymond. *Kempeitai: Japan's Dreaded Military Police*. Phoenix Mill Publishing Limited, 1998.
Lamont-Brown, Raymond. *Ships from Hell: Japanese War Crimes on High Seas*. Sutton Publishing, 2002.
Landrum, Bruce. 'The Yamashita War Crimes Trial: Command Responsibility Then and Now'. *Military Law Review* 149 (1995): 293–302.
Large, Stephen S. *Emperor Hirohito and Showa Japan: A Political Biography*. Routledge, 1992.
Laska, Lewis L., and James S. Smith. 'Hell and the Devil: Andersonville and the Trial of Captain Wirz, C.S.A. 1865'. *Military Law Review* 68 (1975): 77–132.
Lebra, Joyce C. *Japanese-Trained Armies in Southeast Asia*. Heinemann Education Books, 1977.
Lee, Geok Boi. *The Syonan Years: Singapore Under Japanese Rule 1942–1945*. National Archives of Singapore, 2005.
Lemnitzer, Jan Martin. 'International Legal History: From Atrocity Reports to War Crimes Tribunals – The Roots of Modern War Crimes Investigations in Nineteenth Century Legal Activism and First World War Propaganda'. In *War Crimes Trials and Investigations: A Multi-Disciplinary Approach*, edited by Jonathan Waterlow and Jacques Schuhmacher. Palgrave Macmillan, 2018.
Li, Peter. 'The Nanking Holocaust: Memory, Trauma and Reconciliation'. In *Japanese War Crimes: The Search for Justice*, edited by Peter Li. Transaction Publishers, 2003.
Linton, Suzannah, ed. *Hong Kong's War Crimes Trials*. Oxford University Press, 2013.
Linton, Suzannah. 'Introduction'. In *Hong Kong's War Crimes Trials*, edited by Suzannah Linton. Oxford University Press, 2013.
Looman, Richard C. 'Escape from Palawan'. *Leatherneck: Magazine of the Marines* 28 (1945): 66–68.
Lyon, Alan B. *Japanese War Crimes: The Trial of the Naoetsu Camp Guards*. Australian Military History Publications, 2000.
MacGuire, Peter. *Law and War: International Law and American History*. Columbia University Press, 2010.
Maddox, Kelly. 'An Island of Killing and Slaughter: Anti-Guerrilla Warfare in Panay, 1943'. *Journal of Contemporary History* 55, no. 3 (2019): 535–56.
Manchester, William. *Goodbye Darkness: A Memoir of the Pacific War*. Little, Brown and Company, 2008.
Mant, Gilbert. *Massacre at Parit Sulong*. Kangaroo Press, 1995.
Matthäus, Jürgen. 'The Lessons of Leipzig: Punishing German War Criminals after the First World War'. In *Atrocities on Trial: Historical Perspectives on the Politic of Prosecuting War Crimes*, edited by Patricia Heberer and Jürgen Matthäus. University of Nebraska Press, 2008.
Mauch, Peter. 'The Showa Political Crisis, July 1940: The Imperial Japanese Army Courts a Breach with its Sovereign'. *War in History* 27 (2020): 670–88.
McCormack, Gavan. 'Apportioning the Blame: Australian Trials for Railway Crimes'. In *The Burma-Thailand Railway*, edited by Gavan McCormack and Hank Nelson. Allen & Unwin, 1993.

McCormack, Timothy. 'From Sun Tzu to the Sixth Committee: The Evolution of an International Criminal Law Regime'. In *The Law of War Crimes: National and International Approaches*, edited by Timothy McCormack and Gerry Simpson. Kluwer Law International, 1997.

McCoubrey, Hilaire. *International Humanitarian Law: The Regulation of Armed Conflicts*. Dartmouth Publishing Company, 1990.

Meloni, Chantal. 'Command Responsibility: Mode of Liability for the Crimes of Subordinates or Separate Offence of the Superior?' *Journal of International Criminal Justice* 5 (2007): 619–37.

Mettraux, Guénaël. *The Law of Command* Responsibility. Oxford University Press, 2009.

Michiko, Nakahara. 'Malayan Labour on the Thailand Burma Railway'. In *Asian Labour in the Wartime Japanese Empire: Unknown Histories*, edited by Paul H. Kratoska. M.E. Sharpe, 2005.

Michno, Gregory F. *Death on the Hellships: Prisoners at Sea in the Pacific War*. Naval Institute Press, 2001.

Miranda, Miguel. *Battle of Manila: Nadir of Japanese Barbarism, 3 February 1945–3 March 1945*. Pen and Sword Military, 2019.

Mitchell, Andrew D. 'Failure to Halt, Prevent, or Punish: The Doctrine of Command Responsibility for War Crimes'. *Sydney Law Review* 22 (2000): 381–400.

Moore, Aaron William. 'An Insatiable Parasite: Eating and Drinking in WWII Armies of the Asia-Pacific Theatre (1937–1945)'. *Food and War in Mid-Twentieth-Century East Asia*, edited by Katarzyna J. Cwiertka. Ashgate Publishing Limited, 2013.

Morris, Narrelle. *Japanese War Crimes in the Pacific: Australia's Investigations and Prosecutions*. National Archives of Australia, 2019.

Moss, Tristan, and Georgina Fitzpatrick. 'Crimes Against Captured Airmen'. In *Australia's War Crimes Trials 1945–51*, edited by Georgina Fitzpatrick, Timothy McCormack, and Narrelle Morris. Brill-Nijhoff, 2016.

Munemiya, Shinji. *The Account of Legal Proceedings of Court for War Criminal Suspects*. Translated by Kazuo Yoshioka. Horitzu Shimpo Press, 1946.

Murphy, Kevin C. *Inside the Bataan Death March: Defeat, Travail and Memory*. MacFarland and Company, 2014.

Nelson, Hank. 'Measuring the Railway: From Individual Lives to National History'. In *The Burma-Thailand Railway*, edited by Gavan McCormack and Hank Nelson. Allen & Unwin, 1993.

Nurick, Lester, and Roger W. Barrett. 'Legality of Guerrilla Forces Under International Law'. *The American Journal of International Law* 40 (1946): 563–83.

Onishi, Satoru. *Hiroku Shōnan Kakyō Shukusei*. Kongo Shuppan, 1977.

Oppenheim, Lassa. *International Law: A Treatise* Vol. 2, *War and Neutrality*, 2nd Edition. Longmans, Green and Co., 1912.

Orbach, Danny. *Curse on This Country: The Rebellious Army of Imperial Japan*. Cornell University Press, 2017.

O'Reilly, Arthur. 'Command Responsibility: A Call to Realign the Doctrine with Principles of Individual Accountability and Retributive Justice'. *Gonzaga Law Review* 40 (2005): 127–55.

Pappas, Caroline. 'Law and Politics: Australia's War Crimes Trials in the Pacific, 1943–1961'. Unpublished PhD thesis, University of New South Wales, 1998.
Parks, W. H. 'Command Responsibility for War Crimes'. *Military Law Review* 62 (1973): 1–104.
Petrossian, Gurgen. 'Elements of Superior Responsibility for Sexual Violence by Subordinates'. *Manitoba Law Review* 42, no. 3 (2019): 123–52.
Post, Peter. 'Policing Society'. In *The Encyclopedia of Indonesia in the Second World War*, edited by Peter Post. Brill, 2009.
Piccigallo, Philip R. *The Japanese on Trial: Allied War Crimes Prosecutions in the Far East, 1945–1951*. University of Texas Press, 1979.
Prévost, Anne-Marie. 'Race and War Crimes: The 1945 Trial of General Tomoyuki Yamashita'. *Human Rights Quarterly* 14 (1992): 303–38.
Pringle, H. F. *Bridge House Survivor: Experiences of a Civilian Prisoner-of-War in Shanghai and Beijing, 1942–5*. Earnshaw Books, 2010.
Pritchard, R. John. 'The Historical Experience of British War Crimes Courts in the Far East, 1946–1948'. *International Relations* 6 (1978): 311–26.
Pritchard, John. 'The Parameters of Justice: The Evolution of British Civil and Military Perspectives on War Crimes Trials and Their Legal Context (1942–1956)'. In *International Humanitarian Law: Prospects*, edited by John Carey, William V. Dunlop, and R. John Pritchard. Brill, 2006.
Ralph, William W. 'Improvised Destruction: Arnold, LeMay, and the Firebombing of Japan'. *War in History* 14, no. 4 (2006): 495–522.
Reed, A., and B. Fitzpatrick. *Criminal Law*. Sweet & Maxwell, 2009.
Reel, A. Frank. *The Case of General Yamashita*. Octagon Books, 1971.
Reid, Richard. *Laden, Fevered, Starved: The POWs of Sandakan, North Borneo*. Commonwealth Department of Veteran Affairs, 1999.
Report of Robert H. Jackson, U.S. Representative to the International Conference on Military Trials, London, 1945. US Department of State, 1949.
Rogers, A. P. V. 'War Crimes Trials Under the British Royal Warrant: British Practice, 1945–1949'. *The International and Comparative Law Quarterly* 39, no. 4 (1990): 780–800.
Rogers, A. P. V. *Law on the Battlefield*. Manchester University Press, 1996.
Rohfleisch, Kramer J. 'Drawing the Battle Lines in the Pacific'. In *The Army Air Force in World War II: Plans and Early Operations January 1939 to August 1942*, Vol. 1, edited by Wesley F. Craven and James L. Cate. University of Chicago Press, 1983.
Rowland, Robin. 'Command Ability and Command Responsibility: Lt. Col. Hirateru Banno and the 'F Force' Trials'. Master's thesis, York University, 2003.
Russell, E. F. L. *The Knights of Bushido: A Short History of Japanese War Crimes*. Cassell, 1958.
Ryan, Allan A. *Yamashita's Ghost: War Crimes, MacArthur's Justice, and Command Accountability*. University Press of Kansas, 2012.
Sadurski, Wojciech. *Giving Desert Its Due: Social Justice and Legal Theory*. Reidel 1985.
Schaller, Michale. *Altered States: The United States and Japan Since the Occupation*. Oxford University Press, 1997.

Schouten, Lisette. 'Colonial Justice in the Netherlands Indies War Crimes Trials'. In *Trials for International Crimes in Asia*, edited by Kirsten Sellars. Cambridge University Press, 2016.

Scott, James M. *Rampage: MacArthur, Yamashita, and the Battle of Manila*. W. W. Norton and Co., 2018.

Searle, Thomas R. 'It Made a Lot of Sense to Kill Skilled Workers: The Firebombing of Tokyo in March 1945'. *The Journal of Military History* 66 (2002): 103–33.

Shennan, Margaret. *Out in the Midday Sun: The British in Malaya 1880–1960*. John Murray, 2010.

Shephard, Ben. 'Guerrillas and Counter-Insurgency'. In *The Cambridge History of the Second World War, Volume One: Fighting the War*, edited by John Ferris and Evan Mawdsley. Cambridge University Press, 2015.

Silver, Lynette. *Sandakan: A Conspiracy of Silence*. Sally Milner Publishing, 1998.

Silver, Lynette. *The Bridge at Parit Sulong: An Investigation of Mass Murder*. The Watermark Press, 2004.

Sissons, D. C. S. 'The Australian War Crimes Trials and Investigations (1942–51)'. In *Bridging Australia and Japan Volume 2: The Writings of David Sissons, Historian and Political Scientist*, edited by Keiko Tamura and Arthur Stockwin. ANU Press, 2020.

Sleeman, Colin, ed. *Trial of Gozawa Sadaichi and Nine Others*. William Hodge and Company, 1948.

Sloan, Bill. *Given Up for Dead: America's Heroic Stand at Wake Island*. Bantam Books, 2004.

Smith, S. C. 'Crimes and Punishment: Local Responses to the Trial of Japanese War Criminals in Malaya and Singapore, 1946–48'. *South East Asia Research* 5 (1997): 41–56.

Solis, Gary D. *The Law of Armed Conflict: International Humanitarian Law in War*. Cambridge University Press, 2010.

Spector, Ronald H. *Eagle Against the Sun: The American War with Japan*. Vintage Books, 1985.

Steinberg, Joel. *Philippines Collaboration in World War II*. University of Michigan Press, 1967.

Steinberg, Rafael. *Return to the Philippines*. Time-Life Books, 1979.

Syjuco, Maria Felisa A. *The Kempei Tai in the Philippines: 1941–1945*. New Day Publishers, 1988.

Sturma, Michael. 'Japanese Treatment of Allied Prisoners During the Second World War: Evaluating the Death Toll'. *Journal of Contemporary History* 55 (2020): 514–34.

Sturma, Michael. *Surface and Destroy: The Submarine Gun War in the Pacific*. University of Kentucky Press, 2011.

Takeda, Kayoko. *Interpreting the Tokyo War Crimes Tribunal: A Sociopolitical Analysis*. University of Ottawa Press, 2010.

Takemae, Eiji. *Inside GHQ: The Allied Occupation of Japan and Its Legacy*. Translated by Robert Ricketts and Sebastian Swann. Continuum, 2002.

Tanaka, Yuki. 'Japanese Atrocities on Nauru During the Pacific War: The Murder of Australians, the Massacre of Lepers and the Ethnocide of Nauruans'. *The Asia Pacific Journal* 8 (2010): 1–19.

Taucher, Paul. 'Command Responsibility at the Sandakan-Ranau War Crimes Trials'. Unpublished Honours thesis, Murdoch University, 2016.
Taucher, Paul. 'Escape from Justice: The Prosecution of Baron Takasaki Masamitsu'. *War in History* 28, no. 1 (2021): 184–99.
Taylor, Telford. *Nuremberg and Vietnam: An American Tragedy*. Quadrangle Books, 1970.
Totani, Yuma. *Justice in Asia and the Pacific Region, 1945–1952: Allied War Crimes Prosecutions*. Cambridge University Press, 2015.
Totani, Yuma. *The Tokyo War Crimes Trial: The Pursuit of Justice in the Wake of World War II*. Harvard University Asia Center, 2008.
Triggs, Gillian. 'Australia's War Crimes Trials: All Pity Choked'. In *The Law of War Crimes: National and International Approaches*, edited by Timothy McCormack and Gerry Simpson. Kluwer Law International, 1997.
Twomey, Christina. *Australia's Forgotten Prisoners: Civilians Interned by the Japanese in World War Two*. Cambridge University Press, 2007.
United Nations War Crimes Commission. *History of the United Nations War Crimes Commission and the Development of the Laws of War*. His Majesty's Stationery Office, London, 1948.
United Nations War Crimes Commission. *Law Reports of Trials of War Criminals, Volume One*. His Majesty's Stationery Office, London, 1947.
United Nations War Crimes Commission. *Law Reports of Trials of War Criminals Volume Five*. His Majesty's Stationery Office, London, 1948.
United States Department of State. *Foreign Relations of the United States: Diplomatic Papers: The Conference of Berlin (the Potsdam Conference), 1945*. US Government Printing Office, 1945.
United States Strategic Bombing Survey. *The Campaigns of the Pacific War*. United States Printing Office, 1946.
United States Strategic Bombing Survey. *Summary Report – Pacific War*. Government Printing Office, 1946.
Unwin, George G. W. *Victory in Defeat: The Wake Island Defenders in Captivity*. Naval Institute Press, 2010.
Utsumi, Aiko. 'The Japanese Army and its Prisoners: Relevant Documents and Bureaucratic Institutions'. *Australia-Japan Research Project*, Australian War Memorial.
Utsumi, Aiko. 'Japan's World War II POW Policy: Indifference and Irresponsibility'. *Asia-Pacific Journal: Japan Focus*, 3 no. 5 (2005): 1–4.
Utsumi, Aiko. 'Prisoners of War in the Pacific War: Japan's Policy'. In *The Burma-Thailand Railway*, edited by Gavan McCormack and Hank Nelson. Allen & Unwin, 1993.
Vance, Jonathon F. 'Doolittle Raid'. In *Encyclopedia of Prisoners of War and Internment*, 2nd ed., edited by Jonathon F. Vance. Grey House Publishing, 2006.
Vickers, Adrian. 'Dugas Jepengé/The Japanese Period: Bali Under the Japanese'. In *The Encyclopedia of Indonesia in the Pacific War*, edited by Peter Post, William H. Frederick, Iris Heidebrink, and Shigeru Sato. Koninklijke Brill, 2010.
Wakabayashi, Bob Tadashi. *The Nanking Atrocity, 1937–38: Complicating the Picture*. Berghahn Books, 2017.
Wall, Don. *Singapore and Beyond*. 2/20 Battalion Association, 1985.

Warner, Dennis, and Peggy Warner. *The Sacred Warriors: Japan's Suicide Legions*. Avon, 1984.

Whitney, Courtney. *The Case of General Yamashita: A Memorandum*. Supreme Commander for the Allied Powers, Government Section, 1949.

Wilbanks, Bob. *Last Man Out: Glenn McDole, USMC, Survivor of the Palawan Massacre in WWII*. McFarland and Company, 2004.

Willis, James F. *Prologue to Nuremberg: The Politics and Diplomacy of Punishing War Crimes*. Greenwood Press, 1982.

Willoughby, Charles A. *The Guerrilla Resistance Movement in the Philippines 1941–1945*. Vantage Press, 1972.

Wilner, Alan M. 'Superior Orders as a Defense to Violations of International Law'. *Maryland Law Review* 22 (1966): 127–42.

Wilson, Sandra. 'Koreans in the Trials of Japanese War Crimes Suspects'. In *Debating Collaboration and Complicity in War Crimes Trials in Asia, 1945–1956*, edited by Kerstin von Lingen. Palgrave MacMillan, 2017.

Wilson, Sandra. 'War Crimes Trials and the Politics of Justice: The Case of Kinoshita Eichi, 1945–57'. *Historical Research* 92 (2019): 632–53.

Wilson, Sandra. 'Detention Camps in the Japanese Empire, 1941–1945'. In *Detention Camps in Asia: The Conditions of Confinement in Modern Asian History*, edited by Robert Cribb, Christina Twomey, and Sandra Wilson. Brill, 2022.

Wilson, Sandra, Robert Cribb, Beatrice Trefalt, and Dean Aszkielowicz. *Japanese War Criminals: The Politics of Justice*. Columbia University Press, 2017.

Wilson, Sandra, Michael Sturma, Arjun Subrahmanyan, Dean Aszkielowicz, and J. Charles Schencking. *The U.S. and the War in the Pacific, 1941–1945*. Routledge, 2022.

Wilson, T., and J. A. Reid. 'Malaria Amongst Prisoners of War in Siam ('F' Force)'. *Transactions of the Royal Society of Tropical Medicine and Hygiene* 43, no. 3 (1949): 257–72.

Yanev, Lachezar D. *Theories of Co-Perpetration in International Criminal Law*. Brill-Nijhoff, 2018.

Yang, Daqing. 'Convergence or Divergence? Recent Historical Writings on the Rape of Nanjing'. *The American Historical Review* 104 (1999): 842–65.

Yap, Felicia. 'Prisoner of War and Civilian Internees of the Japanese in British Asia: The Similarities and Contrasts of Experience'. *Journal of Contemporary History* 47, no. 2 (2012): 317–416.

Zamperini, Louis, and David Rensin. *Devil at My Heels: A Heroic Olympian's Astonishing Story of Survival as a Japanese POW in World War II*. HarperCollins, 2003.

Index

www.ingramcontent.com/pod-product-compliance
Ingram Content Group UK Ltd.
Pitfield, Milton Keynes, MK11 3LW, UK
UKHW021838100926
8556IPUK00004B/426

9 789888 946822